CCNA Routing and Switching Portable Command Guide

Fourth Edition

All the ICND1 (100-105), ICND2 (200-105), and CCNA (200-125)
commands in one compact, portable resource

Scott Empson

800 East 96th Street
Indianapolis, Indiana 46240 USA

CCNA Routing and Switching Portable Command Guide

Scott Empson

Copyright© 2016 Cisco Systems, Inc.

Published by:
Cisco Press
800 East 96th Street
Indianapolis, IN 46240 USA

Printed in the United States of America

2 16

Library of Congress Control Number: 2016935767

ISBN-13: 978-1-58720-588-0

ISBN-10: 1-58720-588-2

Publisher
Mark Taub

Business Operation Manager, Cisco Press
Jan Cornelssen

Executive Editor
Mary Beth Ray

Managing Editor
Sandra Schroeder

Senior Development Editor
Christopher Cleveland

Senior Project Editor
Tonya Simpson

Copy Editor
Gill Editorial Services

Technical Editor
Brian D'Andrea

Editorial Assistant
Vanessa Evans

Cover Designer
Mark Shirar

Composition
Trina Wurst

Indexer
WordWise Publishing Services

Proofreader
Language Logistics

Warning and Disclaimer

This book is designed to provide information about the Cisco Certified Network Associate (CCNA) Routing and Switching composite exam (200-125). Every effort has been made to make this book as complete and as accurate as possible, but no warranty or fitness is implied.

The information is provided on an "as is" basis. The authors, Cisco Press, and Cisco Systems, Inc. shall have neither liability nor responsibility to any person or entity with respect to any loss or damages arising from the information contained in this book or from the use of the discs or programs that may accompany it.

The opinions expressed in this book belong to the author and are not necessarily those of Cisco Systems, Inc.

Trademark Acknowledgments

All terms mentioned in this book that are known to be trademarks or service marks have been appropriately capitalized. Cisco Press or Cisco Systems, Inc., cannot attest to the accuracy of this information. Use of a term in this book should not be regarded as affecting the validity of any trademark or service mark.

Special Sales

For information about buying this title in bulk quantities, or for special sales opportunities (which may include electronic versions; custom cover designs; and content particular to your business, training goals, marketing focus, or branding interests), please contact our corporate sales department at corpsales@pearsoned.com or (800) 382-3419.

For government sales inquiries, please contact governmentsales@pearsoned.com.

For questions about sales outside the U.S., please contact intlcs@pearson.com.

Feedback Information

At Cisco Press, our goal is to create in-depth technical books of the highest quality and value. Each book is crafted with care and precision, undergoing rigorous development that involves the unique expertise of members from the professional technical community.

Readers' feedback is a natural continuation of this process. If you have any comments regarding how we could improve the quality of this book, or otherwise alter it to better suit your needs, you can contact us through email at feedback@ciscopress.com. Please make sure to include the book title and ISBN in your message.

We greatly appreciate your assistance.

Contents at a Glance

Part VI Infrastructure Security

Part VII Infrastructure Management

Part VIII Appendixes

Contents

Part IV WAN Technologies

About the Author

Scott Empson is the chair of the Bachelor of Applied Information Systems Technology degree program at the Northern Alberta Institute of Technology in Edmonton, Alberta, Canada, where he has taught Cisco routing, switching, network design, and leadership courses in a variety of different programs (certificate, diploma, and applied degree) at the postsecondary level. Scott is also the program coordinator of the Cisco Networking Academy Program at NAIT, an Area Support Centre for the province of Alberta. He has a master of education degree along with three undergraduate degrees: a bachelor of arts, with a major in English; a bachelor of education, again with a major in English/language arts; and a bachelor of applied information systems technology, with a major in network management. He currently holds several industry certifications, including CCNP, CCDP, C|EH and Network+. Before instructing at NAIT, he was a junior/senior high school English/language arts/computer science teacher at different schools throughout northern Alberta. Scott lives in Edmonton, Alberta, with his wife, Trina, and two children, Zachariah and Shaelyn.

About the Technical Reviewer

Brian D'Andrea is a senior instructor at www.TrainingCamp.com with more than 14 years of instruction experience. He started and currently consults for multiple medical and financial businesses. Brian maintains Cisco certifications in CCNP Routing and Switching, CCNP Security, and CCNP Data Center. Brian currently resides in northern New Jersey along the Delaware Water Gap.

Dedications

As always, this book is dedicated to Trina, Zach, and Shae.

Acknowledgments

Anyone who has ever had anything to do with the publishing industry knows that it takes many, many people to create a book. It may be my name on the cover, but there is no way that I can take credit for all that occurred to get this book from idea to publication. Therefore, I must thank:

The team at Cisco Press. Once again, you amaze me with your professionalism and the ability to make me look good. Mary Beth, Chris, Tonya: Thank you for your continued support and belief in my little engineering journal.

To my technical reviewer, Brian: Thanks for keeping me on track and making sure that what I wrote was correct and relevant.

Reader Services

Register your copy at www.ciscopress.com/title/9781587205880 for convenient access to downloads, updates, and corrections as they become available. To start the registration process, go to www.ciscopress.com/register and log in or create an account*. Enter the product ISBN 9781587205880 and click Submit. Once the process is complete, you will find any available bonus content under Registered Products.

*Be sure to check the box that you would like to hear from us to receive exclusive discounts on future editions of this product.

Command Syntax Conventions

The conventions used to present command syntax in this book are the same conventions used in the IOS Command Reference. The Command Reference describes these conventions as follows:

- **Boldface** indicates commands and keywords that are entered literally as shown. In actual configuration examples and output (not general command syntax), boldface indicates commands that are manually input by the user (such as a **show** command).
- *Italic* indicates arguments for which you supply actual values.
- Vertical bars (|) separate alternative, mutually exclusive elements.
- Square brackets ([ ]) indicate an optional element.
- Braces ({ }) indicate a required choice.
- Braces within brackets ([{ }]) indicate a required choice within an optional element.

Introduction

Welcome to *CCNA Routing and Switching Portable Command Guide*! The success of the previous editions of this book prompted Cisco Press to approach me with a request to update the book with the necessary new content to help both students and IT professionals in the field study and prepare for the CCNA Routing and Switching exam. For someone who originally thought that this book would be less than 100 pages in length and limited to the Cisco Networking Academy program for its complete audience, I am continually amazed that my little engineering journal has caught on with such a wide range of people throughout the IT community.

I have long been a fan of what I call the "engineering journal," a small notebook that can be carried around and that contains little nuggets of information—commands that you forget, the IP addressing scheme of some remote part of the network, little reminders about how to do something you only have to do once or twice a year (but is vital to the integrity and maintenance of your network). This journal has been a constant companion by my side for the past 15 years; I only teach some of these concepts every second or third year, so I constantly need to refresh commands and concepts and learn new commands and ideas as Cisco releases them. My journals are the best way for me to review because they are written in my own words (words that I can understand). At least, I had better understand them because if I can't, I have only myself to blame.

My first published engineering journal was the *CCNA Quick Command Guide*; it was organized to match the (then) order of the Cisco Networking Academy program. That book then morphed into the *Portable Command Guide*, the fourth edition of which you are reading right now. This book is my "industry" edition of the engineering journal. It contains a different logical flow to the topics, one more suited to someone working in the field. Like topics are grouped together: routing protocols, switches, troubleshooting. More complex examples are given. IPv6 has now been integrated directly into the content chapters themselves. IPv6 is not something new that can be introduced in a separate chapter; it is part of network designs all around the globe, and we need to be as comfortable with it as we are with IPv4. The popular "Create Your Own Journal" appendix is still here (blank pages for you to add in your own commands that you need in your specific job). We all recognize the fact that no network administrator's job can be so easily pigeonholed as to just working with CCNA topics; you all have your own specific jobs and duties assigned to you. That is why you will find those blank pages at the end of the book. Make this book your own; personalize it with what you need to make it more effective. This way your journal will not look like mine.

Networking Devices Used in the Preparation of This Book

To verify the commands in this book, I had to try them out on a few different devices. The following is a list of the equipment I used when writing this book:

- C2821 ISR with PVDM2, CMME, a WIC-2T, FXS and FXO VICs, running 12.4(10a) IPBase IOS

- WS-C2960-24TT-L Catalyst switch, running 12.2(25)SE IOS

- WS-C2950-12 Catalyst switch, running Version C2950-C3.0(5.3)WC(1) Enterprise Edition software

- C1941 ISRG2 router with WIC 2T and HWIC-4ESW, running Version 15.1(1)T Cisco IOS with a technology package of IPBaseK9

Those of you familiar with Cisco devices will recognize that a majority of these commands work across the entire range of the Cisco product line. These commands are not limited to the platforms and Cisco IOS Software versions listed. In fact, these devices are in most cases adequate for someone to continue his or her studies into the CCNP level.

Private Addressing Used in This Book

This book uses RFC 1918 addressing throughout. Because I do not have permission to use public addresses in my examples, I have done everything with private addressing. Private addressing is perfect for use in a lab environment or in a testing situation because it works exactly like public addressing, with the exception that it cannot be routed across a public network.

Who Should Read This Book

This book is for those people preparing for the CCNA Routing and Switching exam, whether through self-study, on-the-job training and practice, or study within the Cisco Networking Academy program. There are also some handy hints and tips along the way to make life a bit easier for you in this endeavor. This book is small enough that you will find it easy to carry around with you. Big, heavy textbooks might look impressive on your bookshelf in your office, but can you really carry them around with you when you are working in some server room or equipment closet somewhere?

Optional Sections

A few sections in this book have been marked as optional. These sections cover topics that are not on the CCNA Routing and Switching certification exam, but they are valuable topics that should be known by someone at a CCNA level. Some of the optional topics might also be concepts that are covered in the Cisco Networking Academy program courses.

Organization of This Book

This book follows a logical approach to configuring a small to mid-size network. It is an approach that I give to my students when they invariably ask for some sort of outline to plan and then configure a network. Specifically, this approach is as follows:

Part I: Network Fundamentals

- **Chapter 1, "How to Subnet"**—An overview of how to subnet, examples of subnetting (both a Class B and a Class C address), the use of the binary AND operation, the Enhanced Bob Maneuver to Subnetting

- **Chapter 2, "VLSM"**—An overview of VLSM, an example of using VLSM to make your IP plan more efficient

- **Chapter 3, "Route Summarization"**—Using route summarization to make your routing updates more efficient, an example of how to summarize a network, necessary requirements for summarizing your network

- **Chapter 4, "Cables and Connections"**—An overview of how to connect to Cisco devices, which cables to use for which interfaces, and the differences between the TIA/EIA 568A and 568B wiring standards for UTP

- **Chapter 5, "The Command-Line Interface"**—How to navigate through Cisco IOS Software: editing commands, keyboard shortcuts, and help commands

Part II: LAN Switching Technologies

- **Chapter 6, "Configuring a Switch"**—Commands to configure Catalyst 2960 switches: names, passwords, IP addresses, default gateways, port speed and duplex, configuring static MAC addresses

- **Chapter 7, "VLANs"**—Configuring static VLANs, troubleshooting VLANs, saving and deleting VLAN information, Voice VLAN configuration with and without trust

- **Chapter 8, "VLAN Trunking Protocol and Inter-VLAN Communication"**— Configuring a VLAN trunk link, configuring VTP, verifying VTP, inter-VLAN communication, router-on-a-stick, subinterfaces, and SVIs

- **Chapter 9, "Spanning Tree Protocol"**—Verifying STP, setting switch priorities, working with the STP Toolkit, enabling Rapid Spanning Tree

- **Chapter 10, "EtherChannel"**—Creating and verifying Layer 2 and Layer 3 EtherChannel groups between switches

Part III: Routing Technologies: IPv4 and IPv6

- **Chapter 11, "Configuring a Cisco Router"**—Commands needed to configure a single router: names, passwords, configuring interfaces, MOTD and login banners, IP host tables, saving and erasing your configurations

- **Chapter 12, "Static Routing"**—Configuring IPv4 and IPv6 static routes in your internetwork

- **Chapter 13, "RIP Next Generation (RIPng)"**—Implementing, verifying, and troubleshooting RIPng

- **Chapter 14, "EIGRP and EIGRPv6"**—Configuring and verifying EIGRP and EIGRPv6

- **Chapter 15, "OSPFv2 and OSPFv3"**—Configuring and verifying OSPFv2 and OSPFv3 in both single-area and multiarea networks

Part IV: WAN Technologies

- **Chapter 16, "Understanding Point-to-Point Protocols"**—Configuring PPP, authenticating PPP using CHAP, compressing in PPP, Multilink PPP, troubleshooting PPP, returning to HDLC encapsulation, configuring a DSL connection using PPPoE

- **Chapter 17, "External Border Gateway Protocol (eBGP)"**—Configuring and verifying eBGP, multihop

- **Chapter 18, "Configuring Generic Routing Encapsulation (GRE) Tunnels"**—Configuring and verifying GRE tunnels

- **Chapter 19, "Quality of Service (QoS)"**—Configuring and verifying basic QoS, configuring and verifying auto-QoS

Part V: Infrastructure Services

- **Chapter 20, "DHCP"**—Configuring and verifying DHCP on a Cisco IOS router, using Cisco IP phones with a DHCP server

- **Chapter 21, "First Hop Redundancy Protocols (FHRP): Hot Standby Router Protocol (HSRP)"**—Configuring and verifying Hot Standby Routing Protocol (HSRP) on a Cisco device

- **Chapter 22, "Network Address Translation (NAT)"**—Configuring and verifying NAT and PAT

Part VI: Infrastructure Security

- **Chapter 23, "Switch Port Security"**—Setting passwords on a switch, switch port security, sticky MAC addresses

- **Chapter 24, "Managing Traffic Using Access Control Lists (ACL)"**—Configuring standard ACLs, wildcard masking, creating extended ACLs, creating named ACLs, using sequence numbers in named ACLs, verifying and troubleshooting ACLs, IPv6 ACLs

- **Chapter 25, "Device Hardening"**—Configuring and encrypting passwords, configuring and verifying SSH, restricting virtual terminal access, disabling unused services

Part VII: Infrastructure Management

- **Chapter 26, "Backing Up and Restoring Cisco IOS Software and Configurations"**—Boot commands for Cisco IOS Software, backing up and restoring Cisco IOS Software using TFTP, Xmodem, and ROMmon environmental variables, Secure Copy

- **Chapter 27, "Password-Recovery Procedures and the Configuration Register"**—The configuration register, password recovery procedure for routers and switches

- **Chapter 28, "Cisco Discovery Protocol (CDP) and Link Layer Discovery Protocol (LLDP)"**—Customizing and verifying CDP, configuring and verifying LLDP

- **Chapter 29, "IOS Tools"**—Commands for both **ping** and extended **ping**, the **traceroute** command

- **Chapter 30, "Device Monitoring"**—Configuring SNMP, working with syslog, severity levels, configuring NetFlow, Network Time Protocol (NTP), using the clock and time stamps

- **Chapter 31, "Cisco IOS Licensing"**—Differences between licensing pre- and post-Cisco IOS Version 15, installing permanent and evaluation licenses, backing up and uninstalling licenses, Cisco Smart Software Manager

- **Chapter 32, "Basic Troubleshooting"**—Various **show** commands used to view the routing table, interpreting the **show** interface command, verifying your IP settings using different operating systems

Part VIII: Appendixes

- **Appendix A, "Binary/Hex/Decimal Chart"**—A chart showing numbers 0 through 255 in the three numbering systems of binary, hexadecimal, and decimal

- **Appendix B, "Create Your Own Journal Here"**—Some blank pages for you to add in your own specific commands that might not be in this book

Did I Miss Anything?

I am always interested to hear how my students, and now readers of my books, do on both certification exams and future studies. If you would like to contact me and let me know how this book helped you in your certification goals, please do so. Did I miss anything? Let me know. Contact me at ccnaguide@empson.ca or through the Cisco Press website, http://www.ciscopress.com.

CHAPTER 1

How to Subnet

Class A–E Addresses

Class	Leading Bit Pattern	First Octet in Decimal	Notes	Formulae	
A	0xxxxxxx	0–127	0 is invalid 127 reserved for loopback testing	2^N Where N is equal to number of bits borrowed	Number of total subnets created
B	10xxxxxx	128–191		$2^N - 2$	Number of valid subnets created
C	110xxxxx	192–223		2^H Where H is equal to number of host bits	Number of total hosts per subnet
D	1110xxxx	224–239	Reserved for multicasting	$2^H - 2$	Number of valid hosts per subnet
E	1111xxxx	240–255	Reserved for future use/ testing		

Class A Address	N	H	H	H
Class B Address	N	N	H	H
Class C Address	N	N	N	H

N = Network bits

H = Host bits

All 0s in host portion = Network or subnetwork address

All 1s in host portion = Broadcast address

Combination of 1s and 0s in host portion = Valid host address

Converting Between Decimal Numbers and Binary

In any given octet of an IP address, the 8 bits can be defined as follows:

2^7	2^6	2^5	2^4	2^3	2^2	2^1	2^0
128	64	32	16	8	4	2	1

To convert a decimal number into binary, you must turn on the bits (make them a 1) that would add up to that number, as follows:

187 = 10111011 = 128+32+16+8+2+1

224 = 11100000 = 128+64+32

To convert a binary number into decimal, you must add the bits that have been turned on (the 1s), as follows:

10101010 = 128+32+8+2 = 170

11110000 = 128+64+32+16 = 240

The IP address 138.101.114.250 is represented in binary as

10001010.01100101.01110010.11111010

The subnet mask of 255.255.255.192 is represented in binary as

11111111.11111111.11111111.11000000

Subnetting a Class C Network Using Binary

You have a Class C address of 192.168.100.0 /24. You need nine subnets. What is the IP plan of network numbers, broadcast numbers, and valid host numbers? What is the subnet mask needed for this plan?

You cannot use N bits, only H bits. Therefore, ignore 192.168.100. These numbers cannot change.

Step 1. Determine how many H bits you need to borrow to create nine valid subnets.

$2^N - 2 \geq 9$

N = 4, so you need to borrow 4 H bits and turn them into N bits.

Start with 8 H bits	HHHHHHHH
Borrow 4 bits	NNNNHHHH

Step 2. Determine the first valid subnet in binary.

0001HHHH	Cannot use subnet 0000 because it is invalid. Therefore, you must start with the bit pattern of 0001
0001**0000**	All 0s in host portion = subnetwork number
0001**0001**	First valid host number
.	
.	
.	
0001**1110**	Last valid host number
0001**1111**	All 1s in host portion = broadcast number

Step 3. Convert binary to decimal.

00010000 = 16	Subnetwork number
00010001 = 17	First valid host number
.	
.	
.	
00011110 = 30	Last valid host number
00011111 = 31	All 1s in host portion = broadcast number

Step 4. Determine the second valid subnet in binary.

0010HHHH	0010 = 2 in binary = second valid subnet
0010**0000**	All 0s in host portion = subnetwork number
0010**0001**	First valid host number
.	
.	
.	
0010**1110**	Last valid host number
0010**1111**	All 1s in host portion = broadcast number

Step 5. Convert binary to decimal.

00100000 = 32	Subnetwork number
00100001 = 33	First valid host number
.	
.	
.	
00101110 = 46	Last valid host number
00101111 = 47	All 1s in host portion = broadcast number

Step 6. Create an IP plan table.

Valid Subnet	Network Number	Range of Valid Hosts	Broadcast Number
1	16	17–30	31
2	32	33–46	47
3	**48**	**49–62**	**63**

Notice a pattern? Counting by 16.

Step 7. Verify the pattern in binary. (The third valid subnet in binary is used here.)

0011HHHH	Third valid subnet
00110000 = **48**	Subnetwork number
00110001 = **49**	First valid host number
.	
.	
.	
00111110 = **62**	Last valid host number
00111111 = **63**	Broadcast number

Step 8. Finish the IP plan table.

Subnet	Network Address (0000)	Range of Valid Hosts (0001–1110)	Broadcast Address (1111)
0 (0000) invalid	192.168.100.**0**	192.168.100.**1**– 192.168.100.**14**	192.168.100.**15**
1 (0001)	192.168.100.**16**	192.168.100.**17**– 192.168.100.**30**	192.168.100.**31**
2 (0010)	192.168.100.**32**	192.168.100.**33**– 192.168.100.**46**	192.168.100.**47**
3 (0011)	192.168.100.**48**	192.168.100.**49**– 192.168.100.**62**	192.168.100.**63**
4 (0100)	192.168.100.**64**	192.168.100.**65**– 192.168.100.**78**	192.168.100.**79**
5 (0101)	192.168.100.**80**	192.168.100.**81**– 192.168.100.**94**	192.168.100.**95**
6 (0110)	192.168.100.**96**	192.168.100.**97**– 192.168.100.**110**	192.168.100.**111**
7 (0111)	192.168.100.**112**	192.168.100.**113**– 192.168.100.**126**	192.168.100.**127**
8 (1000)	192.168.100.**128**	192.168.100.**129**– 192.168.100.**142**	192.168.100.**143**
9 (1001)	192.168.100.**144**	192.168.100.**145**– 192.168.100.**158**	192.168.100.**159**

Subnet	Network Address (0000)	Range of Valid Hosts (0001–1110)	Broadcast Address (1111)
10 (1010)	192.168.100.**160**	192.168.100.**161**– 192.168.100.**174**	192.168.100.**175**
11 (1011)	192.168.100.**176**	192.168.100.**177**– 192.168.100.**190**	192.168.100.**191**
12 (1100)	192.168.100.**192**	192.168.100.**193**– 192.168.100.**206**	192.168.100.**207**
13 (1101)	192.168.100.**208**	192.168.100.**209**– 192.168.100.**222**	192.168.100.**223**
14 (1110)	192.168.100.**224**	192.168.100.**225**– 192.168.100.**238**	192.168.100.**239**
15 (1111) invalid	192.168.100.**240**	192.168.100.**241**– 192.168.100.**254**	192.168.100.**255**
Quick Check	**Always an even number**	**First valid host is always an odd # Last valid host is always an even #**	**Always an odd number**

Use any nine subnets—the rest are for future growth.

Step 9. Calculate the subnet mask. The default subnet mask for a Class C network is as follows:

Decimal	Binary
255.255.255.0	11111111.11111111.11111111.00000000

1 = Network or subnetwork bit

0 = Host bit

You borrowed 4 bits; therefore, the new subnet mask is the following:

11111111.11111111.11111111.**1111**0000	255.255.255.**240**

NOTE You subnet a Class B or a Class A network with exactly the same steps as for a Class C network; the only difference is that you start with more H bits.

Subnetting a Class B Network Using Binary

You have a Class B address of 172.16.0.0 /16. You need nine subnets. What is the IP plan of network numbers, broadcast numbers, and valid host numbers? What is the subnet mask needed for this plan?

You cannot use N bits, only H bits. Therefore, ignore 172.16. These numbers cannot change.

Step 1.   Determine how many H bits you need to borrow to create nine valid subnets.

$2^N - 2 \geq 9$

N = 4, so you need to borrow 4 H bits and turn them into N bits.

Start with 16 H bits	HHHHHHHHHHHHHHHH (Remove the decimal point for now)
Borrow 4 bits	**NNNN**HHHHHHHHHHHH

Step 2.   Determine the first valid subnet in binary (without using decimal points).

0001HHHHHHHHHHHH	
0001**000000000000**	Subnet number
0001**000000000001**	First valid host
.	
.	
.	
0001**111111111110**	Last valid host
0001**111111111111**	Broadcast number

Step 3.   Convert binary to decimal (replacing the decimal point in the binary numbers).

0001**0000.00000000** = 16.0	Subnetwork number
0001**0000.00000001** = 16.1	First valid host number
.	
.	
.	
0001**1111.11111110** = 31.254	Last valid host number
0001**1111.11111111** = 31.255	Broadcast number

Step 4.   Determine the second valid subnet in binary (without using decimal points).

0010HHHHHHHHHHHH	
0010**000000000000**	Subnet number
0010**000000000001**	First valid host
.	
.	
.	
0010**111111111110**	Last valid host
0010**111111111111**	Broadcast number

Step 5.   Convert binary to decimal (returning the decimal point in the binary numbers).

00100000.00000000 = 32.0	Subnetwork number
00100000.00000001 = 32.1	First valid host number
.	
.	
.	
00101111.11111110 = 47.254	Last valid host number
00101111.11111111 = 47.255	Broadcast number

Step 6.   Create an IP plan table.

Valid Subnet	Network Number	Range of Valid Hosts	Broadcast Number
1	16.0	16.1–31.254	31.255
2	32.0	32.1–47.254	47.255
3	48.0	48.1–63.254	63.255

Notice a pattern? Counting by 16.

Step 7.   Verify the pattern in binary. (The third valid subnet in binary is used here.)

0011HHHHHHHHHHHH	Third valid subnet
00110000.00000000 = 48.0	Subnetwork number
00110000.00000001 = 48.1	First valid host number
.	
.	
.	
00111111.11111110 = 63.254	Last valid host number
00111111.11111111 = 63.255	Broadcast number

Step 8.   Finish the IP plan table.

Subnet	Network Address (0000)	Range of Valid Hosts (0001–1110)	Broadcast Address (1111)
0 (0000) invalid	172.16.0.0	172.16.0.1–172.16.15.254	172.16.15.255
1 (0001)	172.16.16.0	172.16.16.1–172.16.31.254	172.16.31.255
2 (0010)	172.16.32.0	172.16.32.1–172.16.47.254	172.16.47.255
3 (0011)	172.16.48.0	172.16.48.1–172.16.63.254	172.16.63.255
4 (0100)	172.16.64.0	172.16.64.1–172.16.79.254	172.16.79.255

Subnet	Network Address (0000)	Range of Valid Hosts (0001–1110)	Broadcast Address (1111)
5 (0101)	172.16.**80.0**	172.16.**80.1**– 172.16.**95.254**	172.16.**95.255**
6 (0110)	172.16.**96.0**	172.16.**96.1**– 172.16.**111.254**	172.16.**111.255**
7 (0111)	172.16.**112.0**	172.16.**112.1**– 172.16.**127.254**	172.16.**127.255**
8 (1000)	172.16.**128.0**	172.16.**128.1**– 172.16.**143.254**	172.16.**143.255**
9 (1001)	172.16.**144.0**	172.16.**144.1**– 172.16.**159.254**	172.16.**159.255**
10 (1010)	172.16.**160.0**	172.16.**160.1**– 172.16.**175.254**	172.16.**175.255**
11 (1011)	172.16.**176.0**	172.16.**176.1**– 172.16.**191.254**	172.16.**191.255**
12 (1100)	172.16.**192.0**	172.16.**192.1**– 172.16.**207.254**	172.16.**207.255**
13 (1101)	172.16.**208.0**	172.16.**208.1**– 172.16.**223.254**	172.16.**223.255**
14 (1110)	172.16.**224.0**	172.16.**224.1**– 172.16.**239.254**	172.16.**239.255**
15 (1111) invalid	172.16.**240.0**	172.16.**240.1**– 172.16.**255.254**	172.16.**255.255**
Quick Check	**Always in form even #.0**	**First valid host is always even #.1 Last valid host is always odd #.254**	**Always odd #.255**

Use any nine subnets—the rest are for future growth.

Step 9.   Calculate the subnet mask. The default subnet mask for a Class B network is
as follows:

Decimal	Binary
255.255.0.0	11111111.11111111.00000000.00000000

1 = Network or subnetwork bit

0 = Host bit

You borrowed 4 bits; therefore, the new subnet mask is the following:

11111111.11111111.**1111**0000.00000000	255.255.**240**.0

Binary ANDing

Binary ANDing is the process of performing multiplication to two binary numbers. In the decimal numbering system, ANDing is addition: 2 and 3 equals 5. In decimal, there are an infinite number of answers when ANDing two numbers together. However, in the binary numbering system, the AND function yields only two possible outcomes, based on four different combinations. These outcomes, or answers, can be displayed in what is known as a truth table:

0 and 0 = 0

1 and 0 = 0

0 and 1 = 0

1 and 1 = 1

You use ANDing most often when comparing an IP address to its subnet mask. The end result of ANDing these two numbers together is to yield the network number of that address.

Question 1

What is the network number of the IP address 192.168.100.115 if it has a subnet mask of 255.255.255.240?

Answer

Step 1. Convert both the IP address and the subnet mask to binary:

192.168.100.115 = 11000000.10101000.01100100.01110011

255.255.255.240 = 11111111.11111111.11111111.11110000

Step 2. Perform the AND operation to each pair of bits—1 bit from the address ANDed to the corresponding bit in the subnet mask. Refer to the truth table for the possible outcomes:

192.168.100.115 = 11000000.10101000.01100100.01110011

255.255.255.240 = 11111111.11111111.11111111.11110000

ANDed result   = 11000000.10101000.01100100.01110000

Step 3. Convert the answer back into decimal:

11000000.10101000.01100100.01110000 = 192.168.100.112

The IP address 192.168.100.115 belongs to the 192.168.100.112 network when a mask of 255.255.255.240 is used.

Question 2

What is the network number of the IP address 192.168.100.115 if it has a subnet mask of 255.255.255.192?

(Notice that the IP address is the same as in Question 1, but the subnet mask is different. What answer do you think you will get? The same one? Let's find out!)

Answer

Step 1. Convert both the IP address and the subnet mask to binary:

192.168.100.115 = 11000000.10101000.01100100.01110011

255.255.255.192 = 11111111.11111111.11111111.11000000

Step 2. Perform the AND operation to each pair of bits—1 bit from the address ANDed to the corresponding bit in the subnet mask. Refer to the truth table for the possible outcomes:

192.168.100.115 = 11000000.10101000.01100100.01110011

255.255.255.192 = 11111111.11111111.11111111.11000000

ANDed result   = 11000000.10101000.01100100.01000000

Step 3. Convert the answer back into decimal:

11000000.10101000.01100100.01110000 = 192.168.100.64

The IP address 192.168.100.115 belongs to the 192.168.100.64 network when a mask of 255.255.255.192 is used.

So Why AND?

Good question. The best answer is to save you time when working with IP addressing and subnetting. If you are given an IP address and its subnet, you can quickly find out what subnetwork the address belongs to. From here, you can determine what other addresses belong to the same subnet. Remember that if two addresses are in the same network or subnetwork, they are considered to be *local* to each other and can therefore communicate directly with each other. Addresses that are not in the same network or subnetwork are considered to be *remote* to each other and must therefore have a Layer 3 device (like a router or Layer 3 switch) between them to communicate.

Question 3

What is the broadcast address of the IP address 192.168.100.164 if it has a subnet mask of 255.255.255.248?

Answer

Step 1. Convert both the IP address and the subnet mask to binary:

192.168.100.164 = 11000000.10101000.01100100.10100100

255.255.255.248 = 11111111.11111111.11111111.11111000

Step 2. Perform the AND operation to each pair of bits—1 bit from the address ANDed to the corresponding bit in the subnet mask. Refer to the truth table for the possible outcomes:

192.168.100.164 = 11000000.10101000.01100100.10100100

255.255.255.248 = 11111111.11111111.11111111.11111000

ANDed result   = 11000000.10101000.01100100.10100000

                  = 192.168.100.160 (Subnetwork #)

Step 3. Separate the network bits from the host bits:

255.255.255.248 = /29 = The first 29 bits are network/subnetwork bits; therefore,

*11000000.10101000.01100100.10100*000. The last three bits are host bits.

Step 4. Change all host bits to 1. Remember that all 1s in the host portion are the broadcast number for that subnetwork:

*11000000.10101000.01100100.10100*111

Step 5. Convert this number to decimal to reveal your answer:

11000000.10101000.01100100.10100111 = 192.168.100.167

The broadcast address of 192.168.100.164 is 192.168.100.167 when the subnet mask is 255.255.255.248.

Shortcuts in Binary ANDing

Remember when I said that this was supposed to save you time when working with IP addressing and subnetting? Well, there are shortcuts when you AND two numbers together:

- An octet of all 1s in the subnet mask will result in the answer being the same octet as in the IP address.

- An octet of all 0s in the subnet mask will result in the answer being all 0s in that octet.

Question 4

To what network does 172.16.100.45 belong, if its subnet mask is 255.255.255.0?

Answer

172.16.100.0

Proof

Step 1. Convert both the IP address and the subnet mask to binary:

172.16.100.45 = 10101100.00010000.01100100.00101101

255.255.255.0 = 11111111.11111111.11111111.00000000

Step 2. Perform the AND operation to each pair of bits—1 bit from the address ANDed to the corresponding bit in the subnet mask. Refer to the truth table for the possible outcomes:

172.16.100.45	=	10101100.00010000.01100100.00101101
255.255.255.0	=	11111111.11111111.11111111.00000000
		10101100.00010000.01100100.00000000
	=	172.16.100.0

Notice that the first three octets have the same pattern both before and after they were ANDed. Therefore, any octet ANDed to a subnet mask pattern of 255 is itself! Notice that the last octet is all 0s after ANDing. But according to the truth table, anything ANDed to a 0 is a 0. Therefore, any octet ANDed to a subnet mask pattern of 0 is 0! You should only have to convert those parts of an IP address and subnet mask to binary if the mask is not 255 or 0.

Question 5

To what network does 68.43.100.18 belong if its subnet mask is 255.255.255.0?

Answer

68.43.100.0 (There is no need to convert here. The mask is either 255s or 0s.)

Question 6

To what network does 131.186.227.43 belong if its subnet mask is 255.255.240.0?

Answer

Based on the two shortcut rules, the answer should be

131.186.???.0

So now you only need to convert one octet to binary for the ANDing process:

227   = 11100011

240   = 11110000

11100000 = 224

Therefore, the answer is 131.186.224.0.

The Enhanced Bob Maneuver for Subnetting (or How to Subnet Anything in Under a Minute)

Legend has it that once upon a time a networking instructor named Bob taught a class of students a method of subnetting any address using a special chart. This was known as the Bob Maneuver. These students, being the smart type that networking students usually are, added a row to the top of the chart, and the Enhanced Bob Maneuver was born. The chart and instructions on how to use it follow. With practice, you should be able to subnet any address and come up with an IP plan in under a minute. After all, it's *just* math!

The Bob of the Enhanced Bob Maneuver was really a manager/instructor at SHL. He taught this maneuver to Bruce, who taught it to Chad Klymchuk. Chad and a coworker named Troy added the top line of the chart, enhancing it. Chad was first my instructor in Microsoft, then my coworker here at NAIT, and now is one of my Academy instructors—I guess I am now his boss. And the circle is complete.

The Enhanced Bob Maneuver

	192	224	240	248	252	254	255	Subnet Mask
128	64	32	16	8	4	2	1	Target Number
8	7	6	5	4	3	2	1	Bit Place
	126	62	30	14	6	2	N/A	Number of Valid Subnets

Step 1. On the bottom line (Number of Valid Subnets), move from *right* to *left* and find the closest number that is *bigger* than or *equal* to what you need:

Nine subnets—move to 14.

Step 2. From that number (14), move up to the line called Bit Place.

Above 14 is bit place 4.

Step 3. The dark line is called the *high-order line*. If you cross the line, you have to reverse direction.

You were moving from right to left; now you have to move from left to right.

Step 4. Go to the line called Target Number. Counting *from the left*, move over the number of spaces that the bit place number tells you.

Starting on 128, moving 4 places takes you to 16.

Step 5. This target number is what you need to count by, starting at 0 and going until you hit 255 or greater. Stop before you get to 256:

0

16

32

48

64

80

96

112

128

144

160

176

192

208

224

240

256 Stop—too far!

Step 6.   These numbers are your network numbers. Expand to finish your plan.

Network #	Range of Valid Hosts	Broadcast Number
0 (invalid)	1–14	15
16	17–30 (17 is 1 more than network # 30 is 1 less than broadcast#)	31 (1 less than next network #)
32	33–46	47
48	49–62	63
64	65–78	79
80	81–94	95
96	97–110	111
112	113–126	127
128	129–142	143
144	145–158	159
160	161–174	175
176	177–190	191
192	193–206	207
208	209–222	223
224	225–238	239
240 (invalid)	241–254	255

Notice that there are 14 subnets created from .16 to .224.

Step 7.   Go back to the Enhanced Bob Maneuver chart and look above your target number to the top line. The number above your target number is your subnet mask.

Above 16 is 240. Because you started with a Class C network, the new subnet mask is 255.255.255.240.

CHAPTER 2

VLSM

Variable-length subnet masking (VLSM) is the more realistic way of subnetting a network to make the most efficient use of all of the bits.

Remember that when you perform classful (or what I sometimes call classical) subnetting, all subnets have the same number of hosts because they all use the same subnet mask. This leads to inefficiencies. For example, if you borrow 4 bits on a Class C network, you end up with 14 valid subnets of 14 valid hosts. A serial link to another router only needs 2 hosts, but with classical subnetting, you end up wasting 12 of those hosts. Even with the ability to use NAT and private addresses, where you should never run out of addresses in a network design, you still want to ensure that the IP plan you create is as efficient as possible. This is where VLSM comes into play.

VLSM is the process of "subnetting a subnet" and using different subnet masks for different networks in your IP plan. What you have to remember is that you need to make sure that there is no overlap in any of the addresses.

IP Subnet Zero

When you work with classical subnetting, you always have to eliminate the subnets that contain either all zeros or all ones in the subnet portion. Hence, you always used the formula 2^N-2 to define the number of valid subnets created. However, Cisco devices can use those subnets, as long as the command **ip subnet-zero** is in the configuration. This command is on by default in Cisco IOS Software Release 12.0 and later; if it was turned off for some reason, however, you can reenable it by using the following command:

```
Router(config)#ip subnet-zero
```

Now you can use the formula 2^N rather than $2^N - 2$.

2^N	Number of total subnets created	
2^{N-2}	Number of valid subnets created	No longer needed because you have the **ip subnet-zero** command enabled
2^H	Number of total hosts per subnet	
$2^H - 2$	Number of valid hosts per subnet	

VLSM Example

You follow the same steps in performing VLSM as you did when performing classical subnetting.

Consider Figure 2-1 as you work through an example.

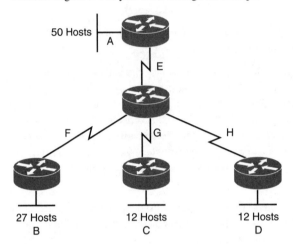

Figure 2-1   Sample Network Needing a VLSM Address Plan

A Class C network—192.168.100.0/24—is assigned. You need to create an IP plan for this network using VLSM.

Once again, you cannot use the N bits—192.168.100. You can use only the H bits. Therefore, ignore the N bits because they cannot change!

The steps to create an IP plan using VLSM for the network illustrated in Figure 2-1 are as follows:

Step 1.   Determine how many H bits will be needed to satisfy the *largest* network.

Step 2.   Pick a subnet for the largest network to use.

Step 3.   Pick the next largest network to work with.

Step 4.   Pick the third largest network to work with.

Step 5.   Determine network numbers for serial links.

The remainder of the chapter details what is involved with each step of the process.

Step 1: Determine How Many H Bits Will Be Needed to Satisfy the *Largest* Network

A is the largest network with 50 hosts. Therefore, you need to know how many H bits will be needed:

If $2^H - 2 =$ Number of valid hosts per subnet

Then $2^H - 2 \geq 50$

Therefore H = 6 (6 is the smallest valid value for H)

You need 6 H bits to satisfy the requirements of Network A.

If you need 6 H bits and you started with 8 N bits, you are left with $8 - 6 = 2$ N bits to create subnets:

Started with: NNNNNNNN (these are the 8 bits in the fourth octet)

Now have: NNHHHHHH

All subnetting will now have to start at this reference point to satisfy the requirements of Network A.

Step 2: Pick a Subnet for the Largest Network to Use

You have 2 N bits to work with, leaving you with 2^N or 2^2 or 4 subnets to work with:

NN = 00HHHHHH (The Hs = The 6 H bits you need for Network A)

01HHHHHH

10HHHHHH

11HHHHHH

If you add all zeros to the H bits, you are left with the network numbers for the four subnets:

00000000 = .0

01000000 = .64

10000000 = .128

11000000 = .192

All of these subnets will have the same subnet mask, just like in classful subnetting.

Two borrowed H bits means a subnet mask of

11111111.11111111.11111111.11000000

or

255.255.255.192

or

/26

The /x notation represents how to show different subnet masks when using VLSM.

/8 means that the first 8 bits of the address are network; the remaining 24 bits are H bits.

/24 means that the first 24 bits are network; the last 8 are host. This is either a traditional default Class C address, a traditional Class A network that has borrowed 16 bits, or even a traditional Class B network that has borrowed 8 bits!

Pick *one* of these subnets to use for Network A. The rest of the networks will have to use the other three subnets.

For purposes of this example, pick the .64 network.

00000000 =	.0	
01000000 =	.64	Network A
10000000 =	.128	
11000000 =	.192	

Step 3: Pick the Next Largest Network to Work With

Network B = 27 hosts

Determine the number of H bits needed for this network:

$$2^H - 2 \geq 27$$

$$H = 5$$

You need 5 H bits to satisfy the requirements of Network B.

You started with a pattern of 2 N bits and 6 H bits for Network A. You have to maintain that pattern.

Pick one of the remaining /26 networks to work with Network B.

For the purposes of this example, select the .128/26 network:

10000000

But you need only 5 H bits, not 6. Therefore, you are left with

10N00000

where

10 represents the original pattern of subnetting.

N represents the extra bit.

00000 represents the 5 H bits you need for Network B.

Because you have this extra bit, you can create two smaller subnets from the original subnet:

> 10**000000**

> 10**100000**

Converted to decimal, these subnets are as follows:

> 10**000000** =.128

> 10**100000** =.160

You have now subnetted a subnet! This is the basis of VLSM.

Each of these sub-subnets will have a new subnet mask. The original subnet mask of /24 was changed into /26 for Network A. You then take one of these /26 networks and break it into two /27 networks:

> 10**000000** and 10**100000** both have 3 N bits and 5 H bits.

The mask now equals:

> 11111111.11111111.11111111.11100000

or

> 255.255.255.224

or

> /27

Pick one of these new sub-subnets for Network B:

> 10**000000** /27 = Network B

Use the remaining sub-subnet for future growth, or you can break it down further if needed.

You want to make sure the addresses are not overlapping with each other. So go back to the original table.

00**000000** =	.0/26	
01**000000** =	.64/26	Network A
10**000000** =	.128/26	
11**000000** =	.192/26	

You can now break the .128/26 network into two smaller /27 networks and assign Network B.

00**000000** =	.0/26	
01**000000** =	.64/26	Network A
10**000000** =	.128/26	Cannot use because it has been subnetted
10**000000** =	.128/27	Network B
101**00000** =	.160/27	
11**000000** =	.192/26	

The remaining networks are still available to be assigned to networks or subnetted further for better efficiency.

Step 4: Pick the Third Largest Network to Work With

Networks C and Network D = 12 hosts each

Determine the number of H bits needed for these networks:

$$2^H - 2 \geq 12$$

$$H = 4$$

You need 4 H bits to satisfy the requirements of Network C and Network D.

You started with a pattern of 2 N bits and 6 H bits for Network A. You have to maintain that pattern.

You now have a choice as to where to put these networks. You could go to a different /26 network, or you could go to a /27 network and try to fit them into there.

For the purposes of this example, select the other /27 network—.160/27:

10**100000** (The 1 in the third bit place is no longer bold because it is part of the N bits.)

But you only need 4 H bits, not 5. Therefore, you are left with

101**N0000**

where

10 represents the original pattern of subnetting.

N represents the extra bit you have.

00000 represents the 5 H bits you need for Networks C and D.

Because you have this extra bit, you can create two smaller subnets from the original subnet:

101**00000**

101**10000**

Converted to decimal, these subnets are as follows:

101**00000** = .160

1011**0000** = .176

These new sub-subnets will now have new subnet masks. Each sub-subnet now has 4 N bits and 4 H bits, so their new masks will be

> 11111111.11111111.11111111.11110000

or

> 255.255.255.240

or

> /28

Pick one of these new sub-subnets for Network C and one for Network D.

00000000 =	.0/26	
01000000 =	.64/26	Network A
10000000 =	.128/26	Cannot use because it has been subnetted
10000000 =	.128/27	Network B
10100000 =	.160/27	Cannot use because it has been subnetted
10100000	.160/28	Network C
10110000	.176/28	Network D
11000000 =	.192/26	

You have now used two of the original four subnets to satisfy the requirements of four networks. Now all you need to do is determine the network numbers for the serial links between the routers.

Step 5: Determine Network Numbers for Serial Links

All serial links between routers have the same property in that they only need two addresses in a network—one for each router interface.

Determine the number of H bits needed for these networks:

> $2^H - 2 \geq 2$
>
> $H = 2$

You need 2 H bits to satisfy the requirements of Networks E, F, G, and H.

You have two of the original subnets left to work with.

For the purposes of this example, select the .0/26 network:

00000000

But you need only 2 H bits, not 6. Therefore, you are left with

00NNNN00

where

00 represents the original pattern of subnetting.

NNNN represents the extra bits you have.

00 represents the 2 H bits you need for the serial links.

Because you have 4 **N** bits, you can create 16 sub-subnets from the original subnet:

00**0000**00 = .0/30

00**0001**00 = .4/30

00**0010**00 = .8/30

00**0011**00 = .12/30

00**0100**00 = .16/30

.

.

.

00**1110**00 = .56/30

00**1111**00 = .60/30

You need only four of them. You can hold the rest for future expansion or recombine them for a new, larger subnet:

00**0100**00 = .16/30

00**0101**00 = .20/30

00**0110**00 = .24/30

00**0111**00 = .32/30

.

.

.

00**1110**00 = .56/30

00**1111**00 = .60/30

The first four of these can be combined into the following:

00**010000** = .16/28

The rest of the /30 subnets can be combined into two /28 networks:

00**100000** = .32/28

00**110000** = .48/28

Or these two subnets can be combined into one larger /27 network

00**010000** = .32/27

Going back to the original table, you now have the following:

00000000 =	.0/26	Cannot use because it has been subnetted
00000000 =	.0/30	Network E
00000100 =	.4/30	Network F
00001000 =	.8/30	Network G
00001100 =	.12/30	Network H
00010000 =	.16/28	Future growth
00100000 =	.32/27	Future growth
01000000 =	.64/26	Network A
10000000 =	.128/26	Cannot use because it has been subnetted
10000000 =	.128/27	Network B
10100000 =	160/27	Cannot use because it has been subnetted
10100000	160/28	Network C
10110000	176/28	Network D
11000000 =	.192/26	Future growth

Looking at the plan, you can see that no number is used twice. You have now created an IP plan for the network and have made the plan as efficient as possible, wasting no addresses in the serial links and leaving room for future growth. This is the power of VLSM!

CHAPTER 3

Route Summarization

Route summarization, or supernetting, is needed to reduce the number of routes that a router advertises to its neighbor. Remember that for every route you advertise, the size of your update grows. It has been said that if there were no route summarization, the Internet backbone would have collapsed from the sheer size of its own routing tables back in 1997!

Routing updates, whether done with a distance vector or link-state protocol, grow with the number of routes you need to advertise. In simple terms, a router that needs to advertise ten routes needs ten specific lines in its update packet. The more routes you have to advertise, the bigger the packet. The bigger the packet, the more bandwidth the update takes, reducing the bandwidth available to transfer data. But with route summarization, you can advertise many routes with only one line in an update packet. This reduces the size of the update, allowing you more bandwidth for data transfer.

Also, when a new data flow enters a router, the router must do a lookup in its routing table to determine which interface the traffic must be sent out. The larger the routing tables, the longer this takes, leading to more used router CPU cycles to perform the lookup. Therefore, a second reason for route summarization is that you want to minimize the amount of time and router CPU cycles that are used to route traffic.

> **NOTE** This example is a very simplified explanation of how routers send updates to each other. For a more in-depth description, I highly recommend you go out and read Jeff Doyle's book *Routing TCP/IP*, Volume I, 2nd edition, Cisco Press. This book has been around for many years and is considered by most to be the authority on how the different routing protocols work. If you are considering continuing on in your certification path to try and achieve the CCIE, you need to buy Doyle's book—and memorize it; it's that good.

Example for Understanding Route Summarization

Refer to Figure 3-1 to assist you as you go through the following explanation of an example of route summarization.

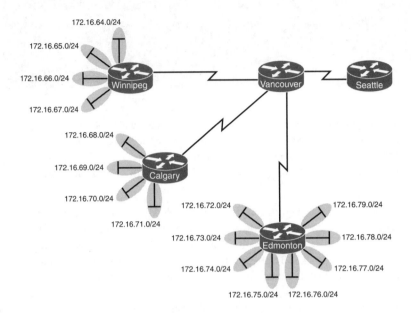

Figure 3-1   Four-City Network Without Route Summarization

As you can see from Figure 3-1, Winnipeg, Calgary, and Edmonton each have to advertise internal networks to the main router located in Vancouver. Without route summarization, Vancouver would have to advertise 16 networks to Seattle. You want to use route summarization to reduce the burden on this upstream router.

Step 1: Summarize Winnipeg's Routes

To do this, you need to look at the routes in binary to see if there are any specific bit patterns that you can use to your advantage. What you are looking for are common bits on the network side of the addresses. Because all of these networks are /24 networks, you want to see which of the first 24 bits are common to all four networks.

  172.16.64.0 = *10101100.00010000.01000000*.00000000

  172.16.65.0 = *10101100.00010000.01000001*.00000000

  172.16.66.0 = *10101100.00010000.01000010*.00000000

  172.16.67.0 = *10101100.00010000.01000011*.00000000

  Common bits: *10101100.00010000.010000*xx

You see that the first 22 bits of the four networks are common. Therefore, you can summarize the four routes by using a subnet mask that reflects that the first 22 bits are common. This is a /22 mask, or 255.255.252.0. You are left with the summarized address of

  172.16.64.0/22

This address, when sent to the upstream Vancouver router, will tell Vancouver: "If you have any packets that are addressed to networks that have the first 22 bits in the pattern of 10101100.00010000.010000xx.xxxxxxxx, then send them to me here in Winnipeg."

By sending one route to Vancouver with this supernetted subnet mask, you have advertised four routes in one line instead of using four lines. Much more efficient!

Step 2: Summarize Calgary's Routes

For Calgary, you do the same thing that you did for Winnipeg—look for common bit patterns in the routes:

    172.16.68.0 = *10101100.00010000.010001*00.00000000

    172.16.69.0 = *10101100.00010000.010001*01.00000000

    172.16.70.0 = *10101100.00010000.010001*10.00000000

    172.16.71.0 = *10101100.00010000.010001*11.00000000

    Common bits: *10101100.00010000.010001*xx

Once again, the first 22 bits are common. The summarized route is therefore

    172.16.68.0/22

Step 3: Summarize Edmonton's Routes

For Edmonton, you do the same thing that we did for Winnipeg and Calgary—look for common bit patterns in the routes:

    172.16.72.0 = *10101100.00010000.01001*000.00000000

    172.16.73.0 = *10101100.00010000.01001*001.00000000

    172.16.74.0 = *10101100.00010000 01001*010.00000000

    172.16.75.0 = *10101100.00010000 01001*011.00000000

    172.16.76.0 = *10101100.00010000.01001*100.00000000

    172.16.77.0 = *10101100.00010000.01001*101.00000000

    172.16.78.0 = *10101100.00010000.01001*110.00000000

    172.16.79.0 = *10101100.00010000.01001*111.00000000

    Common bits: *10101100.00010000.01001*xxx

For Edmonton, the first 21 bits are common. The summarized route is therefore

    172.16.72.0/21

Figure 3-2 shows what the network looks like, with Winnipeg, Calgary, and Edmonton sending their summarized routes to Vancouver.

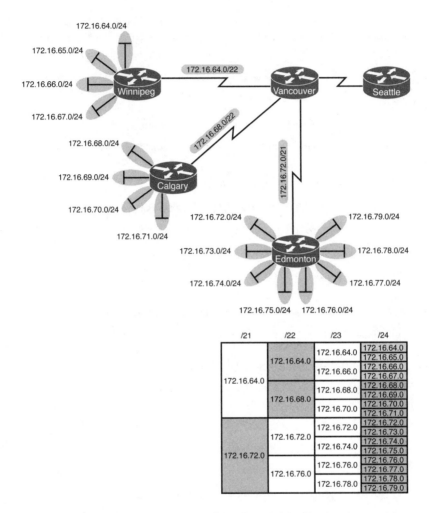

Figure 3-2   Four-City Network with Edge Cities Summarizing Routes

Step 4: Summarize Vancouver's Routes

Yes, you can summarize Vancouver's routes to Seattle. You continue in the same format as before. Take the routes that Winnipeg, Calgary, and Edmonton sent to Vancouver, and look for common bit patterns:

172.16.64.0 = *10101100.00010000.01000000.00000000*

172.16.68.0 = *10101100.00010000.01000100.00000000*

172.16.72.0 = *10101100.00010000.01001000.00000000*

Common bits: *10101100.00010000.0100*xxxx

Because there are 20 bits that are common, you can create one summary route for Vancouver to send to Seattle:

172.16.64.0/20

Vancouver has now told Seattle that in one line of a routing update, 16 different networks are being advertised. This is much more efficient than sending 16 lines in a routing update to be processed.

Figure 3-3 shows what the routing updates would look like with route summarization taking place.

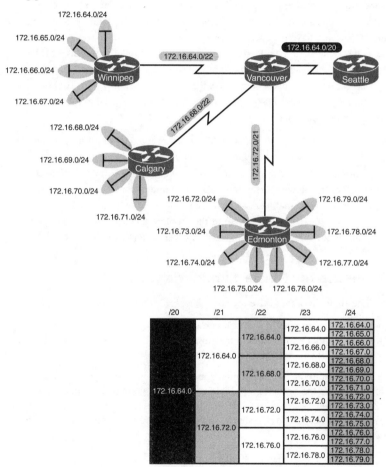

Figure 3-3 Four-City Network with Complete Route Summarization

Route Summarization and Route Flapping

Another positive aspect of route summarization has to do with route flapping. *Route flapping* is when a network, for whatever reason (such as interface hardware failure or misconfiguration), goes up and down on a router, causing that router to constantly advertise changes about that network. Route summarization can help insulate upstream neighbors from these problems.

Consider router Edmonton from Figure 3-1. Suppose that network 172.16.74.0/24 goes down. Without route summarization, Edmonton would advertise Vancouver to remove that network. Vancouver would forward that same message upstream to Calgary, Winnipeg, Seattle, and so on. Now assume the network comes back online a few seconds later. Edmonton would have to send another update informing Vancouver of the change. Each time a change needs to be advertised, the router must use CPU resources. If that route were to flap, the routers would constantly have to update their own tables, as well as advertise changes to their neighbors. In a CPU-intensive protocol such as OSPF, the constant hit on the CPU might make a noticeable change to the speed at which network traffic reaches its destination.

Route summarization enables you to avoid this problem. Even though Edmonton would still have to deal with the route constantly going up and down, no one else would notice. Edmonton advertises a single summarized route, 172.16.72.0/21, to Vancouver. Even though one of the networks is going up and down, this does not invalidate the route to the other networks that were summarized. Edmonton will deal with its own route flap, but Vancouver will be unaware of the problem downstream in Edmonton. Summarization can effectively protect or insulate other routers from route flaps.

Requirements for Route Summarization

To create route summarization, there are some necessary requirements:

- Routers need to be running a classless routing protocol, as they carry subnet mask information with them in routing updates. (Examples are RIP v2, OSPF, EIGRP, IS-IS, and BGP.)

- Addresses need to be assigned in a hierarchical fashion for the summarized address to have the same high-order bits. It does no good if Winnipeg has network 172.16.64.0 and 172.16.67.0 while 172.16.65.0 resides in Calgary and 172.16.66.0 is assigned in Edmonton. No summarization could take place from the edge routers to Vancouver.

TIP   Because most networks use NAT and the ten networks internally, it is important when creating your network design that you assign network subnets in a way that they can be easily summarized. A little more planning now can save you a lot of grief later.

CHAPTER 4

Cables and Connections

This chapter provides information and commands concerning the following topics:

- Connecting a rollover cable to your router or switch
- Using a USB cable to connect to your router or switch
- Determining what your terminal settings should be
- Understanding the setup of different LAN connections
- Identifying different serial cable types
- Determining which cable to use to connect your router or switch to another device
- 568A versus 568B cables

Connecting a Rollover Cable to Your Router or Switch

Figure 4-1 shows how to connect a rollover cable from your PC to a router or switch.

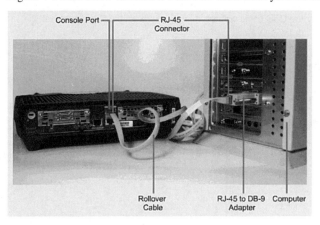

Figure 4-1   Rollover Cable Connection

Using a USB Cable to Connect to Your Router or Switch

On newer Cisco devices, a USB serial console connection is also supported. A USB cable (USB type A to 5-pin mini type B) and operating system driver are needed to establish connectivity. Figure 4-2 shows a Cisco device that can use either a mini-USB connector or a traditional RJ-45 connector.

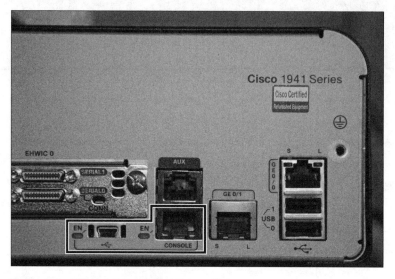

Figure 4-2   Different Console Port Connections

NOTE   Only one console port can be active at a time. If a cable is plugged into the USB port, the RJ-45 port becomes inactive.

NOTE   The OS driver for the USB cable connection is available on the Cisco.com website.

Terminal Settings

Figure 4-3 illustrates the settings that you should configure to have your PC connect to a router or switch.

Figure 4-3   PC Settings to Connect to a Router or Switch

LAN Connections

Table 4-1 shows the various port types and connections between LAN devices.

TABLE 4-1   LAN Connections

Port or Connection	Port Type	Connected To	Cable
Ethernet	RJ-45	Ethernet switch	RJ-45
T1/E1 WAN	RJ-48C/CA81A	T1 or E1 network	Rollover
Console	8 pin	Computer COM port	Rollover
Console	USB	Computer USB port	USB
AUX	8 pin	Modem	RJ-45

Serial Cable Types

Figure 4-4 shows the DB-60 end of a serial cable that connects to a 2500 series router.

Figure 4-5 shows the newer smart serial end of a serial cable that connects to a smart serial port on your router. Smart serial ports are found on modular routers, such as the newest ISR2 series (x900), ISR (x800) series, or on older modular routers such as the 1700 or 2600 series.

Figure 4-6 shows examples of the male DTE and the female DCE ends that are on the other side of a serial or smart serial cable.

Most laptops available today come equipped with USB ports, not serial ports. For these laptops, you need a USB-to-serial connector, as shown in Figure 4-7.

Figure 4-4   Serial Cable (2500)

Figure 4-5   Smart Serial Cable (1700, 2600, ISR, ISR2)

Figure 4-6   V.35 DTE and DCE Cables

NOTE   CCNA focuses on *V.35 cables* for back-to-back connections between routers.

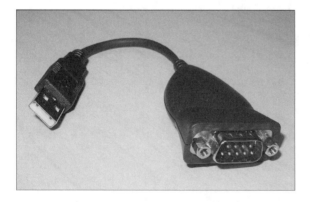

Figure 4-7   USB-to-Serial Connector for Laptops

Which Cable to Use?

Table 4-2 describes which cable should be used when wiring your devices together. It is important to ensure you have proper cabling; otherwise, you might be giving yourself problems before you even get started.

TABLE 4-2 Determining Which Cables to Use When Wiring Devices Together

If Device A Has a:	And Device B Has a:	Then Use This Cable:
Computer COM port	RJ-45 Console of router/switch	Rollover
Computer USB port	USB Console of router/switch	USB type A to 5-pin mini type B with appropriate OS drivers
Computer NIC	Switch	Straight-through
Computer NIC	Computer NIC	Crossover
Switch port	Router's Ethernet port	Straight-through
Switch port	Switch port	Crossover (check for uplink button or toggle switch to defeat this)
Router's Ethernet port	Router's Ethernet port	Crossover
Computer NIC	Router's Ethernet port	Crossover
Router's serial port	Router's serial port	Cisco serial DCE/DTE cables

Table 4-3 lists the pinouts for straight-through, crossover, and rollover cables.

TABLE 4-3 Pinouts for Different Cables

Straight-Through Cable	Crossover Cable	Rollover Cable
Pin 1 – Pin 1	Pin 1 – Pin 3	Pin 1 – Pin 8
Pin 2 – Pin 2	Pin 2 – Pin 6	Pin 2 – Pin 7
Pin 3 – Pin 3	Pin 3 – Pin 1	Pin 3 – Pin 6
Pin 4 – Pin 4	Pin 4 – Pin 4	Pin 4 – Pin 5
Pin 5 – Pin 5	Pin 5 – Pin 5	Pin 5 – Pin 4
Pin 6 – Pin 6	Pin 6 – Pin 2	Pin 6 – Pin 3
Pin 7 – Pin 7	Pin 7 – Pin 7	Pin 7 – Pin 2
Pin 8 – Pin 8	Pin 8 – Pin 8	Pin 8 – Pin 1

568A Versus 568B Cables

There are two different standards released by the EIA/TIA group about UTP wiring: 568A and 568B. Although 568B is newer and is the recommended standard, either one can be used. The difference between these two standards is pin assignments, not in the use of the different colors (see Table 4-4). The 568A standard is more compatible with voice connections and the Universal Service Order Codes (USOC) standard for telephone infrastructure in the United States. In both 568A and USOC standards, the blue and orange pairs are now on the center four pins; therefore, the colors match more closely with 568A than with the 568B standard. So, which one is preferred? Information here from the standards bodies on this matter is sketchy at best. 568B was traditionally widespread in the United States, whereas places such as Canada and Australia use a lot of 568A. However, 568A is now becoming more dominant in the United States, too.

TIP   Use 568A in new installations and 568B if connecting to an existing 568B system.

TABLE 4-4   UTP Wiring Standards

568A Standard				568B Standard			
Pin	**Color**	**Pair**	**Description**	**Pin**	**Color**	**Pair**	**Description**
1	White/green	3	RecvData +	1	White/orange	2	TxData +
2	Green	3	RecvData -	2	Orange	2	TxData -
3	White/orange	2	Txdata +	3	White/green	3	RecvData +
4	Blue	1	Unused	4	Blue	1	Unused
5	White/blue	1	Unused	5	White/blue	1	Unused
6	Orange	2	TxData -	6	Green	3	RecvData -
7	White/brown	4	Unused	7	White/brown	4	Unused
8	Brown	4	Unused	8	Brown	4	Unused

TIP   Odd pin numbers are always the striped wires.

A straight-through cable is one with both ends using the same standard (A or B). A crossover cable is one that has 568A on one end and 568B on the other end.

CHAPTER 5

The Command-Line Interface

This chapter provides information and commands concerning the following topics:

- Shortcuts for entering commands
- Using the [Tab⇆] key to enter complete commands
- Console error messages
- Using the question mark for help
- **enable** command
- **exit** command
- **disable** command
- **logout** command
- Setup mode
- Keyboard help
- History commands
- **terminal** commands
- **show** commands
- Using the pipe parameter (|) with the **show** command

Shortcuts for Entering Commands

To enhance efficiency, Cisco IOS Software has some shortcuts for entering commands. Although these are great to use in the real world, when it comes time to write a vendor exam, make sure you know the full commands, not just the shortcuts.

`Router>`**`enable`** `=` `Router>`**`enab`** `= Router>`**`en`**	Entering a shortened form of a command is sufficient as long as there is no confusion about which command you are attempting to enter.
`Router#`**`configure`** **`terminal`** `is the same` `as Router#`**`config t`**	

Using the [Tab⇆] Key to Complete Commands

When you are entering a command, you can use the [Tab⇆] key to complete the command. Enter the first few characters of a command and press the [Tab⇆] key. If the characters are unique to the command, the rest of the command is entered in for you. This is helpful if you are unsure about the spelling of a command.

```
Router#sh Tab↵ = Router#show
```

Console Error Messages

You may see three types of console error messages when working in the CLI:

- Ambiguous command
- Incomplete command
- Incorrect command

Error Message	Meaning	What to Do
% Ambiguous Command: "show con"	Not enough characters were entered to allow device to recognize the command.	Reenter the command with a question mark (?) immediately after the last character. **show con?** All possible keywords will be displayed.
% Incomplete Command	More parameters need to be entered to complete the command.	Reenter the command followed by a question mark (?). Include a space between the command and the question mark (?).
% Invalid input detected at ^ marker	The command entered has an error. The ^ marks the location of the error.	Reenter the command, correcting the error at the location of the ^. If you are unsure what the error is, reenter the command with a question mark (?) at the point of the error to display the commands or parameters available.

Using the Question Mark for Help

The following output shows you how using the question mark can help you work through a command and all its parameters.

`Router#?`	Lists all commands available in the current command mode
`Router#c? clear clock`	Lists all the possible choices that start with the letter *c*
`Router#cl? clear clock`	Lists all the possible choices that start with the letters *cl*
`Router#clock% Incomplete Command`	Tells you that more parameters need to be entered
`Router#clock ? Set`	Shows all subcommands for this command (in this case, **Set**, which sets the time and date)

`Router#clock set`
`19:50:00 14 July`
`2007 ?` ⏎Enter
	Pressing the ⏎Enter key confirms the time and date configured.

`Router#`	No error message/Incomplete command message means the command was entered successfully.

enable Command

`Router>enable` `Router#`	Moves the user from user mode to privileged mode

exit Command

`Router#exit`
or
`Router>exit`
	Logs a user off

`Router(config-if)#exit` `Router(config)#`	Moves you back one level
`Router(config)#exit` `Router#`	Moves you back one level

disable Command

`Router#disable` `Router>`	Moves you from privileged mode back to user mode

logout Command

`Router#logout`	Performs the same function as **exit**

Setup Mode

Setup mode starts automatically if there is no startup configuration present.

`Router#setup`	Enters startup mode from the command line

NOTE The answer inside the square brackets, [ ], is the default answer. If this is the answer you want, just press ⏎Enter. Pressing Ctrl-C at any time will end the setup process, shut down all interfaces, and take you to user mode (Router>).

NOTE   You *cannot* use setup mode to configure an entire router. It does only the basics. For example, you can only turn on RIPv1, but not Open Shortest Path First Protocol (OSPF) or Enhanced Interior Gateway Routing Protocol (EIGRP). You cannot create access control lists (ACL) here or enable Network Address Translation (NAT). You can assign an IP address to an interface but not to a subinterface. All in all, setup mode is very limiting.

Entering setup mode is not a recommended practice. Instead, you should use the command-line interface (CLI), which is more powerful:

Would you like to enter the initial configuration dialog? [yes]: **no**

Would you like to enable autoinstall? [yes]: **no**

Autoinstall is a feature that tries to broadcast out all interfaces when attempting to find a configuration. If you answer **yes**, you must wait for a few minutes while it looks for a configuration to load. Very frustrating. Answer **no**.

Keyboard Help

The keystrokes in the following table are meant to help you edit the configuration. Because you'll want to perform certain tasks again and again, Cisco IOS Software provides certain keystroke combinations to help make the process more efficient.

^	Shows you where you made a mistake in entering a command
```Router#confog t ^ % Invalid input detected at '^' marker. Router#config t Router(config)#```	
Ctrl-A	Moves cursor to beginning of line
Ctrl-B	Moves cursor back one word
Ctrl-B (or ←)	Moves cursor back one character
Ctrl-E	Moves cursor to end of line
Ctrl-F (or →)	Moves cursor forward one character
Ctrl-F	Moves cursor forward one word
Ctrl-⇧Shift-6	Allows the user to interrupt an IOS process such as ping or traceroute
Ctrl-Z	Moves you from any prompt back down to privileged mode
$	Indicates that the line has been scrolled to the left
```Router#terminal no editing Router#```	Turns off the ability to use the previous keyboard shortcuts
```Router#terminal editing Router#```	Reenables enhanced editing mode (can use above keyboard shortcuts)

History Commands

Ctrl-P (or ↑)	Recalls commands in the history buffer in a backward sequence, beginning with the most recent command
Ctrl-N (or ↓)	Returns to more recent commands in the history buffer after recalling commands with the Ctrl-P key sequence

terminal Commands

Router#**terminal no editing** Router#	Turns off the ability to use keyboard shortcuts.
Router#**terminal editing** Router#	Reenables enhanced editing mode (can use keyboard shortcuts).
Router#**terminal length** *x*	Sets the number of lines displayed in a **show** command to *x*, where *x* is a number between 0 and 512. The default is 24.

NOTE   The default value of the **terminal length** *x* command is 24.

NOTE   If you set the **terminal length** *x* command to zero (0), the router will not pause between screens of output.

Router#**terminal history size_** *number* See the next row for an example.	Sets the number of commands in the buffer that can be recalled by the router (maximum 256)
Router#**terminal history size 25**	Causes the router to now remember the last 25 commands in the buffer
Router#**no terminal history size 25**	Sets the history buffer back to 10 commands, which is the default

NOTE   The **history size** command provides the same function as the **terminal history size** command.

Be careful when you set the size to something larger than the default. By telling the router to keep the last 256 commands in a buffer, you are taking memory away from other parts of the router. What would you rather have: a router that remembers what you last typed in or a router that routes as efficiently as possible?

show Commands

Router#**show version**	Displays information about the current Cisco IOS Software
Router#**show flash**	Displays information about flash memory
Router#**show history**	Lists all commands in the history buffer

NOTE   The last line of output from the **show version** command tells you what the configuration register is set to.

Using the Pipe Parameter (|) with the show Command

By using a pipe (|) character in conjunction with a **show** command, you can filter out specific information that you are interested in.

`Router#show running-config	include hostname`	Displays configuration information that includes the specific word *hostname*
`Router#show running-config	section FastEthernet 0/1`	Displays configuration information about the section FastEthernet 0/1
`The Pipe Parameter (|)` `OptionsParameter`	**Description**
`begin`	Shows all output from a certain point, starting with the line that matches the filtering expression.
`Router#show running-config	begin line con 0`	Output begins with the first line that has the expression "line con 0."
`exclude`	Excludes all output lines that match the filtering expression.
`Router#show running-config	exclude interface`	Any line with the expression "interface" will not be shown as part of the output.
`include`	Includes all output lines that match the filtering expression.
`Router#show running-config	include duplex`	Any line that has the expression "duplex" will be shown as part of the output.
`section`	Shows the entire section that starts with the filtering expression.
`Router#show running-config	section interface GigabitEthernet0/0`	Displays information about interface GigabitEthernet0/0.

NOTE You can use the pipe parameter and filters with any **show** command.

NOTE The filtering expression has to match *exactly* with the output you want to filter. You cannot use shortened forms of the items you are trying to filter. For example, the command

`Router#show running-config | section gig0/0`

will not work because there is no section in the running-config called gig0/0. You must use the expression GiagbitEthernet0/0 with no spelling errors or extra spaces added in.

CHAPTER 6

Configuring a Switch

This chapter provides information and commands concerning the following topics:

- Help commands
- Command modes
- Verifying commands
- Resetting switch configuration
- Setting host names
- Setting passwords
- Setting IP addresses and default gateways
- Setting interface descriptions
- The **mdix auto** command
- Setting duplex operation
- Setting operation speed
- Managing the MAC address table
- Configuration example

Help Commands

`switch>?`	Lists all commands available in the current command mode.
	TIP The **?** works here the same as in a router.

`switch#c?`
`cd clear clock cns`
`configure`
`connect copy`
	Lists all the possible choices that start with the letter *c*.

`switch#`**show ?**	Shows all parameters for this command.

Command Modes

switch>**enable**	Moves the user from user mode to privileged mode. **TIP** This is the same command as used in a router.
switch#	Privileged mode.
switch#**disable**	Leaves privileged mode.
switch>**exit**	Leaves user mode.

Verifying Commands

switch#**show version**	Displays information about software and hardware.
switch#**show flash:**	Displays information about flash memory.
switch#**show** **mac-address-table**	Displays the current MAC address forwarding table.
switch#**show controllers** **ethernet-controller**	Displays information about the Ethernet controller.
switch#**show running-config**	Displays the current configuration in DRAM.
switch#**show startup-config**	Displays the current configuration in NVRAM.
switch#**show post**	Displays whether the switch passed POST.
switch#**show vlan**	Displays the current VLAN configuration.
switch#**show interfaces**	Displays the interface configuration and status of line: up/up, up/down, admin down.
	NOTE This command is unsupported in some Cisco IOS Software releases, such as 12.2(25)FX.
switch#**show interfaces** **vlan1**	Displays setting of virtual interface VLAN 1, the default VLAN on the switch.
	NOTE This command is unsupported in some earlier Cisco IOS Software releases, such as 12.2(25)FX.

Resetting Switch Configuration

Switch#**delete flash:vlan.dat**	Removes the VLAN database from flash memory.
Delete filename [vlan.dat]?	Press ⏎Enter).
Delete flash:vlan.dat? [confirm]	Reconfirm by pressing ⏎Enter).
Switch#**erase startup-config**	Erases the file from NVRAM.
<output omitted>	
Switch#**reload**	Restarts the switch.

Setting Host Names

Switch#**configure terminal**	Moves to global configuration mode.
Switch(config)#**hostname Switch2960**	Creates a locally significant host name of the switch. This is the same command as the router.
Switch2960(config)#	

> **TIP**   If you set a hostname that begins with a number, you receive a warning about using illegal characters. However, the switch accepts the name.
>
> Switch(config)#**hostname 2960**
>
> % Hostname contains one or more illegal characters.
>
> 2960(config)#

Setting Passwords

Setting passwords for the 2960 series switches is the same method as used for a router.

Switch2960(config)#**enable password cisco**	Sets the enable password to *cisco*
Switch2960(config)#**enable secret class**	Sets the encrypted secret password to *class*
Switch2960(config)#**line console 0**	Enters line console mode
Switch2960(config-line)#**login**	Enables password checking
Switch2960(config-line)#**password cisco**	Sets the password to *cisco*
Switch2960(config-line)#**exit**	Exits line console mode
Switch2960(config-line)#**password cisco**	Sets the password to *cisco*
Switch2960(config-line)#**line vty 0 15**	Enters line vty mode for all 15 virtual ports
Switch2960(config-line)#**login**	Enables password checking
Switch2960(config-line)#**password cisco**	Sets the password to *cisco*
Switch2960(config-line)#**exit**	Exits line vty mode
Switch2960(config)#	

Setting IP Addresses and Default Gateways

Switch2960(config)#**interface vlan1**	Enters the virtual interface for VLAN 1, the default VLAN on the switch
Switch2960(config-if)#**ip address 172.16.10.2 255.255.255.0**	Sets the IP address and netmask to allow for remote access to the switch
Switch2960(config-if)#**exit**	Returns to Global Configuration mode
Switch2960(config)#**ip default-gateway 172.16.10.1**	Allows IP information an exit past the local network

TIP   For the 2960 series switches, the IP address of the switch is just that—the IP address for the *entire* switch. That is why you set the address in VLAN 1 (the default VLAN of the switch) and not in a specific Ethernet interface. If you choose to make your management VLAN a different number, you would use these commands in that VLAN using the *interface vlan x* command, where *x* is the number of your management VLAN.

Setting Interface Descriptions

`Switch2960(config)#interface fastethernet 0/1`	Enters interface configuration mode.
`Switch2960(config-if)#description Finance VLAN`	Adds a description of the interface. The description is locally significant only.

TIP   The 2960 series switches have ports ranging from 8 to 48 Fast Ethernet ports named fa0/1, fa0/2, ... fa0/48—there is no fastethernet 0/0. This is true for the 2960G series, in which all ports are Gigabit Ethernet ports named gi0/0, gi0/2...gi0/48. Again, there is no GigabitEthernet 0/0 port.

The mdix auto Command

`Switch2960(config)#interface fastethernet 0/1`	Enters interface configuration mode
`Switch2960(config-if)#mdix auto`	Enables Auto-MDIX on the interface
`Switch2960(config-if)#no mdix auto`	Disables Auto-MDIX on the interface

TIP   When automatic medium-dependent interface crossover (Auto-MDIX) is enabled on an interface, the interface automatically detects the required cable connection type (straight-through or crossover) and configures the connection appropriately. When connecting switches without the Auto-MDIX feature, you must use straight-through cables to connect to devices such as servers, workstations, or routers and crossover cables to connect to other switches or repeaters. With Auto-MDIX enabled, you can use either type of cable to connect to other devices, and the interface automatically corrects for incorrect cabling.

TIP   The Auto-MDIX feature is enabled by default on switches running Cisco IOS Release 12.2(18)SE or later. For releases between Cisco IOS Release 12.1(14)EA1 and 12.2(18)SE, the Auto-MDIX feature is disabled by default.

TIP   If you are working on a device where Auto-MDIX is enabled by default, the command does *not* show up when you enter **show running-config**.

CAUTION   When you enable Auto-MDIX, you must also set the interface speed and duplex to auto so that the feature operates correctly. In other words, if you use Auto-MDIX to give you the flexibility to use either type of cable to connect your switches, you lose the ability to hard-set the speed/duplex on both sides of the link.

The following table shows the different link state results from Auto-MDIX settings with correct and incorrect cabling.

Local Side Auto-MDIX	Remote Side Auto-MDIX	With Correct Cabling	With Incorrect Cabling
On	On	Link up	Link up
On	Off	Link up	Link up
Off	On	Link up	Link up
Off	Off	Link up	Link down

Setting Duplex Operation

Switch2960(config)#**interface fastethernet 0/1**	Moves to interface configuration mode
Switch2960(config-if)#**duplex full**	Forces full-duplex operation
Switch2960(config-if)#**duplex auto**	Enables auto-duplex config
Switch2960(config-if)#**duplex half**	Forces half-duplex operation

Setting Operation Speed

Switch2960(config)#**interface fastethernet 0/1**	Moves to interface configuration mode
Switch2960(config-if)#**speed 10**	Forces 10-Mbps operation
Switch2960(config-if)#**speed 100**	Forces 100-Mbps operation
Switch2960(config-if)#**speed auto**	Enables autospeed configuration

Managing the MAC Address Table

switch#**show mac address-table**	Displays current MAC address forwarding table
switch#**clear mac address-table**	Deletes all entries from current MAC address forwarding table
switch#**clear mac address-table dynamic**	Deletes only dynamic entries from table

Configuration Example

Figure 6-1 shows the network topology for the basic configuration of a 2960 series switch using commands covered in this chapter.

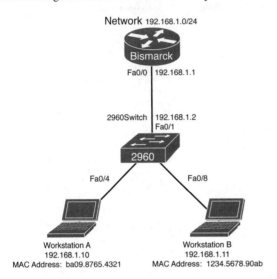

Figure 6-1 Network Topology for 2960 Series Switch Configuration

`switch>enable`	Enters privileged mode.
`switch#configure terminal`	Enters global configuration mode.
`switch(config)#no ip domain-lookup`	Turns off Domain Name System (DNS) queries so that spelling mistakes do not slow you down.
`switch(config)#hostname Switch2960`	Sets the host name.
`Switch2960(config)#enable secret cisco`	Sets the encrypted secret password to *cisco*.
`Switch2960(config)#line console 0`	Enters line console mode.
`Switch2960(config-line)#logging synchronous`	Appends commands to a new line; switch information will not interrupt.
`Switch2960(config-line)#login`	User must log in to console before use.
`Switch2960(config-line)#password switch`	Sets the console password to *switch*.
`Switch2960(config-line)#exec-timeout 0 0`	The console line will not log out because of the connection to the console being idle.

`Switch2960(config-line)#exit`	Moves back to global configuration mode.
`Switch2960(config)#line vty 0 15`	Moves to configure all 16 vty ports at the same time.
`Switch2960(config-line)#login`	User must log in to vty port before use.
`Switch2960(config-line)#password class`	Sets the vty password to *class*.
`Switch2960(config-line)#exit`	Moves back to global configuration mode.
`Switch2960(config)#ip default-gateway 192.168.1.1`	Sets default gateway address.
`Switch2960(config)#interface vlan 1`	Moves to virtual interface VLAN 1 configuration mode.
`Switch2960(config-if)#ip address 192.168.1.2 255.255.255.0`	Sets the IP address and netmask for switch.
`Switch2960(config-if)#no shutdown`	Turns the virtual interface on.
`Switch2960(config-if)#interface fastethernet 0/1`	Moves to interface configuration mode for fastethernet 0/1.
`Switch2960(config-if)#description Link to Bismarck Router`	Sets a local description.
`Switch2960(config-if)#interface fastethernet 0/4`	Moves to interface configuration mode for fastethernet 0/4.
`Switch2960(config-if)#description Link to Workstation A`	Sets a local description.
`Switch2960(config-if)#interface fastethernet 0/8`	Moves to interface configuration mode for fastethernet 0/8.
`Switch2960(config-if)#description Link to Workstation B`	Sets a local description.
`Switch2960(config-if)#exit`	Returns to global configuration mode.
`Switch2960(config)#exit`	Returns to privileged mode.
`Switch2960#copy running-config startup-config`	Saves the configuration to NVRAM.
`Switch2960#`	

CHAPTER 7

VLANs

This chapter provides information and commands concerning the following topics:

- Creating static VLANs
    - Using VLAN configuration mode
    - Using VLAN database mode
- Assigning ports to VLANs
- Using the **range** command
- Configuring a voice VLAN
    - Configuring voice and data with trust
    - Configuring voice and data without trust
- Verifying VLAN information
- Saving VLAN configurations
- Erasing VLAN configurations
- Configuration example: VLANs

Creating Static VLANs

Static VLANs occur when a switch port is manually assigned by the network administrator to belong to a VLAN. Each port is associated with a specific VLAN. By default, all ports are originally assigned to VLAN 1. You can create VLANs in two different ways:

- Using the VLAN configuration mode, which is the recommended way to create VLANs
- Using the VLAN database mode (which should not be used but is still available on some older models)

Using VLAN Configuration Mode

Switch(config)#**vlan 3**	Creates VLAN 3 and enters VLAN configuration mode for further definitions.
Switch(config-vlan)#**name Engineering**	Assigns a name to the VLAN. The length of the name can be from 1 to 32 characters.
Switch(config-vlan)#**exit**	Applies changes, increases the revision number by 1, and returns to global configuration mode.
Switch(config)#	

NOTE   This method is the only way to configure extended-range VLANs (VLAN IDs from 1006 to 4094).

NOTE   VLANs 1006 to 4094 can only be created in transparent mode.

NOTE   Regardless of the method used to create VLANs, the VLAN Trunking Protocol (VTP) revision number is increased by 1 each time a VLAN is created or changed.

NOTE   Transparent mode does not increment the VTP revision number.

Using VLAN Database Mode

CAUTION   The VLAN database mode has been deprecated and will be removed in some future Cisco IOS Software release. It is recommended to use only VLAN configuration mode.

Switch#**vlan database**	Enters VLAN database mode.
Switch(vlan)#**vlan 4 name Sales**	Creates VLAN 4 and names it Sales. The length of the name can be from 1 to 32 characters.
Switch(vlan)#**vlan 10**	Creates VLAN 10 and gives it a name of VLAN0010 as a default.
Switch(vlan)#**apply**	Applies changes to the VLAN database and increases the revision number by 1.
Switch(vlan)#**exit**	Applies changes to the VLAN database, increases the revision number by 1, *and* exits VLAN database mode.
Switch#	

NOTE   You must apply the changes to the VLAN database for the changes to take effect. You must use either the **apply** command or the **exit** command to do so. Using the Ctrl-Z command to exit out of the VLAN database does not work in this mode because it aborts all changes made to the VLAN database—you must either use **exit** or **apply** and then the **exit** command.

Assigning Ports to VLANs

`Switch(config)#interface fastethernet 0/1`	Moves to interface configuration mode
`Switch(config-if)#switchport mode access`	Sets the port to access mode
`Switch(config-if)#switchport access vlan 10`	Assigns this port to VLAN 10

NOTE   When you use the **switchport mode access** command, the port operates as a nontrunking, single VLAN interface.

TIP   An access port can belong to only one data VLAN.

TIP   By default, all ports are members of VLAN 1.

Using the range Command

`Switch(config)#interface range fastethernet 0/1 - 9`	Enables you to set the same configuration parameters on multiple ports at the same time.
	NOTE Depending on the model of switch, there is a space before and after the hyphen in the **interface range** command. Be careful with your typing.
`Switch(config-if-range)#switchport mode access`	Sets ports 1 to 9 as access ports.
`Switch(config-if-range)#switchport access vlan 10`	Assigns ports 1 to 9 to VLAN 10.

Configuring a Voice VLAN

The voice VLAN feature permits switch ports to carry voice traffic with Layer 3 precedence and Layer 2 class of service (CoS) values from an IP Phone.

You can configure the switch port, which is connected to an IP Phone, to use one VLAN for voice traffic and another VLAN for data traffic originating from a device that is connected to the access port of the IP Phone.

Cisco switches use Cisco Discovery Protocol (CDP) packets to communicate with the IP Phone. CDP must be enabled on any switch port that is to be connected to an IP Phone.

NOTE   Voice VLANs are disabled by default.

NOTE   By default, a switch port drops any tagged frames in hardware.

Configuring Voice and Data with Trust

NOTE   This configuration is used for Cisco IP Phones that trust data traffic using CoS coming from the laptop or PC connected to the IP Phone's access port. Data traffic uses the native VLAN.

`Switch#configure terminal`	Enters global configuration mode.
`Switch(config)#mls qos`	Enables QoS functionality globally.
`Switch(config)#interface` `fastethernet 0/6`	Moves to interface configuration mode.
`Switch(config-if)#mls qos` `trust cos`	Has the interface enter into a state of trust and classifies traffic by examining the incoming Class of Service (CoS).
`Switch(config-if)#mls qos` `trust dscp`	Has the interface enter into a state of trust and classifies traffic by examining the incoming Differentiated Services Code Point (DSCP) value.

`Switch(config-if)`
`#switchport voice vlan`
`dot1p`
	Instructs the switch to use the IEEE 802.1p priority tagging to forward all voice traffic with a higher priority through the native (access) VLAN.

`Switch(config-if)` `#switchport voice vlan 10`	Configures voice VLAN 10.

`Switch(config-if)`
`#switchport priority extend`
`trust`
	Extends the trust state to the device (PC) connected to the access port of the IP Phone.
	
	The switch instructs the phone on how to process data packets from the device (PC) connected to the phone.

`Switch(config-if)` `#priority-queue out`	Gives voice packets head-of-line privileges when trying to exit the port. This helps prevent jitter.
`Switch(config-if)` `#spanning-tree portfast`	Enables PortFast on the interface, which removes the interface from the Spanning Tree Protocol (STP).

`Switch(config-if)`
`#spanning-tree bpduguard`
`enable`
	Enables bridge protocol data unit (BPDU) Guard on the interface.

`Switch(config-if)#exit`	Exits interface configuration mode and returns to global configuration mode.
`Switch(config)#`	

Configuring Voice and Data Without Trust

NOTE   This configuration is used for Cisco IP Phones without trusting the laptop or PC connected to the IP Phone's access port. Data traffic uses the 802.1Q frame type.

`Switch#configure terminal`	Enters global configuration mode.
`Switch(config)#mls qos`	Enables QoS functionality globally.
`Switch(config)#interface fastethernet 0/8`	Moves to interface configuration mode.
`Switch(config-if)#mls qos trust cos`	Has the interface enter into a state of trust and classifies traffic by examining the incoming Class of Service (CoS) value.
`Switch(config-if)#mls qos trust dscp`	Has the interface enter into a state of trust and classifies traffic by examining the incoming Differentiated Services Code Point (DSCP) value.
`Switch(config-if) #switchport voice vlan 10`	Configures voice VLAN 10.
`Switch(config-if) #switchport access vlan 20`	Configures data VLAN 20.
`Switch(config-if) #priority-queue out`	Gives voice packets head-of-line privileges when trying to exit the port. This helps prevent jitter.
`Switch(config-if) #spanning-tree portfast`	Enables PortFast on the interface, which removes the interface from the Spanning Tree Protocol (STP).
`Switch(config-if) #spanning-tree bpduguard enable`	Enables BPDU Guard on the interface.
`Switch(config-if)#exit`	Exits interface configuration mode and returns to global configuration mode.
`Switch(config)#`	

Verifying VLAN Information

`Switch#show vlan`	Displays VLAN information
`Switch#show vlan brief`	Displays VLAN information in brief
`Switch#show vlan id 2`	Displays information about VLAN 2 only
`Switch#show vlan name marketing`	Displays information about VLAN named marketing only
`Switch#show interfaces vlan x`	Displays interface characteristics for the specified VLAN
`Switch#show interfaces switchport`	Displays VLAN information for all interfaces
`Switch#show interfaces fastethernet 0/6 switchport`	Displays VLAN information (including voice VLAN information) for the specified interface

Saving VLAN Configurations

The configurations of VLANs 1 to 1005 are always saved in the VLAN database. As long as the **apply** or the **exit** command is executed in VLAN database mode, changes are saved. If you are using VLAN configuration mode, the **exit** command saves the changes to the VLAN database, too.

If the VLAN database configuration is used at startup, and the startup configuration file contains extended-range VLAN configuration, this information is lost when the system boots.

If you are using VTP transparent mode, the configurations are also saved in the running configuration and can be saved to the startup configuration using the **copy running-config startup-config** command.

If the VTP mode is transparent in the startup configuration, and the VLAN database and the VTP domain name from the VLAN database match that in the startup configuration file, the VLAN database is ignored (cleared), and the VTP and VLAN configurations in the startup configuration file are used. The VLAN database revision number remains unchanged in the VLAN database.

Erasing VLAN Configurations

`Switch#`**`delete flash:vlan.dat`**	Removes the entire VLAN database from flash.

	CAUTION Make sure there is *no* space between the colon (:) and the characters *vlan.dat*. You can potentially erase the entire contents of the flash with this command if the syntax is not correct. Make sure you read the output from the switch. If you need to cancel, press Ctrl-C to escape back to privileged mode:
	
	`(Switch#)`
	`Switch#`**`delete flash:vlan.dat`**
	`Delete filename [vlan.dat]?`
	`Delete flash:vlan.dat? [confirm]`
	`Switch#`

`Switch(config)#`**`interface fastethernet 0/5`**	Moves to interface configuration mode.
`Switch(config-if)#`**`no switchport access vlan 5`**	Removes port from VLAN 5 and reassigns it to VLAN 1—the default VLAN.
`Switch(config-if)#`**`exit`**	Moves to global configuration mode.
`Switch(config)#`**`no vlan 5`**	Removes VLAN 5 from the VLAN database.
`Or`	
`Switch#`**`vlan database`**	Enters VLAN database mode.
`Switch(vlan)#`**`no vlan 5`**	Removes VLAN 5 from the VLAN database.
`Switch(vlan)#`**`exit`**	Applies changes, increases the revision number by 1, and exits VLAN database mode.

NOTE   When you delete a VLAN from a switch that is in VTP server mode, the VLAN is removed from the VLAN database for all switches in the VTP domain. When you delete a VLAN from a switch that is in VTP transparent mode, the VLAN is deleted only on that specific switch.

NOTE   You cannot delete the default VLANs for the different media types: Ethernet VLAN 1 and FDDI or Token Ring VLANs 1002 to 1005.

CAUTION   When you delete a VLAN, any ports assigned to that VLAN become inactive. They remain associated with the VLAN (and thus inactive) until you assign them to a new VLAN. Therefore, it is recommended that you reassign ports to a new VLAN or the default VLAN before you delete a VLAN from the VLAN database.

Configuration Example: VLANs

Figure 7-1 illustrates the network topology for the configuration that follows, which shows how to configure VLANs using the commands covered in this chapter.

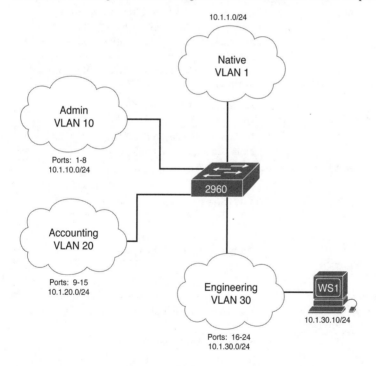

Figure 7-1   Network Topology for VLAN Configuration Example

2960 Switch

`Switch>enable`	Moves to privileged mode.
`Switch#configure terminal`	Moves to global configuration mode.
`Switch(config)#hostname Switch2960`	Sets the host name.
`Switch2960(config)#vlan 10`	Creates VLAN 10 and enters VLAN configuration mode.
`Switch2960(config-vlan) #name Admin`	Assigns a name to the VLAN.
`Switch2960(config-vlan)#exit`	Increases the revision number by 1 and returns to global configuration mode.
`Switch2960(config)#vlan 20`	Creates VLAN 20 and enters VLAN configuration mode.
`Switch2960(config-vlan)#name Accounting`	Assigns a name to the VLAN.
`Switch2960(config-vlan) #vlan 30`	Creates VLAN 30 and enters VLAN configuration mode. Note that you do not have to exit back to global configuration mode to execute this command. This also increases the revision number by 1 because you moved from VLAN 20 to VLAN 30.
`Switch2960(config-vlan) #name Engineering`	Assigns a name to the VLAN.
`Switch2960(config-vlan)#exit`	Increases the revision number by 1 and returns to global configuration mode.
`Switch2960(config)#interface range fasthethernet 0/1 - 8`	Enables you to set the same configuration parameters on multiple ports at the same time.
`Switch2960(config-if-range)#switchport mode access`	Sets ports 1 to 8 as access ports.
`Switch2960(config-if-range)#switchport access vlan 10`	Assigns ports 1 to 8 to VLAN 10.
`Switch2960(config-if-range)#interface range fastethernet 0/9 - 15`	Enables you to set the same configuration parameters on multiple ports at the same time.
`Switch2960(config-if-range)#switchport mode access`	Sets ports 9 to 15 as access ports.
`Switch2960(config-if-range)#switchport access vlan 20`	Assigns ports 9 to 15 to VLAN 20.
`Switch2960(config-if-range)#interface range fastethernet 0/16 - 24`	Enables you to set the same configuration parameters on multiple ports at the same time.

`Switch2960(config-if-range)#`**`switchport mode access`**	Sets ports 16 to 24 as access ports.
`Switch2960(config-if-range)#`**`switchport access vlan 30`**	Assigns ports 16 to 24 to VLAN 30.
`Switch2960(config-if-range)#`**`exit`**	Returns to global configuration mode.
`Switch2960(config)#`**`exit`**	Returns to privileged mode.
`Switch2960#`**`copy running-config startup-config`**	Saves the configuration in NVRAM.

CHAPTER 8

VLAN Trunking Protocol and Inter-VLAN Communication

This chapter provides information and commands concerning the following topics:

- Dynamic Trunking Protocol (DTP)
- Setting the VLAN encapsulation type
- VLAN Trunking Protocol (VTP)
- Verifying VTP
- Inter-VLAN communication using an external router: router-on-a-stick
- Inter-VLAN communication on a multilayer switch through a switch virtual interface (SVI)
- Remove L2 switchport capability of an interface on an L3 switch
- Configuring Inter-VLAN communication on an L3 switch
- Inter-VLAN communication tips
- Configuration example: Inter-VLAN communication

Dynamic Trunking Protocol (DTP)

`Switch(config)#interface fastethernet 0/1`	Moves to interface configuration mode.
`Switch(config-if)#switchport mode dynamic desirable`	Makes the interface actively attempt to convert the link to a trunk link.
	NOTE With the **switchport mode dynamic desirable** command set, the interface becomes a trunk link if the neighboring interface is set to **trunk, desirable,** or **auto.**
`Switch(config-if)#switchport mode dynamic auto`	Makes the interface able to convert into a trunk link.
	NOTE With the **switchport mode dynamic auto** command set, the interface becomes a trunk link if the neighboring interface is set to **trunk** or **desirable.**
`Switch(config-if)#switchport nonegotiate`	Prevents the interface from generating DTP frames.
	NOTE Use the **switchport mode nonegotiate** command only when the interface switchport mode is **access** or **trunk.** You must manually configure the neighboring interface to establish a trunk link.

| Switch(config-if)#**switchport mode trunk** | Puts the interface into permanent trunking mode and negotiates to convert the link into a trunk link. |
| | **NOTE**   With the **switchport mode trunk** command set, the interface becomes a trunk link even if the neighboring interface is not a trunk link. |

TIP   The default mode is dependent on the platform. For the 2960, the default mode is dynamic auto.

TIP   On a 2960 switch, the default for all ports is to be an access port. However, with the default DTP mode being dynamic auto, an access port can be converted into a trunk port if that port receives DTP information from the other side of the link if that other side is set to **trunk** or **desirable**. It is therefore recommended that you hard-code all access ports as access ports with the **switchport mode access** command. This way, DTP information will not inadvertently change an access port to a trunk port. Any port set with the **switchport mode access** command ignores any DTP requests to convert the link.

TIP   VLAN Trunking Protocol (VTP) domain names must match for a DTP to negotiate a trunk.

Setting the VLAN Encapsulation Type

Depending on the series of switch that you are using, you might have a choice as to what type of VLAN encapsulation you want to use: the Cisco proprietary Inter-Switch Link (ISL) or the IEEE Standard 802.1Q (dot1q). The 2960 switch supports only dot1q trunking.

CAUTION   Cisco ISL has been deprecated. Depending on the age and model of your Cisco switch, you may be able to change the encapsulation type between dot1q and ISL.

Switch3560(config)#**interface fastethernet 0/1**	Moves to interface configuration mode
Switch3560(config-if)#**switchport mode trunk**	Puts the interface into permanent trunking mode and negotiates to convert the link into a trunk link
Switch3560(config-if)#**switchport trunk encapsulation isl**	Specifies ISL encapsulation on the trunk link
Switch3560(config-if)#**switchport trunk encapsulation dot1q**	Specifies 802.1q tagging on the trunk link
Switch3560(config-if)#**switchport trunk encapsulation negotiate**	Specifies that the interface negotiate with the neighboring interface to become either an ISL or dot1q trunk, depending on the capabilities or configuration of the neighboring interface

TIP   With the **switchport trunk encapsulation negotiate** command set, the preferred trunking method is ISL.

CAUTION   Both the 2960 and the 2960-x series of switches support only dot1q trunking.

VLAN Trunking Protocol (VTP)

VTP is a Cisco proprietary protocol that allows for VLAN configuration (addition, deletion, or renaming of VLANs) to be consistently maintained across a common administrative domain.

Switch(config)#**vtp mode client**	Changes the switch to VTP client mode.
Switch(config)#**vtp mode server**	Changes the switch to VTP server mode.
Switch(config)#**vtp mode transparent**	Changes the switch to VTP transparent mode.
	NOTE By default, all Catalyst switches are in server mode.
Switch(config)#**no vtp mode**	Returns the switch to the default VTP server mode.
Switch(config)#**vtp domain** *domain-name*	Configures the VTP domain name. The name can be from 1 to 32 characters long.
	NOTE All switches operating in VTP server or client mode must have the same domain name to ensure communication.
Switch(config)#**vtp password** *password*	Configures a VTP password. In Cisco IOS Software Release 12.3 and later, the password is an ASCII string from 1 to 32 characters long. If you are using a Cisco IOS Software release earlier than 12.3, the password length ranges from 8 to 64 characters long.
	NOTE To communicate with each other, all switches must have the same VTP password set.
Switch(config)#**vtp v2-mode**	Sets the VTP domain to Version 2. This command is for Cisco IOS Software Release 12.3 and later. If you are using a Cisco IOS Software release earlier than 12.3, the command is **vtp version 2**.
	NOTE VTP Versions 1 and 2 are not interoperable. All switches must use the same version. The biggest difference between Versions 1 and 2 is that Version 2 has support for Token Ring VLANs.
Switch(config)#**vtp pruning**	Enables VTP pruning.
	NOTE By default, VTP pruning is disabled. You need to enable VTP pruning on only 1 switch in VTP server mode.

NOTE   Only VLANs included in the pruning-eligible list can be pruned. VLANs 2 through 1001 are pruning eligible by default on trunk ports. Reserved VLANs and extended-range VLANs cannot be pruned. To change which eligible VLANs can be pruned, use the interface-specific **switchport trunk pruning vlan** command:

```
Switch(config-if)#switchport trunk pruning vlan remove 4,20-30
! Removes VLANs 4 and 20-30
Switch(config-if)#switchport trunk pruning vlan except 40-50
! All VLANs are added to the pruning list except for 40-50
```

Verifying VTP

Switch#**show vtp status**	Displays general information about VTP configuration
Switch#**show vtp counters**	Displays the VTP counters for the switch

NOTE   If trunking has been established before VTP is set up, VTP information is propagated throughout the switch fabric almost immediately. However, because VTP information is advertised only every 300 seconds (5 minutes), unless a change has been made to force an update, it can take several minutes for VTP information to be propagated.

Inter-VLAN Communication Using an External Router: Router-on-a-Stick

Router(config)#**interface fastethernet 0/0**	Moves to interface configuration mode.
Router(config-if)#**duplex full**	Sets the interface to full duplex.
Router(config-if)#**no shutdown**	Enables the interface.
Router(config-if)#**interface fastethernet 0/0.1**	Creates subinterface 0/0.1 and moves to subinterface configuration mode.
Router(config-subif)#**description Management VLAN 1**	(Optional) Sets the locally significant description of the subinterface.
Router(config-subif)#**encapsulation dot1q 1 native**	Assigns VLAN 1 to this subinterface. VLAN 1 will be the native VLAN. This subinterface uses the 802.1q tagging protocol.
Router(config-subif)#**ip address 192.168.1.1 255.255.255.0**	Assigns the IP address and netmask.
Router(config-subif)#**interface fastethernet 0/0.10**	Creates subinterface 0/0.10 and moves to subinterface configuration mode.
Router(config-subif)#**description Accounting VLAN 10**	(Optional) Sets the locally significant description of the subinterface.
Router(config-subif)#**encapsulation dot1q 10**	Assigns VLAN 10 to this subinterface. This subinterface uses the 802.1q tagging protocol.
Router(config-subif)#**ip address 192.168.10.1 255.255.255.0**	Assigns the IP address and netmask.

`Router(config-subif)#exit`	Returns to interface configuration mode.
`Router(config-if)#exit`	Returns to global configuration mode.
`Router(config)#`	

NOTE   The networks of the VLANs are directly connected to the router. Routing between these networks does not require a dynamic routing protocol. In a more complex topology, these routes need to either be advertised with whatever dynamic routing protocol is being used or be redistributed into whatever dynamic routing protocol is being used.

NOTE   Routes to the networks associated with these VLANs appear in the routing table as directly connected networks.

NOTE   In production environments, VLAN 1 should not be used as the management VLAN because it poses a potential security risk; all ports are in VLAN 1 by default, and it is an easy mistake to add a nonmanagement user to the management VLAN.

Inter-VLAN Communication on a Multilayer Switch Through a Switch Virtual Interface

NOTE   Rather than using an external router to provide inter-VLAN communication, a multilayer switch can perform the same task through the use of a switched virtual interface (SVI).

Remove L2 Switchport Capability of an Interface on an L3 Switch

`Switch3750(config)#interface fastethernet 0/1`	Moves to interface configuration mode.
`Switch3750(config-if)#no switchport`	Creates a Layer 3 port on the switch.
	NOTE You can use the **no switchport** command on physical ports only on a Layer 3-capable switch.

Configuring Inter-VLAN Communication on an L3 Switch

`Switch3560(config)#interface vlan 1`	Creates a virtual interface for VLAN 1 and enters interface configuration mode
`Switch3560(config-if)#ip address 172.16.1.1 255.255.255.0`	Assigns IP address and netmask
`Switch3560(config-if)#no shutdown`	Enables the interface
`Switch3560(config)#interface vlan 10`	Creates a virtual interface for VLAN 10 and enters interface configuration mode
`Switch3560(config-if)#ip address 172.16.10.1 255.255.255.0`	Assigns an IP address and netmask
`Switch3560(config-if)#no shutdown`	Enables the interface

`Switch3560(config)#interface vlan 20`	Creates a virtual interface for VLAN 20 and enters interface configuration mode
`Switch3560(config-if)#ip address` `172.16.20.1 255.255.255.0`	Assigns an IP address and netmask
`Switch3560(config-if)#no shutdown`	Enables the interface
`Switch3560(config-if)#exit`	Returns to global configuration mode
`Switch3560(config)#ip routing`	Enables routing on the switch

NOTE For an SVI to go to up/up and be added to the routing table, the VLAN for the SVI must be created, an IP address must be assigned, and at least one interface must support it.

Inter-VLAN Communication Tips

- Although most routers (routers running IOS 12.2 and earlier) support both ISL and dot1q, some switch models support only dot1q, such as the 2960 and 2960-x series. Check with the version of IOS you are using to determine whether ISL or dot1q is supported.

- If you need to use ISL as your trunking protocol, use the command **encapsulation isl** *x*, where *x* is the number of the VLAN to be assigned to that subinterface.

- Recommended best practice is to use the same number of the VLAN number for the subinterface number. It is easier to troubleshoot VLAN 10 on subinterface fa0/0.10 than on fa0/0.2.

- The native VLAN (usually VLAN 1) cannot be configured on a subinterface for Cisco IOS Software releases that are earlier than 12.1(3)T. Therefore, native VLAN IP addresses must be configured on the physical interface. Other VLAN traffic is configured on subinterfaces:

  ```
  Router(config)#interface fastethernet 0/0
  Router(config-if)#encapsulation dot1q 1 native
  Router(config-if)#ip address 192.168.1.1 255.255.255.0
  Router(config-if)#interface fastethernet 0/0.10
  Router(config-subif)#encapsulation dot1q 10
  Router(config-subif)#ip address 192.168.10.1 255.255.255.0
  ```

Configuration Example: Inter-VLAN Communication

Figure 8-1 illustrates the network topology for the configuration that follows, which shows how to configure inter-VLAN communication using commands covered in this chapter. Some commands used in this configuration are from other chapters.

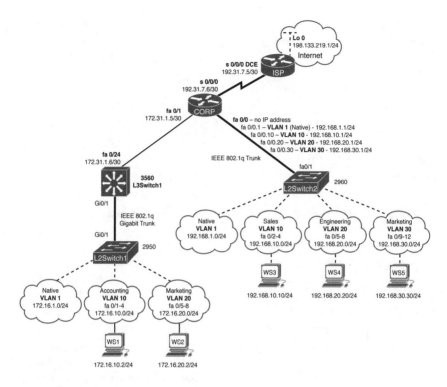

Figure 8-1 Network Topology for Inter-VLAN Communication Configuration

ISP Router

Router>**enable**	Moves to privileged mode
Router>#**configure terminal**	Moves to global configuration mode
Router(config)#**hostname ISP**	Sets the host name
ISP(config)#**interface loopback 0**	Moves to interface configuration mode
ISP(config-if)#**description simulated address representing remote website**	Sets the locally significant interface description
ISP(config-if)#**ip address 198.133.219.1 255.255.255.0**	Assigns an IP address and netmask
ISP(config-if)#**interface serial 0/0/0**	Moves to interface configuration mode
ISP(config-if)#**description WAN link to the Corporate Router**	Sets the locally significant interface description
ISP(config-if)#**ip address 192.31.7.5 255.255.255.252**	Assigns an IP address and netmask
ISP(config-if)#**clock rate 56000**	Assigns a clock rate to the interface; DCE cable is plugged into this interface
ISP(config-if)#**no shutdown**	Enables the interface

ISP(config-if)#**exit**	Returns to global configuration mode
ISP(config-if)#**router eigrp 10**	Creates Enhanced Interior Gateway Routing Protocol (EIGRP) routing process 10
ISP(config-router)#**network 198.133.219.0**	Advertises directly connected networks (classful address only)
ISP(config-router)#**network 192.31.7.0**	Advertises directly connected networks (classful address only)
ISP(config-router)#**no auto-summary**	Disables automatic summarization
ISP(config-router)#**exit**	Returns to global configuration mode
ISP(config)#**exit**	Returns to privileged mode
ISP#**copy running-config startup-config**	Saves the configuration to NVRAM

CORP Router

Router>**enable**	Moves to privileged mode.
Router>#**configure terminal**	Moves to global configuration mode.
Router(config)#**hostname CORP**	Sets the host name.
CORP(config)#**no ip domain-lookup**	Turns off DomainName System (DNS) resolution to avoid wait time due to DNS lookup of spelling errors.
CORP(config)#**interface serial 0/0/0**	Moves to interface configuration mode.
CORP(config-if)#**description link to ISP**	Sets the locally significant interface description.
CORP(config-if)#**ip address 192.31.7.6 255.255.255.252**	Assigns an IP address and netmask.
CORP(config-if)#**no shutdown**	Enables the interface.
CORP(config)#**interface fastethernet 0/1**	Moves to interface configuration mode.
CORP(config-if)#**description link to 3560 Switch**	Sets the locally significant interface description.
CORP(config-if)#**ip address 172.31.1.5 255.255.255.252**	Assigns an IP address and netmask.
CORP(config-if)#**no shutdown**	Enables the interface.
CORP(config-if)#**exit**	Returns to global configuration mode.
CORP(config)#**interface fastethernet 0/0**	Enters interface configuration mode.
CORP(config-if)#**duplex full**	Enables full-duplex operation to ensure trunking takes effect between here and L2Switch2.
CORP(config-if)#**no shutdown**	Enables the interface.

`CORP(config-if)#interface` `fastethernet 0/0.1`	Creates a virtual subinterface and moves to subinterface configuration mode.
`CORP(config-subif)#description` `Management VLAN 1 - Native VLAN`	Sets the locally significant interface description.
`CORP(config-subif)#encapsulation` `dot1q 1 native`	Assigns VLAN 1 to this subinterface. VLAN 1 is the native VLAN. This subinterface uses the 802.1q trunking protocol.
`CORP(config-subif)#ip address` `192.168.1.1 255.255.255.0`	Assigns an IP address and netmask.
`CORP(config-subif)#interface` `fastethernet 0/0.10`	Creates a virtual subinterface and moves to subinterface configuration mode.
`CORP(config-subif)#description` `Sales VLAN 10`	Sets the locally significant interface description.
`CORP(config-subif)#encapsulation` `dot1q 10`	Assigns VLAN 10 to this subinterface. This subinterface uses the 802.1q tagging protocol.
`CORP(config-subif)#ip address` `192.168.10.1 255.255.255.0`	Assigns an IP address and netmask.
`CORP(config-subif)#interface` `fastethernet 0/0.20`	Creates a virtual subinterface and moves to subinterface configuration mode.
`CORP(config-subif)#description` `Engineering VLAN 20`	Sets the locally significant interface description.
`CORP(config-subif)#encapsulation` `dot1q 20`	Assigns VLAN 20 to this subinterface. This subinterface uses the 802.1q tagging protocol.
`CORP(config-subif)#ip address` `192.168.20.1 255.255.255.0`	Assigns an IP address and netmask.
`CORP(config-subif)#interface` `fastethernet 0/0.30`	Creates a virtual subinterface and moves to subinterface configuration mode.
`CORP(config-subif)#description` `Marketing VLAN 30`	Sets the locally significant interface description.
`CORP(config-subif)#encapsulation` `dot1q 30`	Assigns VLAN 30 to this subinterface. This subinterface uses the 802.1q tagging protocol.
`CORP(config-subif)#ip add 192.168.30.1` `255.255.255.0`	Assigns an IP address and netmask.
`CORP(config-subif)#exit`	Returns to interface configuration mode.
`CORP(config-if)#exit`	Returns to global configuration mode.

CORP(config)#router eigrp 10	Creates EIGRP routing process 10 and moves to router configuration mode.
CORP(config-router)#network 192.168.1.0	Advertises the 192.168.1.0 network.
CORP(config-router)#network 192.168.10.0	Advertises the 192.168.10.0 network.
CORP(config-router)#network 192.168.20.0	Advertises the 192.168.20.0 network.
CORP(config-router)#network 192.168.30.0	Advertises the 192.168.30.0 network.
CORP(config-router)#network 172.31.0.0	Advertises the 172.31.0.0 network.
CORP(config-router)#network 192.31.7.0	Advertises the 192.31.7.0 network.
CORP(config-router)#no auto-summary	Turns off automatic summarization at classful boundary.
CORP(config-router)#exit	Returns to global configuration mode.
CORP(config)#exit	Returns to privileged mode.
CORP#copy running-config startup-config	Saves the configuration in NVRAM.

L2Switch2 (Catalyst 2960)

Switch>enable	Moves to privileged mode.
Switch#configure terminal	Moves to global configuration mode.
Switch(config)#hostname L2Switch2	Sets the host name.
L2Switch2(config)#no ip domain-lookup	Turns off DNS resolution.
L2Switch2(config)#vlan 10	Creates VLAN 10 and enters VLAN-configuration mode.
L2Switch2(config-vlan)#name Sales	Assigns a name to the VLAN.
L2Switch2(config-vlan)#exit	Returns to global configuration mode.
L2Switch2(config)#vlan 20	Creates VLAN 20 and enters VLAN configuration mode.
L2Switch2(config-vlan)#name Engineering	Assigns a name to the VLAN.
L2Switch2(config-vlan)#vlan 30	Creates VLAN 30 and enters VLAN configuration mode. Note that you do not have to exit back to global configuration mode to execute this command.
L2Switch2(config-vlan)#name Marketing	Assigns a name to the VLAN.
L2Switch2(config-vlan)#exit	Returns to global configuration mode.
L2Switch2(config)#interface range fastethernet 0/2 - 4	Enables you to set the same configuration parameters on multiple ports at the same time.

`L2Switch2(config-if-range)#switchport mode access`	Sets ports 2 to 4 as access ports.
`L2Switch2(config-if-range)#switchport access vlan 10`	Assigns ports 2 to 4 to VLAN 10.
`L2Switch2(config-if-range)#interface range fastethernet 0/5 - 8`	Enables you to set the same configuration parameters on multiple ports at the same time.
`L2Switch2(config-if-range)#switchport mode access`	Sets ports 5 to 8 as access ports.
`L2Switch2(config-if-range)#switchport access vlan 20`	Assigns ports 5 to 8 to VLAN 20.
`L2Switch2(config-if-range)#interface range fastethernet 0/9 - 12`	Enables you to set the same configuration parameters on multiple ports at the same time.
`L2Switch2(config-if-range)#switchport mode access`	Sets ports 9 to 12 as access ports.
`L2Switch2(config-if-range)#switchport access vlan 30`	Assigns ports 9 to 12 to VLAN 30.
`L2Switch2(config-if-range)#exit`	Returns to global configuration mode.
`L2Switch2(config)#interface fastethernet 0/1`	Moves to interface configuration mode.
`L2Switch2(config)#description Trunk Link to CORP Router`	Sets the locally significant interface description.
`L2Switch2(config-if)#switchport mode trunk`	Puts the interface into trunking mode and negotiates to convert the link into a trunk link.
`L2Switch2(config-if)#exit`	Returns to global configuration mode.
`L2Switch2(config)#interface vlan 1`	Creates a virtual interface for VLAN 1 and enters interface configuration mode.
`L2Switch2(config-if)#ip address 192.168.1.2 255.255.255.0`	Assigns an IP address and netmask.
`L2Switch2(config-if)#no shutdown`	Enables the interface.
`L2Switch2(config-if)#exit`	Returns to global configuration mode.
`L2Switch2(config)#ip default-gateway 192.168.1.1`	Assigns a default gateway address.
`L2Switch2(config)#exit`	Returns to privileged mode.
`L2Switch2#copy running-config startup-config`	Saves the configuration in NVRAM.

L3Switch1 (Catalyst 3560)

`Switch>enable`	Moves to privileged mode
`Switch#configure terminal`	Moves to global configuration mode
`Switch(config)#hostname L3Switch1`	Sets the hostname
`L3Switch1(config)#no ip domain-lookup`	Turns off DNS queries so that spelling mistakes do not slow you down
`L3Switch1(config)#vtp mode server`	Changes the switch to VTP server mode
`L3Switch1(config)#vtp domain testdomain`	Configures the VTP domain name to *testdomain*
`L3Switch1(config)#vlan 10`	Creates VLAN 10 and enters VLAN configuration mode
`L3Switch1(config-vlan)#name Accounting`	Assigns a name to the VLAN
`L3Switch1(config-vlan)#exit`	Returns to global configuration mode
`L3Switch1(config)#vlan 20`	Creates VLAN 20 and enters VLAN configuration mode
`L3Switch1(config-vlan)#name Marketing`	Assigns a name to the VLAN
`L3Switch1(config-vlan)#exit`	Returns to global configuration mode
`L3Switch1(config)#interface gigabitethernet 0/1`	Moves to interface configuration mode
`L3Switch1(config-if)#switchport trunk encapsulation dot1q`	Specifies 802.1q tagging on the trunk link
`L3Switch1(config-if)#switchport mode trunk`	Puts the interface into trunking mode and negotiates to convert the link into a trunk link
`L3Switch1(config-if)#exit`	Returns to global configuration mode
`L3Switch1(config)#ip routing`	Enables IP routing on this device
`L3Switch1(config)#interface vlan 1`	Creates a virtual interface for VLAN 1 and enters interface configuration mode
`L3Switch1(config-if)#ip address 172.16.1.1 255.255.255.0`	Assigns an IP address and netmask
`L3Switch1(config-if)#no shutdown`	Enables the interface
`L3Switch1(config-if)#interface vlan 10`	Creates a virtual interface for VLAN 10 and enters interface configuration mode
`L3Switch1(config-if)#ip address 172.16.10.1 255.255.255.0`	Assigns an IP address and mask
`L3Switch1(config-if)#no shutdown`	Enables the interface
`L3Switch1(config-if)#interface vlan 20`	Creates a virtual interface for VLAN 20 and enters interface configuration mode
`L3Switch1(config-if)#ip address 172.16.20.1 255.255.255.0`	Assigns an IP address and mask

`L3Switch1(config-if)#no shutdown`	Enables the interface
`L3Switch1(config-if)#exit`	Returns to global configuration mode
`L3Switch1(config)#interface fastethernet 0/24`	Enters interface configuration mode
`L3Switch1(config-if)#no switchport`	Creates a Layer 3 port on the switch
`L3Switch1(config-if)#ip address 172.31.1.6 255.255.255.252`	Assigns an IP address and netmask
`L3Switch1(config-if)#exit`	Returns to global configuration mode
`L3Switch1(config)#router eigrp 10`	Creates EIGRP routing process 10 and moves to router configuration mode
`L3Switch1(config-router)#network 172.16.0.0`	Advertises the 172.16.0.0 classful network
`L3Switch1(config-router)#network 172.31.0.0`	Advertises the 172.31.0.0 classful network
`L3Switch1(config-router)#no auto-summary`	Turns off automatic summarization at classful boundary
`L3Switch1(config-router)#exit`	Applies changes and returns to global configuration mode
`L3Switch1(config)#exit`	Returns to privileged mode
`L3Switch1#copy running-config startup-config`	Saves configuration in NVRAM

L2Switch1 (Catalyst 2960)

`Switch>enable`	Moves to privileged mode
`Switch#configure terminal`	Moves to global configuration mode
`Switch(config)#hostname L2Switch1`	Sets the host name
`L2Switch1(config)#no ip domain-lookup`	Turns off DNS queries so that spelling mistakes do not slow you down
`L2Switch1(config)#vtp domain testdomain`	Configures the VTP domain name to *testdomain*
`L2Switch1(config)#vtp mode client`	Changes the switch to VTP client mode
`L2Switch1(config)#interface range fastethernet 0/1 - 4`	Enables you to set the same configuration parameters on multiple ports at the same time
`L2Switch1(config-if-range)#switchport mode access`	Sets ports 1 to 4 as access ports
`L2Switch1(config-if-range)#switchport access vlan 10`	Assigns ports 1 to 4 to VLAN 10
`L2Switch1(config-if-range)#interface range fastethernet 0/5 - 8`	Enables you to set the same configuration parameters on multiple ports at the same time

L2Switch1(config-if-range)#**switchport mode access**	Sets ports 5 to 8 as access ports
L2Switch1(config-if-range)#**switchport access vlan 20**	Assigns ports 5 to 8 to VLAN 20
L2Switch1(config-if-range)#**exit**	Returns to global configuration mode
L2Switch1(config)#**interface gigabitethernet 0/1**	Moves to interface configuration mode
L2Switch1(config-if)#**switchport mode trunk**	Puts the interface into trunking mode and negotiates to convert the link into a trunk link
L2Switch1(config-if)#**exit**	Returns to global configuration mode
L2Switch1(config)#**interface vlan 1**	Creates a virtual interface for VLAN 1 and enters interface configuration mode
L2Switch1(config-if)#**ip address 172.16.1.2 255.255.255.0**	Assigns an IP address and netmask
L2Switch1(config-if)#**no shutdown**	Enables the interface
L2Switch1(config-if)#**exit**	Returns to global configuration mode
L2Switch1(config)#**ip default-gateway 172.16.1.1**	Assigns the default gateway address
L2Switch1(config)#**exit**	Returns to privileged mode
L2Switch1#**copy running-config startup-config**	Saves the configuration in NVRAM

CHAPTER 9

Spanning Tree Protocol

This chapter provides information and commands concerning the following topics:

- Spanning Tree Protocol Definition
- Enabling Spanning Tree Protocol
- Configuring the root switch
- Configuring a secondary root switch
- Configuring port priority
- Configuring the path cost
- Configuring the switch priority of a VLAN
- Configuring STP timers
- Verifying STP
- Cisco STP Toolkit
  - PortFast
  - BPDU Guard
- Changing the spanning-tree mode
- Extended System ID
- Enabling Rapid Spanning Tree
- Troubleshooting Spanning Tree
- Configuration example: PVST+

Spanning Tree Protocol Definition

The spanning tree standards offer the same safety that routing protocols provide in Layer 3 forwarding environments to Layer 2 bridging environments. A single best path to a main bridge is found and maintained in the Layer 2 domain, and other redundant paths are managed by selective port blocking. Appropriate blocked ports begin forwarding when primary paths to the main bridge are no longer available.

The IEEE published the first Spanning Tree Protocol (STP) standard, 802.1d, in 1990. The last version of 802.1d was published in 2004 and included several enhancements. The 802.1d standard supported a single common spanning tree.

In 2001 the IEEE published the Rapid Spanning Tree Protocol (RSTP) standard, 802.1w. This standard relied less upon state machine timers and more upon "loop protecting" real time switch to switch negotiation after a topology change. The selection of ports for blocking or forwarding was fast, as was the flushing of invalid MAC addresses in the affected switches. The 802.1w standard, like the 802.1d standard, supported a single common spanning tree instance.

Multiple Instance Spanning Tree Protocol (MISTP), IEEE 802.1s, allows several VLANs to be mapped to a reduced number of spanning-tree instances. Cisco curriculums refer to IEEE 802.1s as Multiple Spanning Tree (MST). Each MST instance handles multiple VLANs that have the same Layer 2 topology.

NOTE   Enabling MST enables RSTP.

Two Cisco proprietary spanning tree protocols are in common use: Per VLAN Spanning Tree Plus (PVST+) and Per VLAN Rapid Spanning Tree Plus (PVRST+). Both protocols allow an instance of either STP or RSTP to run on each VLAN configured on the switch. PVST+ is based on the IEEE 802.1D standard and includes Cisco proprietary extensions such as BackboneFast, UplinkFast, and PortFast. PVRST+ is based on the IEEE 802.1w standard and has a faster convergence than 802.1D.

NOTE   Default spanning tree implementation for Catalyst 2950, 2960, 3550, 3560, and 3750 switches is Per VLAN Spanning-Tree Plus (PVST+). This is a per-VLAN implementation of 802.1d.

Enabling Spanning Tree Protocol

`Switch(config)#spanning-tree vlan 5`	Enables STP on VLAN 5
`Switch(config)#no spanning-tree vlan 5`	Disables STP on VLAN 5

NOTE   Many access switches such as the Catalyst, 2960, 3550, 3560, and 3750 support a maximum 128 spanning trees using any combination of PVST+ or PVRST+. The 2950 model supports only 64 instances. Any VLANs created in excess of 128 cannot have a spanning tree instance running in them. There is a possibility of an L2 loop that could not be broken in the case where a VLAN without spanning tree is transported across a trunk. It is recommended that you use Multiple Spanning Tree Protocol (MSTP) if the number of VLANs in a common topology is high.

Configuring the Root Switch

`Switch(config)`
`#spanning-tree vlan 5 root`
`{primary | secondary}`
	Modifies the switch priority from the default 32768 to a lower value to allow the switch to become the primary or secondary root switch for VLAN 5 (depending on which argument is chosen).

	NOTE This switch sets its priority to 24576. If any other switch has a priority set to below 24576 already, this switch sets its own priority to 4096 *less* than the lowest switch priority. If by doing this the switch has a priority of less than 1, this command fails.

Switch(config)#**spanning-tree vlan 5 root primary**	Configures the switch to become the root switch for VLAN 5.
	NOTE The maximum switch topology width and the hello-time can be set within this command.
	TIP The root switch should be a backbone or distribution switch.
Switch(config) #**spanning-tree vlan 5 root primary diameter 7**	Configures the switch to be the root switch for VLAN 5 and sets the network diameter to 7.
	TIP The **diameter** keyword defines the maximum number of switches between any two end stations. The range is from 2 to 7 switches.
	TIP The **hello-time** keyword sets the hello-interval timer to any amount between 1 and 10 seconds. The default time is 2 seconds.

Configuring a Secondary Root Switch

Switch(config)#**spanning-tree vlan 5 root secondary**	Configures the switch to become the root switch for VLAN 5 should the primary root switch fail.
	NOTE This switch resets its priority to 28672. If the root switch fails and all other switches are set to the default priority of 32768, this becomes the new root switch.
Switch(config)#**spanning-tree vlan 5 root secondary diameter 7**	Configures the switch to be the secondary root switch for VLAN 5 and sets the network diameter to 7.

Configuring Port Priority

Switch(config)#**interface gigabitethernet 0/1**	Moves to interface configuration mode.
Switch(config-if) #**spanning-tree port-priority 64**	Configures the port priority for the interface that is an access port.
Switch(config-if) #**spanning-tree vlan 5 port-priority 64**	Configures the VLAN port priority for an interface that is a trunk port.
	NOTE If a loop occurs, spanning tree uses the port priority when selecting an interface to put into the forwarding state. Assign a higher priority value (lower numerical number) to interfaces you want selected first and a lower priority value (higher numerical number) to interfaces you want selected last.
	The number can be between 0 and 240 in increments of 16. The default port priority is 128.

NOTE   The **port priority** setting supersedes the physical port number in spanning tree calculations.

Configuring the Path Cost

`Switch(config)#interface` `gigabitethernet 0/1`	Moves to interface configuration mode.
`Switch(config-if)#spanning-` `tree cost 100000`	Configures the cost for the interface that is an access port.
`Switch(config-if)#spanning-` `tree vlan 5 cost 1000000`	Configures the VLAN cost for an interface that is a trunk port.
	NOTE If a loop occurs, STP uses the path cost when trying to determine which interface to place into the forwarding state. A higher path cost means a lower speed transmission. The range of the cost keyword is 1 through 200000000. The default is based on the media speed of the interface.

Configuring the Switch Priority of a VLAN

`Switch(config)#spanning-tree` `vlan 5 priority 12288`	Configures the switch priority of VLAN 5 to 12288

NOTE   With the **priority** keyword, the range is 0 to 61440 in increments of 4096. The default is 32768. The lower the priority, the more likely the switch will be chosen as the root switch. Only the following numbers can be used as priority values:

0	4096	8192	12288
16384	20480	24576	28672
32768	36864	40960	45056
49152	53248	57344	61440

CAUTION   Cisco recommends caution when using this command. Cisco further recommends that the **spanning-tree vlan** *x* **root primary** or the **spanning-tree vlan** *x* **root secondary** command be used instead to modify the switch priority.

Configuring STP Timers

`Switch(config)#spanning-tree` `vlan 5 hello-time 4`	Changes the hello-delay timer to 4 seconds on VLAN 5
`Switch(config)#spanning-tree` `vlan 5 forward-time 20`	Changes the forward-delay timer to 20 seconds on VLAN 5
`Switch(config)#spanning-tree` `vlan 5 max-age 25`	Changes the maximum-aging timer to 25 seconds on VLAN 5

NOTE   For the **hello-time** command, the range is 1 to 10 seconds. The default is 2 seconds.

For the **forward-time** command, the range is 4 to 30 seconds. The default is 15 seconds.

For the **max-age** command, the range is 6 to 40 seconds. The default is 20 seconds.

Verifying STP

`Switch#show spanning-tree`	Displays STP information
`Switch#show spanning-tree active`	Displays STP information on active interfaces only
`Switch#show spanning-tree bridge`	Displays status and configuration of the STP
`Switch#show spanning-tree detail`	Displays a detailed summary of interface information
`Switch#show spanning-tree interface gigabitethernet 0/1`	Displays STP information for interface gigabitethernet 0/1
`Switch#show spanning-tree summary`	Displays a summary of port states
`Switch#show spanning-tree summary totals`	Displays the total lines of the STP section
`Switch#show spanning-tree vlan 5`	Displays STP information for VLAN 5

Cisco STP Toolkit

Although the following commands are not mandatory for STP to work, you might find these helpful to fine-tune your network.

PortFast

`Switch(config)#interface fastethernet 0/10`	Moves to interface configuration mode.
`Switch(config-if)#spanning-tree portfast`	Enables PortFast on an access port.
`Switch(config-if)#spanning-tree portfast trunk`	Enables PortFast on a trunk port.
	CAUTION Use the PortFast command only when connecting a single end station to an access or trunk port. Using this command on a port connected to a switch or hub might prevent spanning tree from detecting loops.
	NOTE If you enable the voice VLAN feature, PortFast is enabled automatically. If you disable voice VLAN, PortFast is still enabled.
`Switch(config)#spanning-tree portfast default`	Globally enables PortFast on all switchports that are nontrunking.
	NOTE You can override the **spanning-tree portfast default** global configuration command by using the **spanning-tree portfast disable** interface configuration command.
`Switch#show spanning-tree interface fastethernet 0/10 portfast`	Displays PortFast information on interface fastethernet 0/10.

BPDU Guard

`Switch(config)#spanning-tree portfast bpduguard default`	Globally enables BPDU Guard on ports where **portfast** is enabled.
`Switch(config)#interface range fastethernet 0/1 - 5`	Enters interface range configuration mode.
`Switch(config-if-range)#spanning-tree portfast`	Enables PortFast on all interfaces in the range.
`Switch(config-if-range)#spanning-tree bpduguard enable`	Enables BPDU Guard on the interface.
	NOTE By default, BPDU Guard is disabled.
`Switch(config-if)#spanning-tree bpduguard disable`	Disables BPDU Guard on the interface.
`Switch(config)#errdisable recovery cause bpduguard`	Allows port to reenable itself if the cause of the error is BPDU Guard by setting a recovery timer.
`Switch(config)#errdisable recovery interval 400`	Sets recovery timer to 400 seconds. The default is 300 seconds. The range is from 30 to 86,400 seconds.
`Switch#show spanning-tree summary totals`	Verifies whether BPDU Guard is enabled or disabled.
`Switch#show errdisable recovery`	Displays errdisable recovery timer information.

Changing the Spanning-Tree Mode

You can configure different types of spanning trees on a Cisco switch. The options vary according to the platform:

- **Per-VLAN Spanning Tree (PVST)**—One instance of spanning tree exists for each VLAN with ISL trunking. This is a Cisco proprietary protocol.

- **PVST+**—One instance of spanning tree exists for each VLAN with 802.1Q trunking. Also Cisco proprietary. Has added extensions to the PVST protocol.

- **Rapid PVST+**—This mode is the same as PVST+ except that it uses a rapid convergence based on the 802.1w standard.

- **MSTP**—IEEE 802.1s. Extends the 802.1w Rapid Spanning Tree (RST) algorithm to multiple spanning trees. Multiple VLANs can map to a single instance of RST. You cannot run MSTP and PVST at the same time.

`Switch(config)#spanning-tree mode mst`	Enables MSTP. This command is available only on a switch running the EI software image.
`Switch(config)#spanning-tree mode pvst`	Enables PVST+. This is the default setting.
`Switch(config)#spanning-tree mode rapid-pvst`	Enables Rapid PVST+.

Extended System ID

`Switch(config)#spanning-tree extend system-id`	Enables extended system ID, also known as MAC address reduction.
	NOTE Catalyst switches running software earlier than Cisco IOS Software Release 12.1(8) EA1 do not support the extended system ID.
`Switch#show spanning-tree summary`	Verifies that extended system ID is enabled.
`Switch#show spanning-tree bridge`	Displays the extended system ID as part of the bridge ID.
	NOTE The 12-bit extended system ID is the VLAN number for the instance of PVST+ and PVRST+ spanning tree. In MST, these 12 bits carry the instance number.

Enabling Rapid Spanning Tree

`Switch(config)#spanning-tree mode rapid-pvst`	Enables Rapid PVST+.
`Switch(config)#clear spanning-tree detected-protocols`	
	NOTE When a current switch running MST or PVRST+ receives a legacy switch 802.1d BPDU, it responds with only IEEE 802.1D BPDUs on that port using a built-in protocol migration mechanism. When the legacy switch is replaced with one running MST or PVRST+, the previous MST/PVRST+ switch still expects to receive 802.1d BPDUs. The **clear spanning-tree detected-protocols** command forces the renegotiation with neighboring switches to restart the protocol migration mechanism.
`Switch#show spanning-tree`	Displays mode, root and bridge IDs, participating ports, and their spanning tree states.
`Switch#show spanning-tree summary`	Displays summary of configured port states including spanning tree mode.
`Switch#show spanning-tree detail`	Displays a detailed summary of spanning tree interface information including mode, priority, system ID, MAC address, timers, and role in the spanning tree for each VLAN and port.

Troubleshooting Spanning Tree

Switch#**debug spanning-tree all**	Displays all spanning-tree debugging events
Switch#**debug spanning-tree events**	Displays spanning-tree debugging topology events
Switch#**debug spanning-tree backbonefast**	Displays spanning-tree debugging BackboneFast events
Switch#**debug spanning-tree uplinkfast**	Displays spanning-tree debugging UplinkFast event
Switch#**debug spanning-tree mstp all**	Displays all MST debugging events
Switch#**debug spanning-tree switch state**	Displays spanning-tree port state changes
Switch#**debug spanning-tree pvst+**	Displays PVST+ events

Configuration Example: PVST+

Figure 9-1 shows the network topology for the configuration of PVST+ using commands covered in this chapter. Assume that other commands needed for connectivity have already been configured.

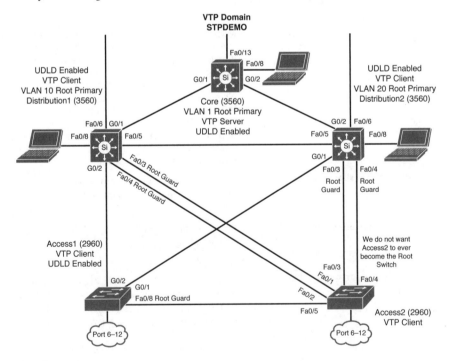

Figure 9-1 Network Topology for STP Configuration Example

Core Switch (3560)

`Switch>`**`enable`**	Moves to privileged mode.
`Switch#`**`configure terminal`**	Moves to global config mode.
`Switch(config)#`**`hostname Core`**	Sets host name.
`Core(config)#`**`no ip domain-lookup`**	Turns off Dynamic Name System (DNS) queries so that spelling mistakes do not slow you down.
`Core(config)#`**`vtp mode server`**	Changes the switch to VTP server mode. This is the default mode.
`Core(config)#`**`vtp domain STPDEMO`**	Configures the VTP domain name to *STPDEMO*.
`Core(config)#`**`vlan 10`**	Creates VLAN 10 and enters VLAN-config mode.
`Core(config-vlan)#`**`name Accounting`**	Assigns a name to the VLAN.
`Core(config-vlan)#`**`exit`**	Returns to global config mode.
`Core(config)#`**`vlan 20`**	Creates VLAN 20 and enters VLAN-config mode.
`Core(config-vlan)#`**`name Marketing`**	Assigns a name to the VLAN.
`Core(config-vlan)#`**`exit`**	Returns to global config mode.
`Core(config)#`**`spanning-tree vlan 1 root primary`**	Configures the switch to become the root switch for VLAN 1.
`Core(config)#`**`exit`**	Returns to privileged mode.
`Core#`**`copy running-config startup-config`**	Saves the configuration to NVRAM.

Distribution 1 Switch (3560)

`Switch>`**`enable`**	Moves to privileged mode
`Switch#`**`configure terminal`**	Moves to global config mode
`Switch(config)#`**`hostname Distribution1`**	Sets host name
`Distribution1(config)#`**`no ip domain-lookup`**	Turns off DNS queries so that spelling mistakes do not slow you down
`Distribution1(config)#`**`vtp domain STPDEMO`**	Configures the VTP domain name to *STPDEMO*

`Distribution1(config)#`**`vtp mode client`**	Changes the switch to VTP client mode
`Distribution1(config)#`**`spanning-tree vlan 10 root primary`**	Configures the switch to become the root switch of VLAN 10
`Distribution1(config)#`**`exit`**	Returns to privileged mode
`Distribution1#`**`copy running-config startup-config`**	Saves the configuration to NVRAM

Distribution 2 Switch (3560)

`Switch>`**`enable`**	Moves to privileged mode
`Switch#`**`configure terminal`**	Moves to global config mode
`Switch(config)#`**`hostname Distribution2`**	Sets the host name
`Distribution2(config)#`**`no ip domain-lookup`**	Turns off DNS queries so that spelling mistakes do not slow you down
`Distribution2(config)#`**`vtp domain STPDEMO`**	Configures the VTP domain name to *STPDEMO*
`Distribution2(config)#`**`vtp mode client`**	Changes the switch to VTP client mode
`Distribution2(config)#`**`spanning-tree vlan 20 root primary`**	Configures the switch to become the root switch of VLAN 20
`Distribution2(config)#`**`exit`**	Returns to privileged mode
`Distribution2#`**`copy running-config startup-config`**	Saves the configuration to NVRAM

Access 1 Switch (2960)

`Switch>`**`enable`**	Moves to privileged mode
`Switch#`**`configure terminal`**	Moves to global config mode
`Switch(config)#`**`hostname Access1`**	Sets the host name
`Access1(config)#`**`no ip domain-lookup`**	Turns off DNS queries so that spelling mistakes do not slow you down
`Access1(config)#`**`vtp domain STPDEMO`**	Configures the VTP domain name to *STPDEMO*
`Access1(config)#`**`vtp mode client`**	Changes the switch to VTP client mode

`Access1(config)#`**`interface range`** **`fastethernet 0/6 - 12`**	Moves to interface range config mode
`Access1(config-if-range)` `#`**`switchport mode access`**	Places all interfaces in access mode
`Access1(config-if-range)` `#`**`spanning-tree portfast`**	Places all ports directly into forwarding mode
`Access1(config-if-range)` `#`**`spanning-tree bpduguard enable`**	Enables BPDU Guard
`Access1(config-if-range)#`**`exit`**	Moves back to global config mode
`Access1(config)#`**`exit`**	Returns to privileged mode
`Access1#`**`copy running-config`** **`startup-config`**	Saves the configuration to NVRAM

Access 2 Switch (2960)

`Switch>`**`enable`**	Moves to privileged mode
`Switch#`**`configure terminal`**	Moves to global config mode
`Switch(config)#`**`hostname Access2`**	Sets the host name
`Access2(config)#`**`no ip domain-lookup`**	Turns off DNS queries so that spelling mistakes do not slow you down
`Access2(config)#`**`vtp domain STPDEMO`**	Configures the VTP domain name to *STPDEMO*
`Access2(config)#`**`vtp mode client`**	Changes the switch to VTP client mode
`Access2(config)#`**`interface range`** **`fastethernet 0/6 - 12`**	Moves to interface range config mode
`Access2(config-if-range)#`**`switchport`** **`mode access`**	Places all interfaces in access mode
`Access2(config-if-range)` `#`**`spanning-tree portfast`**	Places all ports directly into forwarding mode
`Access2(config-if-range)` `#`**`spanning-tree bpduguard enable`**	Enables BPDU Guard
`Access2(config-if-range)#`**`exit`**	Moves back to global config mode
`Access2(config)#`**`spanning-tree vlan`** **`1,10,20 priority 61440`**	Ensures this switch does not become the root switch for VLAN 10
`Access2(config)#`**`exit`**	Returns to privileged mode
`Access2#`**`copy running-config`** **`startup-config`**	Saves config to NVRAM

Spanning-Tree Migration Example: PVST+ to Rapid-PVST+

The topology in Figure 9-1 is used for this migration example and adds to the configuration of the previous example.

Rapid-PVST+ uses the same BPDU format as the 802.1D. This interoperability between the two spanning tree protocols enables a longer conversion time in large networks without disrupting services.

The Spanning Tree features UplinkFast and BackboneFast in 802.1d-based PVST+ are already incorporated in the 802.1w-based Rapid-PVST+ and are disabled when you enable Rapid-PVST+. The 802.1d-based features of PVST+ such as PortFast, BPDU Guard, BPDU filter, root guard, and loop guard are applicable in Rapid-PVST+ mode and need not be changed.

> **NOTE**   These features are not part of the CCNA Routing and Switching vendor exam objectives; they are, however, part of the CCNP Routing and Switch SWITCH vendor exam objectives.

Access 1 Switch (2960)

`Access1>`**`enable`**	Moves to privileged mode
`Access1#`**`configure terminal`**	Moves to global config mode
`Access1 (config)#`**`spanning-tree mode rapid-pvst`**	Enables 802.1w-based Rapid-PVST+
`Access1(config)#`**`no spanning-tree uplinkfast`**	Removes UplinkFast programming line
`Access1(config)#`**`no spanning-tree backbonefast`**	Removes BackboneFast programming line

Access 2 Switch (2960)

`Access2>`**`enable`**	Moves to privileged mode
`Access2#`**`configure terminal`**	Moves to global config mode
`Access2 (config)#`**`spanning-tree mode rapid-pvst`**	Enables 802.1w-based Rapid-PVST+

Distribution 1 Switch (3560)

`Distribution1>`**`enable`**	Moves to privileged mode
`Distribution1#`**`configure terminal`**	Moves to global config mode
`Distribution1 (config)#`**`spanning-tree mode rapid-pvst`**	Enables 802.1w-based Rapid-PVST+

Distribution 2 Switch (3560)

`Distribution2>`**`enable`**	Moves to privileged mode
`Distribution2#`**`configure terminal`**	Moves to global config mode
`Distribution2 (config)#`**`spanning-tree mode rapid-pvst`**	Enables 802.1w-based Rapid-PVST+

Core Switch (3560)

`Core>`**`enable`**	Moves to privileged mode
`Core#`**`configure terminal`**	Moves to global config mode
`Core(config)#`**`spanning-tree mode rapid-pvst`**	Enables 802.1w-based Rapid-PVST+

CHAPTER 10

EtherChannel

This chapter provides information and commands concerning the following topics:

- EtherChannel
    - Interface modes in EtherChannel
    - Guidelines for configuring EtherChannel
    - Configuring Layer 2 EtherChannel
    - Configuring Layer 3 EtherChannel
    - Verifying EtherChannel
- Configuration example: EtherChannel

EtherChannel

EtherChannel provides fault-tolerant, high-speed links between switches, routers, and servers. An EtherChannel consists of individual Fast Ethernet or Gigabit Ethernet links bundled into a single logical link. If a link within an EtherChannel fails, traffic previously carried over that failed link changes to the remaining links within the EtherChannel.

Interface Modes in EtherChannel

Mode	Protocol	Description
On	None	Forces the interface into an EtherChannel without Port Aggregation Protocol (PAgP) or Link Aggregation Control Protocol (LACP). Channel only exists if connected to another interface group also in On mode.
Auto	PAgP (Cisco)	Places the interface into a passive negotiating state (will respond to PAgP packets but will not initiate PAgP negotiation).
Desirable	PAgP (Cisco)	Places the interface into an active negotiating state (will send PAgP packets to start negotiations).
Passive	LACP (IEEE)	Places the interface into a passive negotiating state (will respond to LACP packets but will not initiate LACP negotiation).
Active	LACP (IEEE)	Places the interface into an active negotiating state (will send LACP packets to start negotiations).

Guidelines for Configuring EtherChannel

- PAgP is Cisco proprietary and not compatible with LACP.

- LACP is defined in 802.3ad.

- A single EtherChannel can be made by combining anywhere from two to eight parallel links.

- All ports must be identical:

  - Same speed and duplex

  - Cannot mix Fast Ethernet and Gigabit Ethernet

  - Cannot mix PAgP and LACP

  - Must all be VLAN trunk or nontrunk operational status

- All links must be either Layer 2 or Layer 3 in a single channel group.

- To create a channel in PAgP, sides must be set to one of the following:

  - Auto-Desirable

  - Desirable-Desirable

- To create a channel in LACP, sides must be set to either:

  - Active-Active

  - Active-Passive

- To create a channel without using PAgP or LACP, sides must be set to On-On.

- Do *not* configure a GigaStack gigabit interface converter (GBIC) as part of an EtherChannel.

- An interface that is already configured to be a Switched Port Analyzer (SPAN) destination port will not join an EtherChannel group until SPAN is disabled.

- Do *not* configure a secure port as part of an EtherChannel.

- Interfaces with different native VLANs cannot form an EtherChannel.

- When using trunk links, ensure that all trunks are in the same mode—Inter-Switch Link (ISL) or dot1q.

Configuring Layer 2 EtherChannel

Switch(config)#**interface port-channel** {*number*}	Specifies the port-channel interface.
Switch(config-if)#**interface** {*parameters*}	Once in the interface configuration mode, you can configure additional parameters.
Switch(config)#**interface range fastethernet 0/1 - 4**	Moves to interface range config mode.
Switch(config-if-range)#**channel-group 1 mode on**	Creates channel group 1 as an EtherChannel and assigns interfaces 01 to 04 as part of it.

Switch(config-if-range) #**channel-group 1 mode desirable**	Creates channel group 1 as a PAgP channel and assigns interfaces 01 to 04 as part of it.
Switch(config-if-range) #**channel-group 1 mode active**	Creates channel group 1 as an LACP channel and assigns interfaces 01 to 04 as part of it.

NOTE If you enter in the **channel-group** command in the physical port interface mode without first setting a **port channel** command in global configuration mode, the port channel will automatically be created for you.

Configuring L3 EtherChannel

Switch3560(config)#**interface port-channel 1**	Creates the port-channel logical interface and moves to interface config mode. Valid channel numbers are 1 to 48 for a 3560 series. For a 2960 series switch with L3 capabilities, the valid channel numbers are 1 to 6.
Switch3560(config-if)#**no switchport**	Puts the interface into Layer 3 mode.
Switch3560(config-if)#**ip address 172.16.10.1 255.255.255.0**	Assigns the IP address and netmask.
Switch3560(config-if)#**exit**	Moves to global config mode.
Switch3560(config)#**interface range fastethernet 0/20 - 24**	Moves to interface range config mode.
Switch3560(config-if)#**no switchport**	Puts the interface into Layer 3 mode.
Switch3560(config-if-range)#**no ip address**	Ensures that no IP addresses are assigned on the interfaces.
Switch3560(config-if-range)#**channel-group 1 mode on**	Creates channel group 1 as an EtherChannel and assigns interfaces 20 to 24 as part of it.
Switch3560(config-if-range)#**channel-group 1 mode desirable**	Creates channel group 1 as a PAgP channel and assigns interfaces 20 to 24 as part of it.
Switch3560(config-if-range)#**channel-group 1 mode active**	Creates channel group 1 as an LACP channel and assigns interfaces 20 to 24 as part of it.
	NOTE The channel group number must match the port channel number.

Verifying EtherChannel

Switch#**show running-config**	Displays a list of what is currently running on the device
Switch#**show running-config interface fastethernet 0/12**	Displays interface fastethernet 0/12 information
Switch#**show interfaces fastethernet 0/12 etherchannel**	Displays EtherChannel information for specified interface
Switch#**show etherchannel**	Displays all EtherChannel information
Switch#**show etherchannel 1 port-channel**	Displays port channel information
Switch#**show etherchannel summary**	Displays a summary of EtherChannel information
Switch#**show interface port-channel 1**	Displays the general status of EtherChannel 1
Switch#**show pagp neighbor**	Shows PAgP neighbor information
Switch#**clear pagp 1 counters**	Clears PAgP channel group 1 information
Switch#**clear lacp 1 counters**	Clears LACP channel group 1 information

Configuration Example: EtherChannel

Figure 10-1 shows the network topology for the configuration that follows, which shows how to configure EtherChannel using commands covered in this chapter.

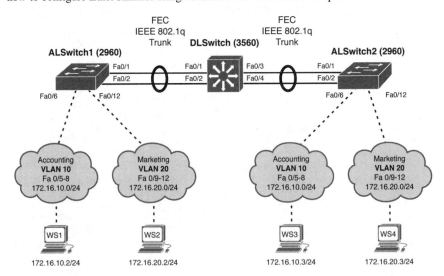

Figure 10-1   Network Topology for EtherChannel Configuration

DLSwitch (3560)

`Switch>enable`	Moves to privileged mode
`Switch#configure terminal`	Moves to global config mode
`Switch(config)#hostname DLSwitch`	Sets the host name
`DLSwitch(config)#no ip domain-lookup`	Turns off DNS queries so that spelling mistakes do not slow you down
`DLSwitch(config)#vtp mode server`	Changes the switch to VTP server mode
`DLSwitch(config)#vtp domain testdomain`	Configures the VTP domain name to *testdomain*
`DLSwitch(config)#vlan 10`	Creates VLAN 10 and enters VLAN-config mode
`DLSwitch(config-vlan)#name Accounting`	Assigns a name to the VLAN
`DLSwitch(config-vlan)#exit`	Returns to global config mode
`DLSwitch(config)#vlan 20`	Creates VLAN 20 and enters VLAN-config mode
`DLSwitch(config-vlan)#name Marketing`	Assigns a name to the VLAN
`DLSwitch(config-vlan)#exit`	Returns to global config mode
`DLSwitch(config)#interface range fastethernet 0/1 - 4`	Moves to interface range config mode
`DLSwitch(config-if)#switchport trunk encapsulation dot1q`	Specifies 802.1Q tagging on the trunk link
`DLSwitch(config-if)#switchport mode trunk`	Puts the interface into permanent trunking mode and negotiates to convert the link into a trunk link
`DLSwitch(config-if)#exit`	Returns to global config mode
`DLSwitch(config)#interface range fastethernet 0/1 - 2`	Moves to interface range config mode
`DLSwitch(config-if)#channel-group 1 mode desirable`	Creates channel group 1 and assigns interfaces 01 to 02 as part of it
`DLSwitch(config-if)#exit`	Moves to global config mode
`DLSwitch(config)#interface range fastethernet 0/3 - 4`	Moves to interface range config mode
`DLSwitch(config-if)#channel-group 2 mode desirable`	Creates channel group 2 and assigns interfaces 03 to 04 as part of it
`DLSwitch(config-if)#exit`	Moves to global config mode
`DLSwitch(config)#port-channel load-balance dst-mac`	Configures load balancing based on destination MAC address
`DLSwitch(config)#exit`	Moves to privileged mode
`DLSwitch#copy running-config startup-config`	Saves the configuration to NVRAM

ALSwitch1 (2960)

`Switch>`**`enable`**	Moves to privileged mode
`Switch#`**`configure terminal`**	Moves to global config mode
`Switch(config)#`**`hostname ALSwitch1`**	Sets host name
`ALSwitch1(config)#`**`no ip domain-lookup`**	Turns off DNS queries so that spelling mistakes do not slow you down
`ALSwitch1(config)#`**`vtp mode client`**	Changes the switch to VTP client mode
`ALSwitch1(config)#`**`vtp domain testdomain`**	Configures the VTP domain name to *testdomain*
`ALSwitch1(config)#`**`interface range fastethernet 0/5 - 8`**	Moves to interface range config mode
`ALSwitch1(config-if-range)#`**`switchport mode access`**	Sets ports 05 to 08 as access ports
`ALSwitch1(config-if-range)#`**`switchport access vlan 10`**	Assigns ports to VLAN 10
`ALSwitch1(config-if-range)#`**`exit`**	Moves to global config mode
`ALSwitch1(config)#`**`interface range fastethernet 0/9 - 12`**	Moves to interface range config mode
`ALSwitch1(config-if-range)#`**`switchport mode access`**	Sets ports 09 to 12 as access ports
`ALSwitch1(config-if-range)#`**`switchport access vlan 20`**	Assigns ports to VLAN 20
`ALSwitch1(config-if-range)#`**`exit`**	Moves to global config mode
`ALSwitch1(config)#`**`interface range fastethernet 0/1 - 2`**	Moves to interface range config mode
`ALSwitch1(config-if-range)#`**`switchport mode trunk`**	Puts the interface into permanent trunking mode and negotiates to convert the link into a trunk link
`ALSwitch1(config-if-range)#`**`channel-group 1 mode desirable`**	Creates Channel Group 1 and assigns interfaces 01 to 02 as part of it
`ALSwitch1(config-if-range)#`**`exit`**	Moves to global config mode
`ALSwitch1(config)#`**`exit`**	Moves to privileged mode
`ALSwitch1#`**`copy running-config startup-config`**	Saves the configuration to NVRAM

ALSwitch2 (2960)

`Switch>enable`	Moves to privileged mode
`Switch#configure terminal`	Moves to global config mode
`Switch(config)#hostname ALSwitch2`	Sets host name
`ALSwitch2(config)#no ip domain-lookup`	Turns off DNS queries so that spelling mistakes do not slow you down
`ALSwitch2(config)#vtp mode client`	Changes the switch to VTP client mode
`ALSwitch2(config)#vtp domain testdomain`	Configures the VTP domain name to *testdomain*
`ALSwitch2(config)#interface range fastethernet 0/5 - 8`	Moves to interface range config mode
`ALSwitch2(config-if-range)#switchport mode access`	Sets ports 05 to 08 as access ports
`ALSwitch2(config-if-range)#switchport access vlan 10`	Assigns ports to VLAN 10
`ALSwitch2(config-if-range)#exit`	Moves to global config mode
`ALSwitch2(config)#interface range fastethernet 0/9 - 12`	Moves to interface range config mode
`ALSwitch2(config-if-range)#switchport mode access`	Sets ports 09 to 12 as access ports
`ALSwitch2(config-if-range)#switchport access vlan 20`	Assigns ports to VLAN 20
`ALSwitch2(config-if-range)#exit`	Moves to global config mode
`ALSwitch2(config)#interface range fastethernet 0/1 - 2`	Moves to interface range config mode
`ALSwitch2(config-if-range)#switchport mode trunk`	Puts the interface into permanent trunking mode and negotiates to convert the link into a trunk link
`ALSwitch2(config-if-range)#channel-group 2 mode desirable`	Creates channel group 2 and assigns interfaces 01 to 02 as part of it
	NOTE Although the local channel group number does not have to match the channel group number on a neighboring switch, the numbers are often chosen to be the same for ease of management and documentation purposes.
`ALSwitch2(config-if-range)#exit`	Moves to global config mode
`ALSwitch2(config)#exit`	Moves to privileged mode
`ALSwitch2#copy running-config startup-config`	Saves the configuration to NVRAM

CHAPTER 11

Configuring a Cisco Router

This chapter provides information and commands concerning the following topics:

- Router modes
- Entering global configuration mode
- Configuring a router, specifically
  - Device Name
  - Passwords
  - Password encryption
  - Interface name
  - Moving between interfaces
  - Configuring a serial interface
  - Configuring a Fast Ethernet interface
  - Configuring a Gigabit Ethernet interface
  - Assigning IPv6 addresses to interfaces
  - Creating a message-of-the-day (MOTD) banner
  - Creating a login banner
  - Setting the clock time zone
  - Mapping a local hostname to a remote IP address
  - The **no ip domain-lookup** command
  - The **logging synchronous** command
  - The **exec-timeout** command
  - Saving configurations
  - Erasing configurations
- **show** commands to verify the router configurations
- EXEC commands in configuration mode: the **do** command
- Configuration Example: Basic Router Configuration

Router Modes

`Router>`	User mode
`Router#`	Privileged mode (also known as EXEC-level mode)
`Router(config)#`	Global configuration mode
`Router(config-if)#`	Interface mode
`Router(config-subif)#`	Subinterface mode
`Router(config-line)#`	Line mode
`Router(config-router)#`	Router configuration mode

TIP   There are other modes than these. Not all commands work in all modes. Be careful. If you type in a command that you know is correct—**show running-config**, for example—and you get an error, make sure that you are in the correct mode.

Entering Global Configuration Mode

`Router>`	Limited viewing of configuration. You cannot make changes in this mode.
`Router#`	You can see the configuration and move to make changes.
`Router#`**`configure terminal`** `Router(config)#`	Moves to global configuration mode. This prompt indicates that you can start making changes.

Configuring a Router Name

This command works on both routers and switches.

`Router(config)#`**`hostname Cisco`**	The name can be any word you choose. The name should start with a letter.
`Cisco(config)#`	Notice that the name of the router has changed from the default Router to Cisco.

Configuring Passwords

These commands work on both routers and switches.

`Router(config)#`**`enable password cisco`**	Sets **enable** password
`Router(config)#`**`enable secret class`**	Sets **enable secret** password
`Router(config)#`**`line console 0`**	Enters console line mode
`Router(config-line)#`**`password console`**	Sets console line mode password to *console*
`Router(config-line)#`**`login`**	Enables password checking at login

`Router(config)#line vty 0 4`	Enters vty line mode for all five vty lines
`Router(config-line)#password telnet`	Sets vty password to *telnet*
`Router(config-line)#login`	Enables password checking at login
`Router(config)#line aux 0`	Enters auxiliary line mode **NOTE** This is not available on Cisco switches.
`Router(config-line)#password backdoor`	Sets auxiliary line mode password to *backdoor*
`Router(config-line)#login`	Enables password checking at login

CAUTION   The **enable secret** *password* is encrypted by default. The **enable** *password* is not. For this reason, recommended practice is that you *never* use the **enable** *password* command. Use only the **enable secret** *password* command in a router or a switch configuration. You cannot set both **enable secret** *password* and **enable** *password* to the same password. Doing so defeats the use of encryption.

Password Encryption

`Router(config)#service password-encryption`	Clear text passwords will be hidden using a weak encryption algorithm.
`Router(config)#enable password cisco`	Sets enable password to *cisco*.
`Router(config)#line console 0`	Moves to console line mode.
`Router(config-line)#password Cisco`	Continue setting passwords as above.
	. . .
`Router(config)#no service password-encryption`	Turns off password encryption.

CAUTION   If you have turned on service password encryption, used it, and then turned it off, any passwords that you have encrypted stay encrypted. New passwords remain unencrypted.

Interface Names

One of the biggest problems that new administrators face is the interface names on the different models of routers. With all the different Cisco devices in production networks today, some administrators are becoming confused about the names of their interfaces. Using Cisco devices that are no longer in production but are still valuable in a lab or classroom setting can also complicate matters. Older devices are still a great (and inexpensive) way to learn the basics (and in some cases the more advanced methods) of router configuration.

The following chart is a sample of some of the different interface names for various routers. This is by no means a complete list. Refer to the hardware guide of the specific router that you are working on to see the various combinations, or use the following command to see which interfaces are installed on your particular router:

```
router#show ip interface brief
```

Router Model	Port Location/ Slot Number	Slot/Port Type	Slot Numbering Range	Example
2501	On board	Ethernet	Interface-type number	ethernet0 (e0)
	On board	Serial	Interface-type number	serial0 (s0) and s1
2514	On board	Ethernet	Interface-type number	e0 and e1
	On board	Serial	Interface-type number	s0 and s1
1721	On board	Fast Ethernet	Interface-type number	fastethernet0 (fa0)
	Slot 0	Wireless Access Controller (WAC)	Interface-type number	s0 and s1
1760	On board	Fast Ethernet	Interface-type 0/port	fa0/0
	Slot 0	WAN Interface Card (WIC)/ Voice Interface Card (VIC)	Interface-type 0/port	s0/0 and s0/1 v0/0 and v0/1
	Slot 1	WIC/VIC	Interface-type 1/port	s1/0 and s1/1 v1/0 and v1/1
	Slot 2	VIC	Interface-type 2/port	v2/0 and v2/1
	Slot 3	VIC	Interface-type 3/port	v3/0 and v3/1
2610	On board	Ethernet	Interface-type 0/port	e0/0
	Slot 0	WIC (Serial)	Interface-type 0/port	s0/0 and s0/1
2611	On board	Ethernet	Interface-type 0/port	e0/0 and e0/1
	Slot 0	WIC (Serial)	Interface-type 0/port	s0/0 and s0/1
2620	On board	Fast Ethernet	Interface-type 0/port	fa0/0
	Slot 0	WIC (serial)	Interface-type 0/port	s0/0 and s0/1
2621	On board	Fast Ethernet	Interface-type 0/port	fa0/0 and fa0/1
	Slot 0	WIC (serial)	Interface-type 0/port	s0/0 and s0/1
1841	On board	Fast Ethernet	Interface-type 0/port	fa0/0 and fa0/1
	Slot 0	High-speed WAN interface card (HWIC)/ WIC/ Voice WAN Interface Card (VWIC)	Interface-type 0/slot/ port	s0/0/0 and s0/0/1

Router Model	Port Location/ Slot Number	Slot/Port Type	Slot Numbering Range	Example
1841	Slot 1	HWIC/WIC/ VWIC	Interface-type 0/slot/ port	s0/1/0 and s0/1/1
2801	On board	Fast Ethernet	Interface-type 0/port	fa0/0 and fa0/1
	Slot 0	VIC/VWIC (voice only)	Interface-type 0/slot/ port	voice0/0/0– voice0/0/3
	Slot 1	HWIC/WIC/ VWIC	Interface-type 0/slot/ port	0/1/0–0/1/3 (single-wide HWIC) 0/1/0– 0/1/7 (double- wide HWIC)
	Slot 2	WIC/VIC/VWIC	Interface-type 0/slot/ port	0/2/0–0/2/3
	Slot 3	HWIC/WIC/ VWIC	Interface-type 0/slot/ port	0/3/0–0/3/3 (single-wide HWIC) 0/3/0– 0/3/7 (double- wide HWIC)
2811	Built in to chassis front	USB	Interface-type port	usb0 and usb 1
	Built in to chassis rear	Fast Ethernet Gigabit Ethernet	Interface-type 0/port	fa0/0 and fa0/1 gi0/0 and gi0/1
	Slot 0	HWIC/ HWIC-D/WIC/ VWIC/VIC	Interface-type 0/slot/ port	s0/0/0 and s0/0/1 fa0/0/0 and 0/0/1
	Slot 1	HWIC/High- Speed WAN Interface Card- Double-wide (HWIC-D)/WIC/ VWIC/VIC	Interface-type 0/slot/ port	s0/1/0 and s0/1/1 fa0/1/0 and 0/1/1
	NME slot	Network module (NM)/ network module enhanced (NME)	Interface-type 1/port	gi1/0 and gi1/1 s1/0 and s1/1
1941 / 1941w	On board	Gigabit Ethernet	Interface-type 0/port	gi0/0 and gi0/1
	Slot 0	Enhanced High- Speed WAN Interface Card (EHWIC)	Interface-type 0/slot/ port	s0/0/0 and s0/0/1
	Slot 1	EHWIC	Interface-type 0/slot/ port	s0/1/0 and s0/1/1

Router Model	Port Location/ Slot Number	Slot/Port Type	Slot Numbering Range	Example
	Built in to chassis back	USB	Interface-type port	usb0 and usb 1
2901 2911	On board	Gigabit Ethernet	Interface-type 0/port	gi0/0 and gi0/1 gi0/2 (2911 only)
	Slot 0	EHWIC	Interface-type 0/slot/ port	s0/0/0 and s0/0/1
	Slot 1	EHWIC	Interface-type 0/slot/ port	s0/1/0 and s0/1/1
	Slot 2	EHWIC	Interface-type 0/slot/ port	s0/2/0 and s0/2/1
	Slot 3	EHWIC	Interface-type 0/slot/ port	s0/3/0 and s0/3/1
	Built in to chassis back	USB	Interface-type port	usb0 and usb 1

Moving Between Interfaces

What happens in Column 1 is the same thing occurring in Column 3.

Router(config) #interface serial 0/0/0	Moves to serial interface configuration mode	Router(config) #interface serial 0/0/0	Moves to serial interface configuration mode
Router(config-if)#exit	Returns to global configuration mode	Router(config-if) #interface fastethernet 0/0	Moves directly to Fast Ethernet 0/0 configuration mode
Router(config) # interface fastethernet 0/0	Moves to Fast Ethernet interface configuration mode	Router(config-if)#	In Fast Ethernet 0/0 configuration mode now
Router(config-if)#	In Fast Ethernet 0/0 configuration mode now	Router(config-if)#	Prompt does not change; be careful

Configuring a Serial Interface

Router(config)#interface serial 0/0/0	Moves to serial interface 0/0/0 configuration mode
Router(config-if)#description Link to ISP	Optional descriptor of the link is locally significant
Router(config-if)#ip address 192.168.10.1 255.255.255.0	Assigns address and subnet mask to interface
Router(config-if)#clock rate 56000	Assigns a clock rate for the interface
Router(config-if)#no shutdown	Turns interface on

TIP The **clock rate** command is used only on a *serial* interface that has a *DCE* cable plugged into it. There must be a clock rate on every serial link between routers. It does not matter which router has the DCE cable plugged into it or which interface the cable is plugged into. Serial 0/0/0 on one router can be plugged into Serial 0/0/1 on another router.

Configuring a Fast Ethernet Interface

Router(config)#interface fastethernet 0/0	Moves to Fast Ethernet 0/0 interface configuration mode
Router(config-if)#description Accounting LAN	Optional descriptor of the link is locally significant
Router(config-if)#ip address 192.168.20.1 255.255.255.0	Assigns address and subnet mask to interface
Router(config-if)#no shutdown	Turns interface on

Configuring a Gigabit Ethernet Interface

Router(config)#interface gigabitethernet 0/0	Moves to gigabitethernet 0/0 interface configuration mode
Router(config-if)#description Human Resources LAN	Optional descriptor of the link is locally significant
Router(config-if)#ip address 192.168.30.1 255.255.255.0	Assigns an address and subnet mask to interface
Router(config-if)#no shutdown	Turns interface on

Assigning IPv6 Addresses to Interfaces

`Router(config)#ipv6 unicast-routing`	Enables the forwarding of IPV6 unicast datagrams globally on the router.
`Router(config)#interface gigabitethernet 0/0`	Moves to interface configuration mode.
`Router(config-if)#ipv6 enable`	Automatically configures an IPv6 link-local address on the interface and enables IPv6 processing on the interface.
	NOTE The link-local address that the **ipv6 enable** command configures can be used only to communicate with nodes on the same broadcast segment.
`Router(config-if)#ipv6 address autoconfig`	Router will configure itself with a link-local address using stateless autoconfiguration.
`Router(config-if)#ipv6 address 2001::1/64`	Configures a global IPv6 address on the interface and enables IPv6 processing on the interface.
`Router(config-if)#ipv6 address 2001:db8:0:1::/64 eui-64`	Configures a global IPv6 address with an interface identifier in the low-order 64 bits of the IPv6 address.
`Router(config-if) #ipv6 address fe80::260:3eff:fe47:1530/ 64 link-local`	Configures a specific link-local IPv6 address on the interface instead of the one that is automatically configured when IPv6 is enabled on the interface.
`Router(config-if)#ipv6 unnumbered type/number`	Specifies an unnumbered interface and enables IPv6 processing on the interface. The global IPv6 address of the interface specified by *type/number* will be used as the source address.

Creating a Message-of-the-Day Banner

`Router(config)#banner motd ^` `Building Power will be interrupted` `next Tuesday evening from 8 - 10` `PM. ^` `Router(config)#`	^ is being used as a *delimiting character*. The delimiting character must surround the banner message and can be any character as long as it is not a character used within the body of the message.

TIP The message-of-the-day (MOTD) banner is displayed on all terminals and is useful for sending messages that affect all users. Use the **no banner motd** command to disable the MOTD banner. The MOTD banner displays before the login prompt and the login banner, if one has been created, if you are connected via the console or through Telnet. If you are connecting using SSH, the MOTD banner appears after the SSH connection.

Creating a Login Banner

```Router(config)#banner login```
```^Authorized Personnel Only! Please```
```enter your username and password.```
```^```
```Router(config)#```
	^ is being used as a *delimiting character*. The delimiting character must surround the banner message and can be any character as long as it is not a character used within the body of the message.

TIP The login banner displays before the username and password login prompts. Use the **no banner login** command to disable the login banner. The MOTD banner displays before the login banner.

Setting the Clock Time Zone

```Router(config)#clock``` ```timezone EST -5```	Sets the time zone for display purposes. Based on coordinated universal time. (Eastern standard time is 5 hours behind UTC.)

Mapping a Local Hostname to a Remote IP Address

```Router(config)#ip host``` ```london 172.16.1.3```	Assigns a hostname to the IP address. After this assignment, you can use the hostname rather than an IP address when trying to telnet or ping to that address.

```Router#ping london```
```=```
```Router#ping 172.16.1.3```
	Both commands execute the same objective: sending a ping to address 172.16.1.3.

TIP When in user EXEC or privilege EXEC modes, commands that do not match a valid command default to Telnet. Therefore, you can use a hostname mapping to telnet to a remote device:

```Router#london``` = ```Router#telnet london``` = ```Router#telnet 172.16.1.3```

The no ip domain-lookup Command

```Router(config)#no ip```
```domain-lookup```
```Router(config)#```
	Turns off trying to automatically resolve an unrecognized command to a local hostname

TIP Ever type in a command incorrectly and end up having to wait for what seems to be a minute or two as the router tries to translate your command to a domain server of 255.255.255.255? When in user EXEC or privilege EXEC modes, commands that do not match a valid command default to Telnet. Also, the router is set by default to try to resolve any word that is not a command to a Domain Name System (DNS) server at address 255.255.255.255. If you are not going to set up DNS, turn off this feature to save you time as you type, especially if you are a poor typist.
```

The logging synchronous Command

Router(config)#**line console 0**	Moves to line console configuration mode.
Router(config-line)#**logging synchronous**	Turns on synchronous logging. Information items sent to the console do not interrupt the command you are typing. The command is moved to a new line.

TIP　Ever try to type in a command and an informational line appears in the middle of what you were typing? Lose your place? Do not know where you are in the command, so you just press Enter and start all over? The **logging synchronous** command tells the router that if any informational items get displayed on the screen, your prompt and command line should be moved to a new line, so as not to confuse you. The informational line does not get inserted into the middle of the command you are trying to type. If you were to continue typing, the command would execute properly, even though it looks wrong on the screen.

The exec-timeout Command

Router(config)#**line console 0**	Moves to line console configuration mode.
Router(config-line)#**exec-timeout 0 0**	Sets the limit of idle connection time, after which the console automatically logs off. A setting of **0 0** (minutes seconds) means the console never logs off.
Router(config-line)#	

TIP　The command **exec-timeout 0 0** is great for a lab environment because the console never logs out, regardless of how long the connection remains idle. This is considered to be bad security and is dangerous in the real world. The default for the **exec-timeout** command is 10 minutes and zero (0) seconds (**exec-timeout 10 0**) of idle connection time.

Saving Configurations

Router#**copy running-config startup-config**	Saves the running configuration to local NVRAM
Router#**copy running-config tftp**	Saves the running configuration remotely to a TFTP server

Erasing Configurations

Router#**erase startup-config**	Deletes the startup configuration file from NVRAM

TIP The running configuration is still in dynamic memory. Reload the router to clear the running configuration.

show Commands

Router#**show ?**	Lists all **show** commands available.
Router#**show arp**	Displays the Address Resolution Protocol (ARP) table.
Router#**show clock**	Displays time set on device.
Router#**show controllers serial 0/0/0**	Displays statistics for interface hardware. Statistics display if the clock rate is set and if the cable is Data Communications Equipment (DCE), data terminal equipment (DTE), or not attached.
Router#**show flash**	Displays info about flash memory.
Router#**show history**	Displays the history of commands used at privilege EXEC level.
Router#**show hosts**	Displays the local host-to-IP address cache. These are the names and addresses of hosts on the network to which you can connect.
Router#**show interface serial 0/0/0**	Displays statistics for a specific interface (in this case, serial 0/0/0).
Router#**show interfaces**	Displays statistics for all interfaces.
Router#**show ip interface brief**	Displays a summary of all interfaces, including status and IP address assigned.
Router#**show ip protocols**	Displays the parameters and the current state of the active IPv4 routing protocol processes.
Router#**show ipv6 interface brief**	Displays a summary of all interfaces, including status and IPv6 address assigned.
Router#**show ipv6 protocols**	Displays the parameters and the current state of the active IPv6 routing protocol processes.
Router#**show protocols**	Displays the status of configured Layer 3 protocols.
Router#**show running-config**	Displays the configuration currently running in RAM.
Router#**show startup-config**	Displays the configuration saved in NVRAM.
Router#**show users**	Displays all users connected to the device.
Router#**show version**	Displays info about loaded software version.

EXEC Commands in Configuration Mode: The do Command

`Router(config)#do show running-config`	Executes the privileged-level **show running-config** command while in global configuration mode.
`Router(config)#`	The router remains in global configuration mode after the command has been executed.

TIP   The **do** command is useful when you want to execute EXEC commands, such as **show**, **clear**, or **debug**, while remaining in global configuration mode or in any configuration submode. You cannot use the **do** command to execute the **configure terminal** command because it is the **configure terminal** command that changes the mode to global configuration mode.

Configuration Example: Basic Router Configuration

Figure 11-1 illustrates the network topology for the configuration that follows, which shows a basic router configuration using the commands covered in this chapter.

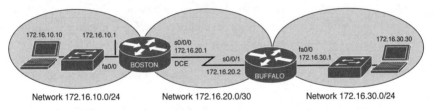

Figure 11-1   Network Topology for Basic Router Configuration

Boston Router

`Router>enable`	Enters privileged mode.
`Router#clock set 18:30:00 15 January 2016`	Sets the local time on the router.
`Router#configure terminal`	Enters global configuration mode.
`Router(config)#hostname Boston`	Sets the router name to Boston.
`Boston(config)#no ip domain-lookup`	Turns off name resolution on unrecognized commands (spelling mistakes).
`Boston(config)#banner login #This is the Boston Router. Authorized Access Only #`	Creates a login banner.
`Boston(config)#clock timezone EST -5`	Sets the time zone to eastern standard time (–5 from UTC).
`Boston(config)#enable secret cisco`	Enables secret password set to *cisco*.

Boston(config)#`service password-encryption`	Clear text passwords will be hidden using a weak encryption algorithm.
Boston(config)#`line console 0`	Enters line console mode.
Boston(config-line)#`logging synchronous`	Commands will not be interrupted by unsolicited messages.
Boston(config-line)#`password class`	Sets the password to *class*.
Boston(config-line)#`login`	Enables password checking at login.
Boston(config-line)#`line vty 0 4`	Moves to virtual Telnet lines 0 through 4.
Boston(config-line)#`password class`	Sets the password to *class*.
Boston(config-line)#`login`	Enables password checking at login.
Boston(config-line)#`line aux 0`	Moves to line auxiliary mode.
Boston(config-line)#`password class`	Sets the password to *class*.
Boston(config-line)#`login`	Enables password checking at login.
Boston(config-line)#`exit`	Moves back to global configuration mode.
Boston(config)#`no service password-encryption`	Turns off password encryption.
Boston(config)#`interface fastethernet 0/0`	Moves to interface Fast Ethernet 0/0 configuration mode.
Boston(config-if)#`description Engineering LAN`	Sets locally significant description of the interface.
Boston(config-if)#`ip address 172.16.10.1 255.255.255.0`	Assigns an IP address and subnet mask to the interface.
Boston(config-if)#`no shutdown`	Turns on the interface.
Boston(config-if)#`interface serial 0/0/0`	Moves directly to interface serial 0/0/0 configuration mode.
Boston(config-if)#`description Link to Buffalo Router`	Sets a locally significant description of the interface.
Boston(config-if)#`ip address 172.16.20.1 255.255.255.252`	Assigns an IP address and subnet mask to the interface.
Boston(config-if)#`clock rate 56000`	Sets a clock rate for serial transmission. The DCE cable must be plugged into this interface.
Boston(config-if)#`no shutdown`	Turns on the interface.
Boston(config-if)#`exit`	Moves back to global configuration mode.
Boston(config)#`ip host buffalo 172.16.20.2`	Sets a local hostname resolution to remote IP address 172.16.20.2.
Boston(config)#`exit`	Moves back to privileged mode.
Boston#`copy running-config startup-config`	Saves the running configuration to NVRAM.

Static Routing

This chapter provides information and commands concerning the following topics:

- Configuring an IPv4 static route on a router
- Static routes and recursive lookups
- The **permanent** keyword (optional)
- Floating static routes and administrative distance (optional)
- Configuring an IPv4 default route on a router
- Verifying IPv4 static routes
- Configuration example: IPv4 Static routes
- Static routes in IPv6
- Floating static routes in IPv6
- Default routes in IPv6
- Verifying and troubleshooting IPv6

Configuring an IPv4 Static Route on a Router

When using the **ip route** command, you can identify where packets should be routed in two ways:

- The next-hop address
- The exit interface

Both ways are shown in the "Configuration Example: IPv4 Static Routes" and the "Configuring an IPv4 Default Route on a Router" sections.

`Router(config)#ip`
`route 172.16.20.0`
`255.255.255.0`
`172.16.10.2`
	172.16.20.0 = destination network.
	
	255.255.255.0 = subnet mask.
	
	172.16.10.2 = next-hop address.
	
	Read this to say, "To get to the destination network of 172.16.20.0, with a subnet mask of 255.255.255.0, send all packets to 172.16.10.2."

`Router(config)#ip`
`route 172.16.20.0`
`255.255.255.0 serial`
`0/0/0`
	172.16.20.0 = destination network.
	
	255.255.255.0 = subnet mask.
	
	Serial 0/0/0 = exit interface.
	
	Read this to say, "To get to the destination network of 172.16.20.0, with a subnet mask of 255.255.255.0, send all packets out interface serial 0/0/0."

Static Routes and Recursive Lookups

A static route that uses a next-hop address (intermediate address) causes the router to look at the routing table twice: once when a packet first enters the router and the router looks up the entry in the table, and a second time when the router has to resolve the location of the intermediate address.

For point-to-point links, always use an exit interface in your static route statements:

`Router(config)#ip route 192.168.10.0 255.255.255.0 serial 0/0/0`

For broadcast links such as Ethernet, Fast Ethernet, or Gigabit Ethernet, use both an exit interface and an intermediate address:

`Router(config)#ip route 192.168.10.0 255.255.255.0 fastethernet 0/0`
`    192.138.20.2`

This saves the router from having to do a recursive lookup for the intermediate address of 192.168.20.2, knowing that the exit interface is FastEthernet 0/0.

Try to avoid using static routes that reference only intermediate addresses.

The permanent Keyword (Optional)

Without the **permanent** keyword in a static route statement, a static route is removed if an interface goes down. A downed interface causes the directly connected network and any associated static routes to be removed from the routing table. If the interface comes back up, the routes are returned.

Adding the **permanent** keyword to a static route statement keeps the static routes in the routing table even if the interface goes down and the directly connected networks are removed. You cannot get to these routes—the interface is down—but the routes remain in the table. The advantage to this is that when the interface comes back up, the static routes do not need to be reprocessed and placed back into the routing table, thus saving time and processing power.

When a static route is added or deleted, this route, along with all other static routes, is processed in 1 second. Before Cisco IOS Software Release 12.0, this processing time was 5 seconds.

The routing table processes static routes every minute to install or remove static routes according to the changing routing table.

To specify that the route will not be removed, even if the interface shuts down, enter the following command, for example:

```
Router(config)#ip route 172.16.20.0 255.255.255.0 172.16.10.2 permanent
```

Floating Static Routes and Administrative Distance (Optional)

To specify that an administrative distance (AD) of 200 has been assigned to a given route, enter the following command, for example:

```
Router(config)#ip route 172.16.20.0 255.255.255.0 172.16.10.2 200
```

By default, a static route is assigned an AD of 1. AD rates the "trustworthiness" of a route. AD is a number from 0 to 255 (or 254 for IPv6), where 0 is absolutely trusted and 255 (254 for IPv6) cannot be trusted at all. Therefore, an AD of 1 is an extremely reliable rating, with only an AD of 0 being better. An AD of 0 is assigned to a directly connected route. Table 12-1 lists the AD for each type of route.

TABLE 12-1   Administrative Distances

Route Type	AD IPv4	AD IPv6
Connected	0	0
Static	1	1
Enhanced Interior Gateway Routing Protocol (EIGRP) summary route	5	5
External Border Gateway Protocol (eBGP)	20	20
EIGRP (internal)	90	90
Open Shortest Path First Protocol (OSPF)	110	110
Intermediate System-to-Intermediate System Protocol (IS-IS)	115	115
RIP	120	120
External Gateway Protocol (EGP) (no longer supported by Cisco IOS)	140	140
On-Demand Routing	160	160
EIGRP (external)	170	170

Route Type	AD IPv4	AD IPv6
Internal Border Gateway Protocol (iBGP) (external)	200	200
Unknown or unbelievable	**255** (Does not pass traffic)	**254** (Does not pass traffic)

By default, a static route is always used rather than a routing protocol. By adding an AD number to your statement, however, you can effectively create a backup route to your routing protocol. If your network is using EIGRP and you need a backup route, add a static route with an AD greater than 90. EIGRP will be used because its AD is better (lower) than the static route. If EIGRP goes down, however, the static route is used in its place. This is known as a *floating static route*.

NOTE   These default ADs are the same for both IPv4 and IPv6 routing with the exception of the Unknown or Unbelievable network—it is 255 in IPv4 but 254 in IPv6.

Configuring an IPv4 Default Route on a Router

Router(config)#**ip route 0.0.0.0 0.0.0.0 172.16.10.2**	Send all packets destined for networks not in my routing table to 172.16.10.2.
Router(config)#**ip route 0.0.0.0 0.0.0.0 serial 0/0/0**	Send all packets destined for networks not in my routing table out my serial 0/0 interface.

NOTE   The combination of the 0.0.0.0 network address and the 0.0.0.0 mask is called a *quad-zero route*.

Verifying IPv4 Static Routes

To display the contents of the IP routing table, enter the following command:

```
Router#show ip route
```

NOTE   The codes to the left of the routes in the table tell you from where the router learned the routes. A static route is described by the letter *S*. A default route learned by a static route is described in the routing table by S*. The asterisk (*) indicates that the last path option is used when forwarding the packet.

Configuration Example: IPv4 Static Routes

Figure 12-1 illustrates the network topology for the configuration that follows, which shows how to configure static routes using the commands covered in this chapter.

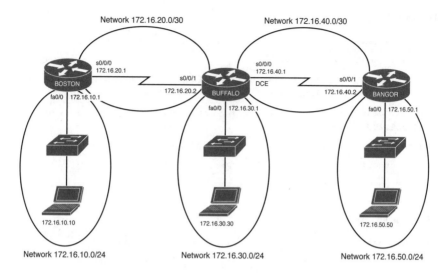

Figure 12-1   Network Topology for Static Route Configuration

NOTE   The hostnames, passwords, and interfaces have all been configured using the commands shown in the configuration example in Chapter 11, "Configuring a Cisco Router."

Boston Router

`Boston>`**`enable`**	Moves to privileged mode
`Boston#`**`configure terminal`**	Moves to global configuration mode
`Boston(config)#`**`ip route`** `172.16.30.0 255.255.255.0` `172.16.20.2`	Configures a static route using the next-hop address
`Boston(config)#`**`ip route`** `172.16.40.0 255.255.255.0` `172.16.20.2`	Configures a static route using the next-hop address
`Boston(config)#`**`ip route`** `172.16.50.0 255.255.255.0` `172.16.20.2`	Configures a static route using the next-hop address
`Boston(config)#`**`exit`**	Moves to privileged mode
`Boston#`**`copy running-config`** **`startup-config`**	Saves the configuration to NVRAM

Buffalo Router

Buffalo>**enable**	Moves to privileged mode
Buffalo#**configure terminal**	Moves to global configuration mode
Buffalo(config)#**ip route 172.16.10.0 255.255.255.0 serial 0/0/1**	Configures a static route using the exit interface
Buffalo(config)#**ip route 172.16.50.0 255.255.255.0 serial 0/0/0**	Configures a static route using the exit interface
Buffalo(config)#**exit**	Moves to privileged mode
Buffalo#**copy running-config startup-config**	Saves the configuration to NVRAM

Bangor Router

Bangor>**enable**	Moves to privileged mode
Bangor#**configure terminal**	Moves to global configuration mode
Bangor(config)#**ip route 0.0.0.0 0.0.0.0 serial 0/0/1**	Configures a static route using the default route
Bangor(config)#**exit**	Moves to privileged mode
Bangor#**copy running-config startup-config**	Saves the configuration to NVRAM

Static Routes in IPv6

NOTE   To create a static route in IPv6, you use the same format as creating a static route in IPv4.

Figure 12-2 illustrates the network topology for the configuration that follows, which shows how to configure static routes with IPv6. Note that only the static routes on the Austin router are displayed.

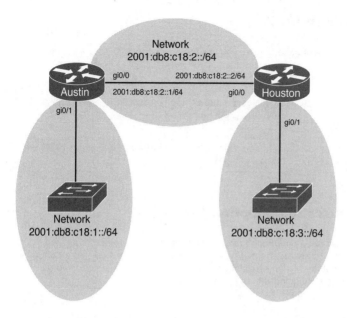

Figure 12-2   Network Topology for IPv6 Static Route Configuration

`Austin(config)#ipv6 route`
`2001:db8:c18:3::/64`
`2001:db8:c18:2::2`
	Creates a static route configured to send all packets addressed to 2001:db8:c18:3::/64 to a next-hop address of 2001:db8:c18:2::2.

`Austin(config)#ipv6 route`
`2001:db8:c18:3::/64`
`gigabitethernet 0/0`
	Creates a directly attached static route configured to send packets out interface gigabitethernet 0/0.

`Austin(config)#ipv6 route`
`2001:db8:c18:3::/64 gigabitethernet`
`0/0 2001:db8:c18:2::2`
	Creates a fully specified static route on a broadcast interface.

	NOTE This is the preferred method for static routes with a broadcast interface as the exit interface.

Floating Static Routes in IPv6

To create a static route with an AD set to 200 as opposed to the default AD of 1, enter the following command, for example:

```
Austin(config)# ipv6 route 2001:db8:c18:3::/64 fastethernet 0/0 200
```

NOTE   The default ADs used in IPv4 are the same for IPv6, with one exception—the AD number for unknown or unbelievable is 254 as opposed to 255. See Table 12-1 for a list of the default ADs.

Default Routes in IPv6

NOTE   To create a default route in IPv6, you use the same format as creating a default route in IPv4.

`Austin(config)#ipv6`
`route ::/0`
`2001:db8:c18:2::2`
	Creates a default route configured to send all packets to a next-hop address of 2001:db8:c18:2::2

`Austin(config)#ipv6` `route ::/0 serial 0/0/0`	Creates a default route configured to send packets out interface serial 0/0/0

Verifying and Troubleshooting IPv6

CAUTION   Using the **debug** command may severely affect router performance and might even cause the router to reboot. Always exercise caution when using the **debug** command, and do not leave it on. Use **debug** long enough to gather needed information, and then disable debugging with the **undebug all** command.

TIP   Send your **debug** output to a syslog server to ensure that you have a copy of it in case your router is overloaded and needs to reboot.

`Router#debug ipv6 packet`	Displays debug messages for IPv6 packets
`Router#debug ipv6 routing`	Displays debug messages for IPv6 routing table updates and route cache updates
`Router#show ipv6 interface`	Displays the status of interfaces configured for IPv6
`Router#show ipv6 interface brief`	Displays a summarized status of interfaces configured for IPv6
`Router#show ipv6 route`	Displays the current IPv6 routing table
`Router#show ipv6 route summary`	Displays a summarized form of the current IPv6 routing table
`Router#show ipv6 static`	Displays only static IPv6 routes installed in the routing table
`Router#show ipv6 static 2001:db8:5555:0/16`	Displays only static route information about the specific address given
`Router#show ipv6 static interface serial 0/0/0`	Displays only static route information with the specified interface as the outgoing interface
`Router#show ipv6 static detail`	Displays a more detailed entry for IPv6 static routes
`Router#show ipv6 traffic`	Displays statistics about IPv6 traffic

RIP Next Generation (RIPng)

This chapter provides information and commands concerning the following topics:

- Implementing RIP Next Generation
- Verifying and troubleshooting RIPng
- Configuration example: RIPng

NOTE   For an excellent overview of IPv6, I strongly recommend you read Rick Graziani's book from Cisco Press: *IPv6 Fundamentals: A Straightforward Approach to Understanding IPv6.*

Implementing RIP Next Generation

This section shows how to implement RIP Next Generation (RIPng) on a router.

`Router(config)#ipv6 unicast-routing`	Enables the forwarding of IPv6 unicast datagrams globally on the router.
`Router(config) #interface serial0/0/0`	Moves to interface configuration mode.
`Router(config-if) #ipv6 rip TOWER enable`	Creates the RIPng process named TOWER and enables RIPng on the interface.
	NOTE Unlike RIPv1 and RIPv2, where you needed to create the RIP routing process with the **router rip** command and then use the **network** command to specify the interfaces on which to run RIP, the RIPng process is created automatically when RIPng is enabled on an interface with the **ipv6 rip** *name* **enable** command.
	TIP Be sure that you do not misspell your process name. If you do misspell the name, you will inadvertently create a second process with the misspelled name.
	NOTE Cisco IOS Software automatically creates an entry in the configuration for the RIPng routing process when it is enabled on an interface.
	NOTE The **ipv6 router rip** *process-name* command is still needed when configuring optional features of RIPng.
	NOTE The routing process name does not need to match between neighbor routers.
`Router(config)#ipv6 router rip TOWER`	Creates the RIPng process named TOWER if it has not already been created and moves to router configuration mode.

Router(config-rtr) #maximum-paths 2	Defines the maximum number of equal-cost routes that RIPng can support.
	NOTE The number of paths that can be used is a number from 1 to 64. The default is 4.
Router(config-if)#ipv6 rip tower default-information originate	Announces the default route along with all other RIPng routes.
Router(config-if) #ipv6 rip tower default-information only	Announces only the default route. Suppresses all other RIPng routes.

Verifying and Troubleshooting RIPng

CAUTION Using the **debug** command may severely affect router performance and might even cause the router to reboot. Always exercise caution when using the **debug** command. Do not leave **debug** on. Use it long enough to gather needed information, and then disable debugging with the **undebug all** command.

TIP Send your **debug** output to a syslog server to ensure you have a copy of it in case your router is overloaded and needs to reboot.

Router#clear ipv6 rip	Deletes routes from the IPv6 RIP routing table and, if installed, routes in the IPv6 routing table.
Router#clear ipv6 route *	Deletes all routes from the IPv6 routing table.
	NOTE Clearing all routes from the routing table causes high CPU utilization rates as the routing table is rebuilt.
Router#clear ipv6 route 2001:db8:c18:3::/64	Clears this specific route from the IPv6 routing table.
Router#clear ipv6 traffic	Resets IPv6 traffic counters.
Router#debug ipv6 packet	Displays debug messages for IPv6 packets.
Router#debug ipv6 rip	Displays debug messages for IPv6 RIP routing transactions.
Router#debug ipv6 routing	Displays debug messages for IPv6 routing table updates and route cache updates.
Router#show ipv6 interface	Displays the status of interfaces configured for IPv6.
Router#show ipv6 interface brief	Displays a summarized status of all interfaces along with assigned IPv6 addresses.
Router#show ipv6 neighbors	Displays IPv6 neighbor discovery cache information.
Router#show ipv6 protocols	Displays the parameters and the current state of the active IPv6 routing protocol processes.

Router#**show ipv6 rip**	Displays information about the current IPv6 RIPng process.
Router#**show ipv6 rip** **database**	Displays the RIPng process database. If more than one RIPng process is running, all are displayed with this command.
Router#**show ipv6 rip** **next-hops**	Displays RIPng processes and, under each process, all next-hop addresses.
Router#**show ipv6 route**	Displays the current IPv6 routing table.
Router#**show ipv6 route rip**	Displays the current RIPng routes in the IPv6 routing table
Router#**show ipv6 route** **summary**	Displays a summarized form of the current IPv6 routing table.
Router#**show ipv6 routers**	Displays IPv6 router advertisement information received from other routers.
Router#**show ipv6 traffic**	Displays statistics about IPv6 traffic.

Configuration Example: RIPng

Figure 13-1 illustrates the network topology for the configuration that follows, which shows how to configure IPv6 and RIPng using the commands covered in this chapter.

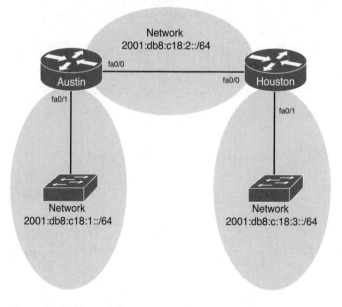

Figure 13-1   Network Topology for IPv6/RIPng Configuration Example

Austin Router

`Router>enable`	Moves to privileged mode
`Router#configure terminal`	Moves to global configuration mode
`Router(config)#hostname Austin`	Assigns a hostname to the router
`Austin(config)#ipv6 unicast-routing`	Enables the forwarding of IPv6 unicast datagrams globally on the router
`Austin(config)#interface fastethernet0/0`	Enters interface configuration mode
`Austin(config-if)#ipv6 address 2001:db8:c18:2::/64 eui-64`	Configures a global IPv6 address with an EUI-64 interface identifier in the low-order 64 bits of the IPv6 address
`Austin(config-if)#ipv6 rip TOWER enable`	Creates the RIPng process named TOWER and enables RIPng on the interface
`Austin(config-if)#no shutdown`	Activates the interface
`Austin(config-if)#interface fastethernet0/1`	Enters interface configuration mode
`Austin(config-if)#ipv6 address 2001:db8:c18:1::/64 eui-64`	Configures a global IPv6 address with an EUI-64 interface identifier in the low-order 64 bits of the IPv6 address
`Austin(config-if)#ipv6 rip TOWER enable`	Creates the RIPng process named TOWER and enables RIPng on the interface
`Austin(config-if)#no shutdown`	Activates the interface
`Austin(config-if)#exit`	Moves to global configuration mode
`Austin(config)#exit`	Moves to privileged mode
`Austin#copy running-config startup-config`	Saves the configuration to NVRAM

Houston Router

`Router>`**`enable`**	Moves to privileged mode
`Router#`**`configure terminal`**	Moves to global configuration mode
`Router(config)#`**`hostname Houston`**	Assigns a hostname to the router
`Houston(config)#`**`ipv6 unicast-routing`**	Enables the forwarding of IPv6 unicast datagrams globally on the router
`Houston(config)#`**`interface fastethernet0/0`**	Enters interface configuration mode
`Houston(config-if)#`**`ipv6 address 2001:db8:c18:2::/64 eui-64`**	Configures a global IPv6 address with an EUI-64 interface identifier in the low-order 64 bits of the IPv6 address
`Houston(config-if)#`**`ipv6 rip TOWER enable`**	Creates the RIPng process named TOWER and enables RIPng on the interface
`Houston(config-if)#`**`no shutdown`**	Activates the interface
`Houston(config-if)#`**`interface fastethernet 0/1`**	Enters interface configuration mode
`Houston(config-if)#`**`ipv6 address 2001:db8:c18:3::/64 eui-64`**	Configures a global IPv6 address with an EUI-64 interface identifier in the low-order 64 bits of the IPv6 address
`Houston(config-if)#`**`ipv6 rip TOWER enable`**	Creates the RIPng process named TOWER and enables RIPng on the interface
`Houston(config-if)#`**`no shutdown`**	Activates the interface
`Houston(config-if)#`**`exit`**	Moves to global configuration mode
`Houston(config)#`**`exit`**	Moves to privileged mode
`Houston#`**`copy running-config startup-config`**	Saves the configuration to NVRAM

EIGRP and EIGRPv6

This chapter provides information and commands concerning the following topics:

- Configuring Enhanced Interior Gateway Routing Protocol (EIGRP) for IPv4
- EIGRP Router ID
- EIGRP Timers
- EIGRP auto-summarization for IPv4
- EIGRP manual summarization for IPv4
- Passive EIGRP interfaces
- Equal-cost load balancing: maximum paths
- Unequal-cost load balancing: **variance**
- Bandwidth use
- Verifying EIGRP and EIGRPv6
- Troubleshooting EIGRP and EIGRPv6
- Configuration example: EIGRP
- Configuration example: EIGRPv6

Configuring Enhanced Interior Gateway Routing Protocol (EIGRP) for IPv4

`Router(config)#router eigrp 100`	Turns on the EIGRP process. 100 is the autonomous system (AS) number, which can be a number between 1 and 65,535.
	All routers must use the same AS number to communicate with each other.
`Router(config-router)#network 10.0.0.0`	Specifies which network to advertise in EIGRP.
`Router(config-if)#bandwidth x`	Sets the bandwidth of this interface to *x* kilobits to allow EIGRP to make a better metric calculation.
	NOTE This command is entered at the interface command prompt (config-if) and not in the router process prompt (config-router). The setting can differ for each interface to which it is applied.
	TIP The **bandwidth** command is used for metric calculations only. It does not change interface performance.

`Router(config-router)#`**`eigrp`** **`log-neighbor-changes`**	Changes with neighbors will be displayed.
`Router(config-router)#`**`no`** **`network 10.0.0.0`**	Removes the network from the EIGRP process.
`Router(config)#`**`no router`** **`eigrp 100`**	Disables routing process 100 and removes the entire EIGRP configuration from the running configuration.
`Router(config-router)#`**`network`** **`10.0.0.0 0.255.255.255`**	Identifies which interfaces or networks to include in EIGRP. Interfaces must be configured with addresses that fall within the wildcard mask range of the **network** statement. Although it is incorrect to do so, a network mask will be accepted here; the IOS is intelligent enough to recognize the difference and correct the error for you.

TIP   The use of a wildcard mask or network mask is optional.

TIP   There is no limit to the number of network statements (that is, **network** commands) that you can configure on a router.

TIP   If you use the **network 172.16.1.0 0.0.0.255** command with a wildcard mask, in this example the command specifies that only interfaces on the 172.16.1.0/24 subnet will participate in EIGRP. EIGRP automatically summarizes routes on the major network boundary when in a discontiguous IP address network topology when the **auto-summary** command is enabled.

TIP   Since IOS version 15.0, EIGRP no longer automatically summarizes networks at the classful boundary by default.

TIP   If you do not use the optional wildcard mask, the EIGRP process assumes that all directly connected networks that are part of the overall major network will participate in the EIGRP process and that EIGRP will attempt to establish neighbor relationships from each interface that is part of that Class A, B, or C major network.

Adjusting the EIGRP for IPv4 Metric Weights

`Router(config-router)#`**`metric weights`** `tos k1 k2 k3 k4 k5`	Changes the default k values used in metric calculation. These are the default values: tos=0, k1=1, k2=0, k3=1, k4=0, k5=0

NOTE   *tos* is a reference to the original Interior Gateway Routing Protocol (IGRP) intention to have IGRP perform type-of-service routing. Because this was never adopted into practice, the *tos* field in this command is always set to zero (0).

NOTE   With default settings in place, the metric of EIGRP is reduced to the slowest bandwidth plus the sum of all the delays of the exit interfaces from the local router to the destination network.

TIP   For two routers to form a neighbor relationship in EIGRP, the *k* values must match.

CAUTION   Unless you are very familiar with what is occurring in your network, it is recommended that you do not change the *k* values.

Adjusting the EIGRPv6 Metric Weights

`Router(config)#`**`ipv6 router eigrp`** **`100`**	Enters router configuration mode and creates an EIGRP IPv6 routing process.
`Router(config-router)#`**`metric`** **`weights`** *`tos k1 k2 k3 k4 k5`* `Router(config-router)#`**`metric`** **`weights 0 1 1 1 1 1`**	Changes the default *k* values used in metric calculation. These are the default values: tos=0, k1=1, k2=0, k3=1, k4=0, k5=0.

Configuring EIGRPv6 on an Interface

No linkage exists between EIGRP for IPv4 and EIGRP for IPv6; the two are configured and managed separately. However, the commands for configuration of EIGRP for IPv4 and IPv6 are similar, making the transition easy.

`Router(config)#`**`ipv6 unicast-routing`**	Enables the forwarding of IPv6 unicast datagrams globally on the router. This command is required before any IPv6 routing protocol can be configured.
`Router(config)#`**`interface serial`** **`0/0/0`**	Moves to interface configuration mode.
`Router(config-if)#`**`ipv6 eigrp 100`**	Enables EIGRP for IPv6 on the interface and creates the EIGRP for IPv6 process.
`Router(config-if)#`**`ipv6 router eigrp`** **`100`**	Enters router configuration mode and creates an EIGRP IPv6 routing process.
`Router(config-rtr)#`**`eigrp router-id`** **`10.1.1.1`**	Enables the use of a fixed router ID.
`Router(config-rtr)#`**`no shutdown`**	Brings up the EIGRP routing process.

NOTE   EIGRP for IPv6 starts in shutdown mode. Use the **no shutdown** command to start the process.

NOTE   The **eigrp router-id w.x.y.z** command is typically used when an IPv4 address is not defined on the router or when manual defining is desired.

NOTE   EIGRP for IPv6 can also be created by entering into router configuration mode and creating the router process, just like you would with EIGRP for IPv4.

```
Router(config)#ipv6 router eigrp 400
Router(config-rtr)#eigrp router-id 10.1.1.1
```

EIGRP Router ID

`Router(config)#router eigrp 100`	Enters into EIGRP router configuration mode for AS 100.
`Router(config-router)#eigrp router-id 172.16.3.3`	Manually sets the router ID to 172.16.3.3. Can be any IP address except for 0.0.0.0 and 255.255.255.255. If not set, the router ID will be the highest IP address of any loopback interfaces. If no loopback interfaces are configured, the router ID will be the highest IP address of your active local interface.
`Router(config-router)#no eigrp router-id 172.16.3.3`	Removes the static router ID from the configuration.

NOTE There is no IPv6 form of the Router ID. Even if a router is using IPv6 exclusively, the router ID will still be in the format of an IPv4 address.

EIGRP Timers

`Router(config)#interface serial 0/0/0`	Moves to interface configuration mode
`Router(config-if)#ip hello-interval eigrp 100 10`	Configures the EIGRP hello time interval for AS 100 to 10 seconds
`Router(config-if)#ip hold-time eigrp 100 30`	Configures the EIGRP hold timer interval for AS 100 to 30 seconds
`Router(config-if)#ipv6 hello-interval eigrp 100 10`	Configures the hello interval for EIGRP for IPv6 process 100 to be 10 seconds
`Router(config-if)#ipv6 hold-time eigrp 100 40`	Configures the hold timer for EIGRP for IPv6 process 100 to be 40 seconds

NOTE   EIGRP hello and hold timers do not have to match between neighbors to successfully establish a neighbor relationship.

NOTE   The AS number in these commands must match the AS number of EIGRP on the router for these changes to take effect.

TIP   It is recommended that you match the timers between neighbors; otherwise, you may experience flapping neighbor relationships or network instability.

EIGRP Auto-Summarization for IPv4

`Router(config-router)#auto-summary`	Enables auto-summarization for the EIGRP process.
	NOTE The behavior of the **auto-summary** command is disabled by default for Cisco IOS Software Versions 15 and later. Earlier software generally has automatic summarization enabled by default.
`Router(config-router)#no auto-summary`	Turns off the auto-summarization feature.

EIGRP Manual Summarization for IPv4

`Router(config)#interface fastethernet 0/0`	Enters interface configuration mode.
`Router(config-if)#ip summary-address eigrp 100 10.10.0.0 255.255.0.0 75`	Enables manual summarization for EIGRP AS 100 on this specific interface for the given address and mask. An administrative distance of 75 is assigned to this summary route.
	NOTE The *administrative-distance* argument is optional in this command. Without it, an administrative distance of 5 is automatically applied to the summary route.

CAUTION   EIGRP automatically summarizes networks at the classful boundary. A poorly designed network with discontiguous subnets could have problems with connectivity if the summarization feature is left on. For instance, you could have two routers advertise the same network—172.16.0.0/16—when in fact they wanted to advertise two different subnets—172.16.10.0/24 and 172.16.20.0/24.

Recommended practice is that you turn off automatic summarization if necessary, use the **ip summary-address** command, and summarize manually what you need to.

EIGRPv6 Summary Addresses

`Router(config)#interface serial0/0/0`	Moves to interface configuration mode.
`Router(config-if)#ipv6 summary-address eigrp 100 2001:0DB8:0:1::/64`	Configures a summary aggregate address for a specified interface. There is an optional administrative distance parameter for this command. This command behaves similarly to the **ip summary-address eigrp** command.

Passive EIGRP Interfaces

`Router(config)#router eigrp 110`	Starts the EIGRP routing process.
`Router(config-router)#network 10.0.0.0`	Specifies a network to advertise in the EIGRP routing process.
`Router(config-router) #passive-interface fastethernet 0/0`	Prevents the sending of hello packets out the Fast Ethernet 0/0 interface. No neighbor adjacency is formed.
`Router(config-router) #passive-interface default`	Prevents the sending of hello packets out all interfaces.
`Router(config)#no passive-interface serial 0/0/1`	Enables hello packets to be sent out interface serial 0/0/1, thereby allowing neighbor adjacencies to form.
`Router(config)#ipv6 router eigrp 110`	Starts the EIGRP for IPv6 routing process.
`Router(config-rtr) #passive-interface fastethernet 0/0`	Prevents the sending of hello packets out the Fast Ethernet 0/0 interface. No neighbor adjacency is formed.
`Router(config-rtr) #passive-interface default`	Prevents the sending of hello packets out all interfaces.
`Router(config-rtr)#no passive-interface serial 0/0/1`	Enables hello packets to be sent out interface serial 0/0/1, thereby allowing neighbor adjacencies to form.

Equal-Cost Load Balancing: Maximum Paths

`Router(config)#router eigrp 100`	Creates routing process 100
`Router(config-router)#network 10.0.0.0`	Specifies which network to advertise in EIGRP
`Router(config-router)#maximum-paths 6`	Set the maximum number of parallel routes that EIGRP will support to 6
`Router(config)#ipv6 router eigrp 100`	Creates routing process 100 for EIGRP for IPv6

`Router(config-rtr)#maximum-paths 6`	Set the maximum number of parallel routes that EIGRP for IPv6 will support to 6

NOTE   With the **maximum-paths** router configuration command, up to 32 equal-cost entries can be in the routing table for the same destination. The default is 4.

NOTE   Setting the **maximum-path** to 1 disables load balancing.

Unequal-Cost Load Balancing: Variance

`Router(config)#router eigrp 100`	Creates routing process 100
`Router(config-router)#network 10.0.0.0`	Specifies which network to advertise in EIGRP
`Router(config-router)#variance n`	Instructs the router to include routes with a metric less than or equal to n times the minimum metric route for that destination, where n is the number specified by the **variance** command
`Router(config)#ipv6 router eigrp 100`	Creates routing process 100 for EIGRP for IPv6
`Router(config-rtr)#variance n`	Instructs the router to include routes with a metric less than or equal to n times the minimum metric route for that destination, where n is the number specified by the **variance** command

NOTE   If a path is not a feasible successor, it is not used in load balancing.

NOTE   EIGRP variance can be set to a number between 1 and 128.

Bandwidth Use

`Router(config)#interface serial 0/0/0`	Enters interface configuration mode.
`Router(config-if)#bandwidth 256`	Sets the bandwidth of this interface to 256 kilobits to allow EIGRP to make a better metric calculation.
`Router(config-if)#ip bandwidth-percent eigrp 50 100`	Configures the percentage of bandwidth that may be used by EIGRP on an interface. 50 is the EIGRP AS number. 100 is the percentage value. 100% * 256 = 256 kbps.

`Router(config-if)#ipv6`
`bandwidth-percent eigrp`
`100 75`
	Configures the percentage of bandwidth (75%) that may be used by EIGRP for IPv6 on the interface.

NOTE   By default, EIGRP is set to use only up to 50 percent of the bandwidth of an interface to exchange routing information. Values greater than 100 percent can be configured. This configuration option might prove useful if the bandwidth is set artificially low for other reasons, such as manipulation of the routing metric or to accommodate an oversubscribed multipoint Frame Relay configuration.

NOTE   The **ip bandwidth-percent** command relies on the value set by the **bandwidth** command.

Verifying EIGRP and EIGRPv6

`Router#clear ip route *`	Deletes all routes from the IPv4 routing table.
`Router#clear ip route` `172.16.10.0`	Clears this specific route from the IPv4 routing table.
`Router#clear ipv6 route *`	Deletes all routes from the IPv6 routing table.
	NOTE Clearing all routes from the routing table causes high CPU utilization rates as the routing table is rebuilt.
`Router#clear ipv6 route` `2001:db8:c18:3::/64`	Clears this specific route from the IPv6 routing table.
`Router#clear ipv6 traffic`	Resets IPv6 traffic counters.
`Router#show ip eigrp neighbors`	Displays the neighbor table.
`Router#show ip eigrp neighbors` `detail`	Displays a detailed neighbor table.
	TIP The **show ip eigrp neighbors detail** command verifies whether a neighbor is configured as a stub router.
`Router#show ip eigrp interfaces`	Shows info for each interface.
`Router#show ip eigrp interfaces` `serial0/0/0`	Shows info for a specific interface.
`Router#show ip eigrp 100` `interfaces`	Shows info for interfaces running process 100.
`Router#show ip eigrp topology`	Displays the topology table.
	TIP The **show ip eigrp topology** command shows you where your feasible successors are.

Router#show ip eigrp topology all-links	Displays all entries in the EIGRP topology table, including nonfeasible-successor sources.
Router#show ip eigrp traffic	Shows the number and type of packets sent and received.
Router#show ip interface	Displays the status of interfaces configured for IPv4.
Router#show ip interface brief	Displays a summarized status of interfaces configured for IPv4.
Router#show ip protocols	Shows the parameters and current state of the active routing protocol process.
Router#show ip route	Shows the complete routing table.
Router#show ip route eigrp	Shows a routing table with only EIGRP entries.
Router#show ipv6 eigrp interfaces	Displays IPv6 info for each interface.
Router#show ipv6 eigrp interfaces serial 0/0/0	Displays IPv6 info for a specific interface.
Router#show ipv6 eigrp 100 interfaces	Displays IPv6 info for interfaces running process 100.
Router#show ipv6 eigrp neighbors	Displays the EIGRPv6 neighbor table.
Router#show ipv6 eigrp neighbors detail	Displays a detailed EIGRPv6 neighbor table.
Router#show ipv6 eigrp topology	Displays the EIGRPv6 topology table.
Router#show ipv6 interface	Displays the status of interfaces configured for IPv6.
Router#show ipv6 interface brief	Displays a summarized status of interfaces configured for IPv6.
Router#show ipv6 neighbors	Displays IPv6 neighbor discovery cache information.
Router#show ipv6 protocols	Displays the parameters and current state of the active IPv6 routing protocol processes.
Router#show ipv6 route	Displays the current IPv6 routing table.
Router#show ipv6 route eigrp	Displays the current IPv6 routing table with only EIGRPv6 routes.
Router#show ipv6 route summary	Displays a summarized form of the current IPv6 routing table.
Router#show ipv6 routers	Displays IPv6 router advertisement information received from other routers.
Router#show ipv6 traffic	Displays statistics about IPv6 traffic.

Troubleshooting EIGRP and EIGRPv6

`Router#debug eigrp fsm`	Displays events/actions related to EIGRP finite state machine (FSM).
`Router#debug eigrp packets`	Displays events/actions related to EIGRP packets.
`Router#debug eigrp neighbor`	Displays events/actions related to your EIGRP neighbors.
`Router#debug ip eigrp`	Displays events/actions related to EIGRP protocol packets.
`Router#debug ip eigrp notifications`	Displays EIGRP event notifications.
`Router#debug ipv6 eigrp`	Displays information about the EIGRP for an IPv6 protocol.
`Router#debug ipv6 eigrp neighbor 2001:db8:c18:3::1`	Displays information about the specified EIGRP for an IPv6 neighbor.
`Router#debug ipv6 eigrp neighbor notification`	Displays EIGRP for IPv6 events and notifications in the console of the router.
`Router#debug ipv6 eigrp neighbor summary`	Displays a summary of EIGRP for IPv6 routing information.
`Router#debug ipv6 packet`	Displays debug messages for IPv6 packets.
	TIP Send your **debug** output to a syslog server to ensure that you have a copy of it in case your router is overloaded and needs to reboot.
`Router#debug ipv6 routing`	Displays debug messages for IPv6 routing table updates and route cache updates.

Configuration Example: EIGRP

Figure 14-1 illustrates the network topology for the configuration that follows, which shows how to configure EIGRP using the commands covered in this chapter.

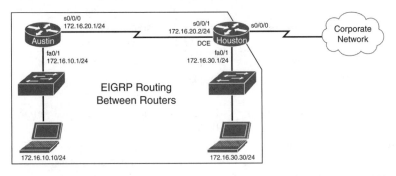

Figure 14-1   Network Topology for EIGRP Configuration

Austin Router

`Austin>enable`	Moves to privileged mode.
`Austin#configure terminal`	Moves to global configuration mode.
`Austin(config)#interface serial 0/0/0`	Enters interface configuration mode.
`Austin(config-if)#ip address 172.16.20.1 255.255.255.0`	Assigns the IP address and netmask.
`Austin(config-if)#no shutdown`	Enables the interface.
`Austin(config-if)#interface fastethernet 0/1`	Enters interface configuration mode.
`Austin(config-if)#ip address 172.16.10.1 255.255.255.0`	Assigns the IP address and netmask.
`Austin(config-if)#no shutdown`	Enables the interface.
`Austin(config-if)#router eigrp 100`	Enables EIGRP routing.
`Austin(config-router)#no auto-summary`	Disables auto-summarization.
`Austin(config-router)#eigrp log-neighbor-changes`	Changes with neighbors will be displayed.
`Austin(config-router)#network 172.16.0.0`	Advertises directly connected networks (classful address only).
`Austin(config-router)#passive interface fastethernet 0/1`	Prevents the sending of hello packets out the Fast Ethernet 0/1 interface. No neighbor adjacency is formed.
`Austin(config)#exit`	Returns to privileged mode.
`Austin#copy running-config startup-config`	Saves the configuration to NVRAM.

Houston Router

`Houston>enable`	Moves to privileged mode.
`Houston#configure terminal`	Moves to global configuration mode.
`Houston(config)#interface serial 0/0/1`	Enters interface configuration mode.
`Houston(config-if)#ip address 172.16.20.2 255.255.255.0`	Assigns the IP address and netmask.
`Houston(config-if)#clock rate 56000`	Sets the clock rate.
`Houston(config-if)#no shutdown`	Enables the interface.
`Houston(config-if)#interface fastethernet 0/1`	Enters interface configuration mode.
`Houston(config-if)#ip address 172.16.30.1 255.255.255.0`	Assigns the IP address and netmask.
`Houston(config-if)#no shutdown`	Enables the interface.
`Houston(config-if)#router eigrp 100`	Enables EIGRP routing.
`Houston(config-router)#no auto-summary`	Disables auto-summarization.

`Houston(config-router)#`**`eigrp`** `log-neighbor-changes`	Changes with neighbors will be displayed.
`Houston(config-router)#`**`network`** `172.16.0.0`	Advertises directly connected networks (classful address only).
`Houston(config-router)#`**`passive interface fastethernet 0/1`**	Prevents the sending of hello packets out the Fast Ethernet 0/1 interface. No neighbor adjacency is formed.
`Houston(config-keychain-key)#`**`exit`**	Returns to global configuration mode.
`Houston(config)#`**`exit`**	Returns to privileged mode.
`Houston#`**`copy running-config startup-config`**	Saves the configuration to NVRAM.

Configuration Example: EIGRPv6

Figure 14-2 shows the network topology for the configuration that follows, which demonstrates how to configure EIGRP for IPv6 using the commands covered in this chapter.

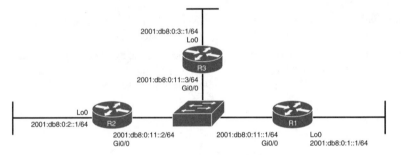

2001:db8:0:0:3::1/64
Lo0

R3

2001:db8:0:11::3/64
Gi0/0

Lo0
2001:db8:0:2::1/64   R2

2001:db8:0:11::2/64
Gi0/0

2001:db8:0:11::1/64
Gi0/0

R1

Lo0
2001:db8:0:1::1/64

Figure 14-2 Network Topology for EIGRP for IPv6 Configuration

R3 Router

`Router>`**`enable`**	Moves to privileged mode
`Router#`**`configure terminal`**	Moves to global configuration mode
`Router(config)#`**`hostname R3`**	Assigns a hostname to the router
`R3(config)#`**`ipv6 unicast-routing`**	Enables the forwarding of IPv6 unicast datagrams globally on the router
`R3(config)#`**`ipv6 router eigrp 1`**	Creates and enters EIGRP router configuration mode with the AS being 1
`R3(config-rtr)#`**`eigrp router-id 10.3.3.3`**	Enables the use of a fixed router ID
`R3(config-rtr)#`**`no shutdown`**	Enables the EIGRP for the IPv6 process
`R3(config-rtr)#`**`exit`**	Returns to global configuration mode

`R3(config)#interface gigabitethernet 0/0`	Moves to interface configuration mode
`R3(config-if)#ipv6 address 2001:db8:0:11::3/64`	Configures a global IPv6 address on the interface and enables IPv6 processing on the interface
`R3(config-if)#ipv6 eigrp 1`	Enables EIGRP for IPv6 on the interface and places this interface into AS 1
`R3(config-if)#no shutdown`	Activates the interface
`R3(config-if)#interface loopback 0`	Moves to interface configuration mode
`R3(config-if)#ipv6 address 2001:db8:0:3::1/64`	Configures a global IPv6 address on the interface and enables IPv6 processing on the interface
`R3(config-if)#ipv6 eigrp 1`	Enables EIGRP for IPv6 on the interface and places this interface into AS 1
`R3(config-if)#exit`	Moves to global configuration mode
`R3(config)#exit`	Moves to privileged mode
`R3#copy running-config startup-config`	Saves the configuration to NVRAM

R2 Router

`Router>enable`	Moves to privileged mode
`Router#configure terminal`	Moves to global configuration mode
`Router(config)#hostname R2`	Assigns a hostname to the router
`R2(config)#ipv6 unicast-routing`	Enables the forwarding of IPv6 unicast datagrams globally on the router
`R2(config)#ipv6 router eigrp 1`	Creates and enters EIGRP router configuration mode with the AS being 1
`R2(config-rtr)#eigrp router-id 10.2.2.2`	Enables the use of a fixed router ID
`R2(config-rtr)#no shutdown`	Enables the EIGRP for the IPv6 process
`R2(config-rtr)#exit`	Returns to global configuration mode
`R2(config)#interface gigabitethernet 0/0`	Moves to interface configuration mode
`R2(config-if)#ipv6 address 2001:db8:0:11::2/64`	Configures a global IPv6 addresses on the interface and enables IPv6 processing on the interface
`R2(config-if)#ipv6 eigrp 1`	Enables EIGRP for IPv6 on the interface and places this interface into AS 1
`R2(config-if)#no shutdown`	Starts the interface
`R2(config-if)#interface loopback 0`	Moves to interface configuration mode
`R2(config-if)#ipv6 address 2001:db8:0:2::1/64`	Configures a global IPv6 address on the interface and enables IPv6 processing on the interface

`R2(config-if)#ipv6 eigrp 1`	Enables EIGRP for IPv6 on the interface and places this interface into AS 1
`R2(config-if)#exit`	Moves to global configuration mode
`R2(config)#exit`	Moves to privileged mode
`R2#copy running-config startup-config`	Saves the configuration to NVRAM

R1 Router

`Router>enable`	Moves to privileged mode
`Router#configure terminal`	Moves to global configuration mode
`Router(config)#hostname R1`	Assigns a hostname to the router
`R1(config)#ipv6 unicast-routing`	Enables the forwarding of IPv6 unicast datagrams globally on the router
`R1(config)#ipv6 router eigrp 1`	Creates and enters EIGRP router configuration mode with the AS being 1
`R1(config-rtr)#eigrp router-id 10.1.1.1`	Enables the use of a fixed router ID
`R1(config-rtr)#no shutdown`	Enables the EIGRP for the IPv6 process
`R1(config)#interface gigabitethernet 0/0`	Moves to interface configuration mode
`R1(config-if)#ipv6 address 2001:db8:0:11::1/64`	Configures a global IPv6 address on the interface and enables IPv6 processing on the interface
`R1(config-if)#ipv6 eigrp 1`	Enables EIGRP for IPv6 on the interface and places this interface into AS 1
`R1(config-if)#no shutdown`	Starts the interface
`R1(config-if)#interface loopback 0`	Moves to interface configuration mode
`R1(config-if)#ipv6 address 2001:db8:0:1::1/64`	Configures a global IPv6 address on the interface and enables IPv6 processing on the interface
`R1(config-if)#ipv6 eigrp 1`	Enables EIGRP for IPv6 on the interface and places this interface into AS 1
`R1(config-if)#exit`	Moves to global configuration mode
`R1(config)#exit`	Moves to privileged mode
`R1#copy running-config startup-config`	Saves the configuration to NVRAM

CHAPTER 15

OSPFv2 and OSPFv3

This chapter provides information about the following topics:

- OSPFv2 versus OSPFv3

- Configuring OSPF

- Using wildcard masks with OSPF areas

- Configuring multiarea OSPF

- Multiarea OSPF Router Types

- Loopback interfaces

- Router ID

- DR/BDR elections

- Passive interfaces

- Modifying cost metrics

- OSPF **auto-cost reference-bandwidth**

- Timers

- Propagating a default route

- Route summarization

    - Interarea route summarization

    - External route summarization

- IPv6 and OSPFv3

    - Enabling OSPF for IPv6 on an interface

    - Interarea OSPFv3 Route Summarization

    - Enabling an IPv4 Router ID for OSPFv3

- Verifying OSPFv2 and OSPFv3 configurations

- Troubleshooting OSPFv2 and OSPFv3

- Configuration example: single-area OSPF

- Configuration example: multiarea OSPF

- Configuration example: IPv6 and OSPFv3

OSPFv2 Versus OSPFv3

The current version of Open Shortest Path First (OSPF), OSPFv2, was developed back in the late 1980s, when some parts of OSPF were designed to compensate for the inefficiencies of routers at that time. Now that router technology has dramatically improved, and with the arrival of IPv6, rather than modify OSPFv2 for IPv6, it was decided to create a new version of OSPF (OSPFv3), not just for IPv6, but for other newer technologies, too.

In most Cisco documentation, if you see something refer to OSPF, it is assumed to be referring to OSPFv2, and working with the IPv4 protocol stack.

The earliest release of the OSPFv3 protocol worked with IPv6 exclusiviely; if you needed to run both OSPF for IPv4 and IPv6, you had to have OSPFv2 and OSPFv3 running concurrently. Newer updates to OSPFv3 are allowing for OSPFv3 to handle both IPv4 and IPv6 addressing. The combining of IPv4 and IPv6 into OSPFv3 is not part of the CCNA vendor exam objectives; it is part of the CCNP ROUTE vendor exam objectives and therefore out of scope for this guide. This guide works with the understanding that anything related to IPv4 will be using OSPFv2, and anything related to IPv6 will be using OSPFv3.

Configuring OSPF

`Router(config)#router` `ospf 123`	Starts OSPF process 123. The process ID is any positive integer value between 1 and 65,535. The process ID is not related to the OSPF area. The process ID merely distinguishes one process from another within the device.

`Router(config-router)`
`#network 172.16.10.0`
`0.0.0.255 area 0`
	OSPF advertises interfaces, not networks. It uses the wildcard mask to determine which interfaces to advertise. Read this line to say, "Any interface with an address of 172.16.10.x is to run OSPF and be put into area 0."

	NOTE The process ID number of one router does not have to match the process ID of any other router. Unlike Enhanced Interior Gateway Routing Protocol (EIGRP), matching this number across all routers does not ensure that network adjacencies will form.

`Router(config-router)`
`#log-adjacency-changes`
`detail`
	Configures the router to send a syslog message when there is a change of state between OSPF neighbors.

	TIP Although the **log-adjacency-changes** command is on by default, only up/down events are reported unless you use the **detail** keyword.

Using Wildcard Masks with OSPF Areas

When compared to an IP address, a wildcard mask identifies what addresses are matched to run OSPF and to be placed into an area:

- A 0 (zero) in a wildcard mask means to check the corresponding bit in the address for an exact match.

- A 1 (one) in a wildcard mask means to ignore the corresponding bit in the address—can be either 1 or 0.

Example 1: 172.16.0.0 0.0.255.255

$$172.16.0.0 \quad = \quad 10101100.00010000.00000000.00000000$$

$$0.0.255.255 \quad = \quad 00000000.00000000.11111111.11111111$$

$$\text{Result} \quad = \quad 10101100.00010000.xxxxxxxx.xxxxxxxx$$

172.16.*x.x* (Anything between 172.16.0.0 and 172.16.255.255 matches the example statement.)

> **TIP** An octet in the wildcard mask of all 0s means that the octet has to match the address exactly. An octet in the wildcard mask of all 1s means that the octet can be ignored.

Example 2: 172.16.8.0 0.0.7.255

$$172.168.8.0 \quad = \quad 10101100.00010000.00001000.00000000$$

$$0.0.0.7.255 \quad = \quad 00000000.00000000.00000111.11111111$$

$$\text{result} \quad = \quad 10101100.00010000.00001xxx.xxxxxxxx$$

$$00001xxx \quad = \quad 00001000 \text{ to } 00001111 = 8\text{--}15$$

$$xxxxxxxx \quad = \quad 00000000 \text{ to } 11111111 = 0\text{--}255$$

Anything between 172.16.8.0 and 172.16.15.255 matches the example statement.

`Router(config-router)#network` `172.16.10.1 0.0.0.0 area 0`	Read this line to say, "Any interface with an exact address of 172.16.10.1 is to run OSPF and be put into area 0."
`Router(config-router)#network` `172.16.0.0 0.0.255.255 area 0`	Read this line to say, "Any interface with an address of 172.16.*x.x* is to run OSPF and be put into area 0."
`Router(config-router)#network` `0.0.0.0 255.255.255.255 area 0`	Read this line to say, "Any interface with any address is to run OSPF and be put into area 0."

Configuring Multiarea OSPF

`Router(config)#router ospf 1`	Starts OSPF process 1.
`Router(config-router)#network` `172.16.10.0 0.0.0.255 area 0`	Read this line to say, "Any interface with an address of 172.16.10.*x* is to run OSPF and be put into area 0."
`Router(config-router)#network` `10.10.10.1 0.0.0.0 area 51`	Read this line to say, "Any interface with an exact address of 10.10.10.1 is to run OSPF and be put into area 51."

CAUTION   Running two different OSPF processes does not create multiarea OSPF; it merely creates two separate instances of OSPF that do not communicate with each other. To create multiarea OSPF, you use two separate **network** statements and advertise two different links into different areas.

NOTE   You can enable OSPF directly on an interface with the **ip ospf** *process ID* **area** *area number* command. Because this command is configured directly on the interface, it takes precedence over the **network area** command entered in router configuration mode.

TIP   If you have problems determining which wildcard mask to use to place your interfaces into an OSPF area, use the **ip ospf** *process ID* **area** *area number* command directly on the interface.

Router(config)#**interface fastethernet 0/0**	Moves to interface configuration mode
Router(config-if)#**ip ospf 1 area 51**	Places this interface into area 51 of OSPF process 1
Router(config-if)#**interface gigabitethernet 0/0**	Moves to interface configuration mode
Router(config-if)#**ip ospf 1 area 0**	Places this interface into area 0 of OSPF process 1

TIP   If you assign interfaces to OSPF areas without first using the **router ospf** *x* command, the router creates the router process for you, and it shows up in a **show running-config** output.

Multiarea OSPF Router Types

There are different types of definitions of routers when working with multiarea OSPF:

- **Internal**—Internal routers have all their interfaces within the same OSPF area.

- **Backbone router**—A router in which at least one of its interfaces is part of the backbone area (Area 0).

- **Area Border Router (ABR)**—An ABR is a router that has at least two interfaces in two different areas. Typically this is designed to be one interface in the backbone area (Area 0) and at least one interface in a different area. It establishes a connection between the backbone area and other areas.

- **Autonomous System Boundary Router (ASBR)**—An ASBR is a router that has at least one interface in one OSPF area and at least one interface in a different routing process (either another dynamic routing protocol or a static route to a remote destination that is being redistributed into OSPF).

It is possible to have a combination of these terms used to describe a router. For example, a router with all of its interfaces belonging to Area 0 could be considered an Internal Backbone router.

These definitions will be used in the Configuration Example: Multiarea OSPF in this chapter to identify the router types.

Loopback Interfaces

`Router(config)#interface loopback0`	Creates a virtual interface named Loopback 0 and then moves the router to interface configuration mode.
`Router(config-if)#ip address 192.168.100.1 255.255.255.255`	Assigns the IP address to the interface.
	NOTE Loopback interfaces are always "up and up" and do not go down unless manually shut down. This makes loopback interfaces great for use as an OSPF router ID.

Router ID

`Router(config)#router ospf 1`	Starts OSPF process 1.
`Router(config-router) #router-id 10.1.1.1`	Sets the router ID to 10.1.1.1. If this command is used on an OSPF router process that is already active (has neighbors), the new router ID is used at the next reload or at a manual OSPF process restart.
`Router(config-router) #no router-id 10.1.1.1`	Removes the static router ID from the configuration. If this command is used on an OSPF router process that is already active (has neighbors), the old router ID behavior is used at the next reload or at a manual OSPF process restart.

NOTE To choose the router ID at the time of OSPF process initialization, the router uses the following criteria in this specific order:

1. Use the router ID specified in the **router-id** *w.x.y.z* command.
2. Use the highest IP address of all active loopback interfaces on the router.
3. Use the highest IP address among all active nonloopback interfaces.

NOTE To have the manually configured router ID take effect, you must clear the OSPF routing process with the **clear ip ospf process** command.

NOTE There is no IPv6 form of router ID. All router IDs are 32-bit numbers in the form of an IPv4 address. Even if a router is running IPv6 exclusiviely, the router ID is still in the form of an IPv4 address.

DR/BDR Elections

`Router(config)#interface fastethernet0/0`	Enters interface configuration mode.
`Router(config-if)#ip ospf priority 50`	Changes the OSPF interface priority to 50.
	NOTE The assigned priority can be between 0 and 255. A priority of 0 makes the router ineligible to become a designated router (DR) or backup designated router (BDR). The highest priority wins the election and becomes the DR; the second highest priority becomes the BDR. A priority of 255 guarantees at least a tie in the election—assuming another router is also set to 255. If all routers have the same priority, regardless of the priority number, they tie. Ties are broken by the highest router ID. The default priority setting is 1.
	TIP Don't assign the same priority value to more than one router.

Passive Interfaces

`Router(config)#router ospf 1`	Starts OSPF process 1.
`Router(config-router)#network 172.16.10.0 0.0.0.255 area 0`	Read this line to say, "Any interface with an address of 172.16.10.x is to be put into area 0."
`Router(config-router)#passive-interface fastethernet0/0`	Disables the sending of any OSPF packets on this interface.
`Router(config-router)#passive-interface default`	Disables the sending of any OSPF packets out all interfaces.
`Router(config-router)#no passive-interface serial 0/0/1`	Enables OSPF packets to be sent out interface serial 0/0/1, thereby allowing neighbor relationships to form.

Modifying Cost Metrics

`Router(config)#interface serial0/0/0`	Enters interface configuration mode.
`Router(config-if) #bandwidth 128`	If you change the bandwidth, OSPF recalculates the cost of the link.
`Or`	
`Router(config-if) #ip ospf cost 1564`	Changes the cost to a value of 1564.
	NOTE The cost of a link is determined by dividing the reference bandwidth by the interface bandwidth. The bandwidth of the interface is a number between 1 and 10,000,000. The unit of measurement is kilobits per second (Kbps). The cost is a number between 1 and 65,535. The cost has no unit of measurement; it is just a number.

OSPF auto-cost reference-bandwidth

`Router(config)#router ospf 1`	Starts OSPF process 1.
`Router(config-router) #auto-cost reference- bandwidth 1000`	Changes the reference bandwidth that OSPF uses to calculate the cost of an interface.
	NOTE The range of the reference bandwidth is 1 to 4,294,967. The default is 100. The unit of measurement is megabits per second (Mbps).
	NOTE The value set by the **ip ospf cost** command over-rides the cost resulting from the **auto-cost** command.
	TIP If you use the command **auto-cost reference-bandwidth** *reference-bandwidth*, you need to configure all the routers to use the same value. Failure to do so results in routers using a different reference cost to calculate the shortest path, creating potential suboptimum routing paths.

Timers

`Router(config-if)#ip ospf hello-interval 20`	Changes the hello interval timer to 20 seconds.
`Router(config-if)#ip ospf dead-interval 80`	Changes the dead interval timer to 80 seconds.

CAUTION   Hello and dead interval timers must match between two routers for those routers to become neighbors.

NOTE   The default hello timer is 10 seconds on multiaccess and point-to-point segments. The default hello timer is 30 seconds on nonbroadcast multiaccess (NBMA) segments such as Frame Relay, X.25, and ATM.

NOTE   The default dead interval timer is 40 seconds on multiaccess and point-to-point segments. The default dead timer is 120 seconds on NBMA segments such as Frame Relay, X.25, and ATM.

NOTE   If you change the hello interval timer, the dead interval timer is automatically adjusted to four times the new hello interval timer.

Propagating a Default Route

`Router(config)#ip route 0.0.0.0 0.0.0.0 serial0/0/0`	Creates a default route.
`Router(config)#router ospf 1`	Starts OSPF process 1.

`Router(config-router)#default-information originate`	Sets the default route to be propagated to all OSPF routers.
`Router(config-router)#default-information originate always`	The **always** option propagates a default "quad-0" route even if this router does not have a default route itself.
	NOTE The **default-information originate** command or the **default-information originate always** command is usually only to be configured on your "entrance" or "gateway" router, the router that connects your network to the outside world—the ASBR.

Route Summarization

> **NOTE**   Route summarization is not part of the CCNA vendor exam objectives.

In OSPF, there are two different types of summarization:

- Interarea route summarization
- External route summarization

The sections that follow provide the commands necessary to configure both types of summarization.

Interarea Route Summarization

`Router(config)#router ospf 1`	Starts OSPF process 1.
`Router(config-router)#area 1 range 192.168.64.0 255.255.224.0`	Summarizes area 1 routes to the specified summary address before injecting them into a different area.
	NOTE This command is to be configured on an ABR only.
	NOTE By default, ABRs do not summarize routes between areas.

External Route Summarization

`Router(config)#router ospf 123`	Starts OSPF process 1.
`Router(config-router)#summary-address 192.168.64.0 255.255.224.0`	Advertises a single route for all the redistributed routes that are covered by a specified network address and netmask.
	NOTE This command is to be configured on an ASBR only.
	NOTE By default, ASBRs do not summarize routes.

IPv6 and OSPFv3

This section covers using IPv6 with OSPFv3. For the purposes of the CCNA vendor exam objectives, OSPFv3 only deals with IPv6 addresses.

NOTE   For an excellent overview of IPv6, I strongly recommend you read Rick Graziani's book from Cisco Press: *IPv6 Fundamentals: A Straightforward Approach to Understanding IPv6.*

Enabling OSPF for IPv6 on an Interface

`Router(config)#ipv6 unicast-routing`	Enables the forwarding of IPv6 unicast datagrams globally on the router.
	NOTE This command is required before any IPv6 routing protocol can be configured.
`Router(config)#interface fastethernet0/0`	Moves to interface configuration mode.
`Router(config-if) #ipv6 address 2001:db8:0:1::1/64`	Configures a global IPv6 address on the interface and enables IPv6 processing on the interface.
`Router(config-if)#ipv6 ospf 1 area 0`	Enables OSPFv3 process 1 on the interface and places this interface into area 0.
	NOTE The OSPFv3 process is created automatically when OSPFv3 is enabled on an interface.
	NOTE The **ipv6 ospf** *x* **area** *y* command has to be configured on each interface that will take part in OSPFv3.
	NOTE If a router ID has not been created first, the router returns a warning stating that the process could not pick a router ID. It then tells you to manually configure a router ID.
`Router(config-if)#ipv6 ospf priority 30`	Assigns a priority number to this interface for use in the DR election. The priority can be a number from 0 to 255. The default is 1. A router interface with a priority set to 0 is ineligible to become the DR or the BDR on the multiaccess segment.
`Router(config-if)#ipv6 ospf cost 20`	Assigns a cost value of 20 to this interface. The cost value can be an integer value from 1 to 65,535.
`Router(config-if)#ospfv3 1 ipv6 area 0`	Enables OSPFv3 instance 1 with the IPv6 address family in area 0.

Interarea OSPFv3 Route Summarization

`Router(config)#ipv6 router ospf 1`	Creates the OSPFv3 process if it has not already been created and moves to router configuration mode
`Router(config-rtr)#area 1 range 2001:db8::/48`	Summarizes area 1 routes to the specified summary address, at an area boundary, before injecting them into a different area

Enabling an IPv4 Router ID for OSPFv3

`Router(config)#ipv6 router ospf 1`	Creates the OSPFv3 process if it has not already been created and moves to router configuration mode.
`Router(config-rtr) #router-id 192.168.254.255`	Creates a 32-bit router ID for this router using an IPv4 address format.
	NOTE In OSPFv3 for IPv6, it is possible that no IPv4 addresses will be configured on an interface. In this case, the user must use the **router-id** command to configure a router ID before the OSPFv3 process will be started. If an IPv4 address does exist when OSPFv3 for IPv6 is enabled on an interface, that IPv4 address is used for the router ID. If more than one IPv4 address is available, a router ID is chosen using the same rules as for OSPFv2.

Verifying OSPFv2 and OSPFv3 Configurations

`Router#show ip protocol`	Displays parameters for all routing protocols running on the router
`Router#show ip route`	Displays a complete IP routing table
`Router#show ip route ospf`	Displays the OSPF routes in the routing table
`Router#show ip route ospfv3`	Displays the OSPFv3 routes in the routing table
`Router#show ip ospf`	Displays basic information about OSPF routing processes
`Router#show ip ospf border-routers`	Displays border and boundary router information
`Router#show ip ospf database`	Displays the contents of the OSPF database
`Router#show ip ospf database summary`	Displays a summary of the OSPF database
`Router#show ip ospf interface`	Displays OSPF info as it relates to all interfaces
`Router#show ip ospf interface fastethernet0/0`	Displays OSPF information for interface fastethernet 0/0
`Router#show ip ospf neighbor`	Lists all OSPF neighbors and their states
`Router#show ip ospf neighbor detail`	Displays a detailed list of neighbors
`Router#show ipv6 interface`	Displays the status of interfaces configured for IPv6
`Router#show ipv6 interface brief`	Displays a summarized status of all interfaces and configured IPv6 addresses
`Router#show ipv6 neighbors`	Displays IPv6 neighbor discovery cache information

`Router#show ipv6 ospf`	Displays general information about the OSPFv3 routing process
`Router#show ipv6 ospf border-routers`	Displays the internal OSPF routing table entries to an ABR or an ASBR
`Router#show ipv6 ospf database`	Displays OSPFv3-related database information
`Router#show ipv6 ospf interface`	Displays OSPFv3-related interface information
`Router#show ipv6 ospf neighbor`	Displays OSPFv3-related neighbor information
`Router#show ipv6 protocols`	Displays the parameters and current state of the active IPv6 routing protocol processes
`Router#show ipv6 route`	Displays the current IPv6 routing table
`Router#show ipv6 route summary`	Displays a summarized form of the current IPv6 routing table
`Router#show ipv6 routers`	Displays IPv6 router advertisement information received from other routers
`Router#show ipv6 traffic`	Displays statistics about IPv6 traffic
`Router#show ospfv3 database`	Displays the OSPFv3 database
`Router#show ospfv3 neighbor`	Displays OSPFv3 neighbor information on a per-interface basis

Troubleshooting OSPFv2 and OSPFv3

`Router#clear ip route *`	Clears the entire routing table, forcing it to rebuild
`Router#clear ip route a.b.c.d`	Clears a specific route to network a.b.c.d
`Router#clear ipv6 route *`	Deletes all routes from the IPv6 routing table
`Router#clear ipv6 route 2001:db8:c18:3::/64`	Clears this specific route from the IPv6 routing table
`Router#clear ipv6 traffic`	Resets IPv6 traffic counters
`Router#clear ip ospf counters`	Resets OSPF counters
`Router#clear ip ospf process`	Resets the *entire* OSPF process, forcing OSPF to re-create neighbors, the database, and the routing table
`Router#clear ip ospf 3 process`	Resets OSPF process 3, forcing OSPF to re-create neighbors, the database, and the routing table

Router#**clear ipv6 ospf process**	Resets the entire OSPFv3 process, forcing OSPFv3 to re-create neighbors, the database, and the routing table
Router#**clear ipv6 ospf 3 process**	Resets OSPFv3 process 3, forcing OSPF to re-create neighbors, the database, and the routing table
Router#**debug ip ospf events**	Displays all OSPF events
Router#**debug ip ospf adj**	Displays various OSPF states and DR/BDR election between adjacent routers
Router#**debug ipv6 ospf adj**	Displays debug messages about the OSPF adjacency process
Router#**debug ipv6 packet**	Displays debug messages for IPv6 packets
Router#**debug ip ospf packets**	Displays OSPF packets
Router#**debug ipv6 routing**	Displays debug messages for IPv6 routing table updates and route cache updates
Router#**undebug all**	Turns off all **debug** commands

Configuration Example: Single-Area OSPF

Figure 15-1 shows the network topology for the configuration that follows, which demonstrates how to configure single-area OSPF using the commands covered in this chapter.

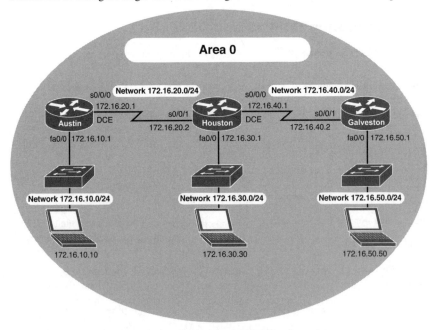

Figure 15-1 Network Topology for Single-Area OSPF Configuration

Austin Router

`Router>`**`enable`**	Moves to privileged mode.
`Router#`**`configure terminal`**	Moves to global configuration mode.
`Router(config)#`**`hostname Austin`**	Sets the hostname.
`Austin(config)#`**`interface fastethernet 0/0`**	Moves to interface configuration mode.
`Austin(config-if)#`**`ip address 172.16.10.1 255.255.255.0`**	Assigns an IP address and a netmask.
`Austin(config-if)#`**`no shutdown`**	Enables the interface.
`Austin(config-if)#`**`interface serial 0/0/0`**	Moves to interface configuration mode.
`Austin(config-if)#`**`ip address 172.16.20.1 255.255.255.0`**	Assigns an IP address and netmask.
`Austin(config-if)#`**`clock rate 56000`**	DCE cable plugged in this side.
`Austin(config-if)#`**`no shutdown`**	Enables the interface.
`Austin(config-if)#`**`exit`**	Returns to global configuration mode.
`Austin(config)#`**`router ospf 1`**	Starts OSPF process 1.
`Austin(config-router)#`**`network 172.16.10.0 0.0.0.255 area 0`**	Read this line to say, "Any interface with an address of 172.16.10.x is to run OSPF and be put into area 0."
`Austin(config-router)#`**`network 172.16.20.0 0.0.0.255 area 0`**	Read this line to say, "Any interface with an address of 172.16.20.x is to run OSPF and be put into area 0.
`Austin(config-router)#`**`<CTRL> z`**	Returns to privileged mode.
`Austin#`**`copy running-config startup-config`**	Saves the configuration to NVRAM.

Houston Router

`Router>`**`enable`**	Moves to privileged mode.
`Router#`**`configure terminal`**	Moves to global configuration mode.
`Router(config)#`**`hostname Houston`**	Sets the hostname.
`Houston(config)#`**`interface fastethernet 0/0`**	Moves to interface configuration mode.
`Houston(config-if)#`**`ip address 172.16.30.1 255.255.255.0`**	Assigns an IP address and netmask.
`Houston(config-if)#`**`no shutdown`**	Enables the interface.

`Houston(config-if)#interface serial0/0/0`	Moves to interface configuration mode.
`Houston(config-if)#ip address 172.16.40.1 255.255.255.0`	Assigns an IP address and netmask.
`Houston(config-if)#clock rate 56000`	DCE cable plugged in this side.
`Houston(config-if)#no shutdown`	Enables the interface.
`Houston(config)#interface serial 0/0/1`	Moves to interface configuration mode.
`Houston(config-if)#ip address 172.16.20.2 255.255.255.0`	Assigns an IP address and netmask.
`Houston(config-if)#no shutdown`	Enables the interface.
`Houston(config-if)#exit`	Returns to global configuration mode.
`Houston(config)#router ospf 1`	Starts OSPF process 1.
`Houston(config-router)#network 172.16.0.0 0.0.255.255 area 0`	Read this line to say, "Any interface with an address of 172.16.x.x is to run OSPF and be put into area 0." One statement now enables OSPF on all three interfaces.
`Houston(config-router)#<CTRL> z`	Returns to privileged mode.
`Houston#copy running-config startup-config`	Saves the configuration to NVRAM.

Galveston Router

`Router>enable`	Moves to privileged mode.
`Router#configure terminal`	Moves to global configuration mode.
`Router(config)#hostname Galveston`	Sets the hostname.
`Galveston(config)#interface fastethernet 0/0`	Moves to interface configuration mode.
`Galveston(config-if)#ip address 172.16.50.1 255.255.255.0`	Assigns an IP address and netmask.
`Galveston(config-if)#no shutdown`	Enables the interface.
`Galveston(config-if)#interface serial 0/0/1`	Moves to interface configuration mode.
`Galveston(config-if)#ip address 172.16.40.2 255.255.255.0`	Assigns an IP address and netmask.
`Galveston(config-if)#no shutdown`	Enables the interface.
`Galveston(config-if)#exit`	Returns to global configuration mode.
`Galveston(config)#router ospf 1`	Starts OSPF process 1.

`Galveston(config-router)#network` `172.16.40.2 0.0.0.0 area 0`	Any interface with an exact address of 172.16.40.2 is to run OSPF and be put into area 0. This is the most precise way to place an exact address into the OSPF routing process.
`Galveston(config-router)#network` `172.16.50.1 0.0.0.0 area 0`	Read this line to say, "Any interface with an exact address of 172.16.50.1 is to be put into area 0."
`Galveston(config-router)#<CTRL> z`	Returns to privileged mode.
`Galveston#copy running-config` `startup-config`	Saves the configuration to NVRAM.

Configuration Example: Multiarea OSPF

Figure 15-2 shows the network topology for the configuration that follows, which demonstrates how to configure multiarea OSPF using the commands covered in this chapter.

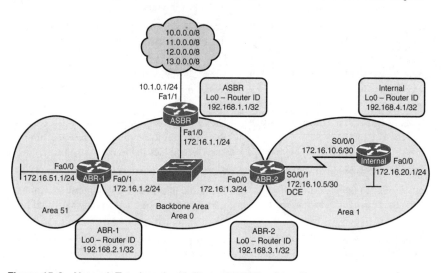

Figure 15-2   Network Topology for Multiarea OSPF Configuration

ASBR Router

`Router> enable`	Moves to privileged mode.
`Router#configure terminal`	Moves to global configuration mode.
`Router(config)#hostname ASBR`	Sets the router hostname.
`ASBR(config)#interface loopback0`	Enters loopback interface mode.
`ASBR(config-if)#ip address` `192.168.1.1 255.255.255.255`	Assigns an IP address and netmask.
`ASBR(config-if)#description` `Router ID`	Sets a locally significant description.

`ASBR(config-if)#exit`	Returns to global configuration mode.
`ASBR(config)#interface` `fastethernet 1/0`	Enters interface configuration mode.
`ASBR(config-if)#ip address` `172.16.1.1 255.255.255.0`	Assigns an IP address and netmask.
`ASBR(config-if)#no shutdown`	Enables the interface.
`ASBR(config-if)#interface` `fastethernet 1/1`	Enters interface configuration mode.
`ASBR(config-if)#ip address` `10.1.0.1 255.255.255.0`	Assigns an IP address and netmask.
`ASBR(config-if)#no shutdown`	Enables the interface.
`ASBR(config-if)#exit`	Returns to global configuration mode.
`ASBR(config)#ip route 0.0.0.0` `0.0.0.0 10.1.0.2 fastethernet1/1`	Creates default route. Using both an exit interface and a next-hop address on a Fast Ethernet interface prevents recursive lookups in the routing table.
`ASBR(config)#ip route 11.0.0.0` `255.0.0.0 null0`	Creates a static route to a null interface. In this example, these routes represent a simulated remote destination.
`ASBR(config)#ip route 12.0.0.0` `255.0.0.0 null0`	Creates a static route to a null interface. In this example, these routes represent a simulated remote destination.
`ASBR(config)#ip route 13.0.0.0` `255.0.0.0 null0`	Creates a static route to a null interface. In this example, these routes represent a simulated remote destination.
`ASBR(config)#router ospf 1`	Starts OSPF process 1.
`ASBR(config-router)#network` `172.16.1.0 0.0.0.255 area 0`	Read this line to say, "Any interface with an address of 172.16.1.x is to run OSPF and be put into area 0."
`ASBR(config-router)#default-` `information originate`	Sets the default route to be propagated to all OSPF routers.
`ASBR(config-router)` `#redistribute static`	Redistributes static routes into the OSPF process. This turns the router into an ASBR because static routes are not part of OSPF, and the definition of an ASBR is a router that sits between OSPF and another routing process—in this case, a redistributed static route.
	NOTE Redistribution is not part of the CCNA Routing & Switching certification exam. It is shown here for informational purposes only.
`ASBR(config-router)#exit`	Returns to global configuration mode.
`ASBR(config)#exit`	Returns to privileged mode.
`ASBR#copy running-config` `startup-config`	Saves the configuration to NVRAM.

ABR-1 Router

`Router> enable`	Moves to privileged mode.
`Router#configure terminal`	Moves to global configuration mode.
`Router(config)#hostname ABR-1`	Sets the router hostname.
`ABR-1(config)#interface loopback0`	Enters loopback interface mode.
`ABR-1(config-if)#ip address 192.168.2.1 255.255.255.255`	Assigns an IP address and netmask.
`ABR-1(config-if)#description Router ID`	Sets a locally significant description.
`ABR-1(config-if)#exit`	Returns to global configuration mode.
`ABR-1(config)#interface fastethernet0/1`	Enters interface configuration mode.
`ABR-1(config-if)#ip address 172.16.1.2 255.255.255.0`	Assigns an IP address and netmask.
`ABR-1(config-if)#ip ospf priority 200`	Sets the priority for the DR/BDR election process. This router will win and become the DR.
`ABR-1(config-if)#no shutdown`	Enables the interface.
`ABR-1(config-if)#exit`	Returns to global configuration mode.
`ABR-1(config)#interface fastethernet 0/0`	Enters interface configuration mode.
`ABR-1(config-if)#ip address 172.16.51.1 255.255.255.0`	Assigns an IP address and netmask.
`ABR-1(config-if)#no shutdown`	Enables the interface.
`ABR-1(config-if)#exit`	Returns to global configuration mode.
`ABR-1(config)#router ospf 1`	Starts OSPF process 1.
`ABR-1(config-router)#network 172.16.1.0 0.0.0.255 area 0`	Read this line to say, "Any interface with an address of 172.16.1.x is to run OSPF and be put into area 0."
`ABR-1(config-router)#network 172.16.51.1 0.0.0.0 area 51`	Read this line to say, "Any interface with an exact address of 172.16.51.1 is to run OSPF and be put into area 51."
`ABR-1(config-router)#exit`	Returns to global configuration mode.
`ABR-1(config)#exit`	Returns to privileged mode.
`ABR-1(config)#copy running-config startup-config`	Saves the configuration to NVRAM.

ABR-2 Router

`Router>enable`	Moves to privileged mode.
`Router#configure terminal`	Moves to global configuration mode.
`Router(config)#hostname ABR-2`	Sets the router hostname.
`ABR-2(config)#interface loopback0`	Enters loopback interface mode.
`ABR-2(config-if)#ip address 192.168.3.1 255.255.255.255`	Assigns an IP address and netmask.
`ABR-2(config-if)#description Router ID`	Sets a locally significant description.
`ABR-2(config-if)#exit`	Returns to global configuration mode.
`ABR-2(config)#interface fastethernet0/0`	Enters interface configuration mode.
`ABR-2(config-if)#ip address 172.16.1.3 255.255.255.0`	Assigns an IP address and netmask.
`ABR-2(config-if)#ip ospf priority 100`	Sets the priority for the DR/BDR election process. This router will become the BDR to ABR-1's DR.
`ABR-2(config-if)#no shutdown`	Enables the interface.
`ABR-2(config-if)#exit`	Returns to global configuration mode.
`ABR-2(config)#interface serial 0/0/1`	Enters interface configuration mode.
`ABR-2(config-if)#ip address 172.16.10.5 255.255.255.252`	Assigns an IP address and netmask.
`ABR-2(config-if)#clock rate 56000`	Assigns a clock rate to the interface.
`ABR-2(config-if)#no shutdown`	Enables the interface.
`ABR-2(config-if)#exit`	Returns to global configuration mode.
`ABR-2(config)#router ospf 1`	Starts OSPF process 1.
`ABR-2(config-router)#network 172.16.1.0 0.0.0.255 area 0`	Read this line to say, "Any interface with an address of 172.16.1.x is to run OSPF and be put into area 0."
`ABR-2(config-router)#network 172.16.10.4 0.0.0.3 area 1`	Read this line to say "Any interface with an address of 172.16.10.4–7 is to run OSPF and be put into area 1."
`ABR-2(config-router)#exit`	Returns to global configuration mode.
`ABR-2(config)#exit`	Returns to privileged mode.
`ABR-2(config)#copy running-config startup-config`	Saves the configuration to NVRAM.

Internal Router

`Router>enable`	Moves to privileged mode.
`Router#configure terminal`	Moves to global configuration mode.
`Router(config)#hostname Internal`	Sets the router hostname.
`Internal(config)#interface loopback0`	Enters loopback interface mode.
`Internal(config-if)#ip address 192.168.4.1 255.255.255.255`	Assigns an IP address and netmask.
`Internal(config-if)#description Router ID`	Sets a locally significant description.
`Internal(config-if)#exit`	Returns to global configuration mode.
`Internal(config)#interface fastethernet0/0`	Enters interface configuration mode.
`Internal(config-if)#ip address 172.16.20.1 255.255.255.0`	Assigns an IP address and netmask.
`Internal(config-if)#no shutdown`	Enables the interface.
`Internal(config-if)#exit`	Returns to global configuration mode.
`Internal(config)#interface serial0/0/0`	Enters interface configuration mode.
`Internal(config-if)#ip address 172.16.10.6 255.255.255.252`	Assigns an IP address and netmask.
`Internal(config-if)#no shutdown`	Enables the interface.
`Internal(config-if)#exit`	Returns to global configuration mode.
`Internal(config)#router ospf 1`	Starts OSPF process 1.
`Internal(config-router)#network 172.16.0.0 0.0.255.255 area 1`	Read this line to say, "Any interface with an address of 172.16.x.x is to run OSPF and be put into area 1."
`Internal(config-router)#exit`	Returns to global configuration mode.
`Internal(config)#exit`	Returns to privileged mode.
`Internal(config)#copy running-config startup-config`	Saves the configuration to NVRAM.

Configuration Example: IPv6 and OSPFv3

Figure 15-3 shows the network topology for the configuration that follows, which demonstrates how to configure IPv6 and OSPFv3 using the commands covered in this chapter.

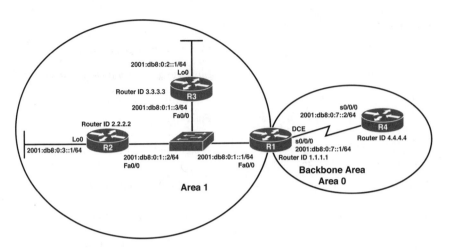

Figure 15-3   Network Topology for IPv6 and OSPFv3 Configuration

R3 Router

Router>**enable**	Moves to privileged mode.
Router#**configure terminal**	Moves to global configuration mode.
Router(config)#**hostname R3**	Assigns a hostname to the router.
R3(config)#**ipv6 unicast-routing**	Enables the forwarding of IPv6 unicast datagrams globally on the router. This command is required before any IPv6 routing protocol can be configured.
R3(config)#**interface fastethernet0/0**	Moves to interface configuration mode.
R3(config-if)#**ipv6 address 2001:db8:0:1::3/64**	Configures a global IPv6 address on the interface and enables IPv6 processing on the interface.
R3(config-if)#**ipv6 ospf 1 area 1**	Enables OSPFv3 on the interface and places this interface into area 1.
R3(config-if)#**no shutdown**	Enables the interface.
R3(config-if)#**interface loopback0**	Moves to interface configuration mode.
R3(config-if)#**ipv6 address 2001:db8:0:2::1/64**	Configures a global IPv6 address on the interface and enables IPv6 processing on the interface.
R3(config-if)#**ipv6 ospf 1 area 1**	Enables OSPFv3 on the interface and places this interface into area 1.
R3(config-if)#**exit**	Moves to global configuration mode.
R3(config)#**ipv6 router ospf 1**	Moves to OSPFv3 router config mode.
R3(config-rtr)#**router-id 3.3.3.3**	Sets a manually configured router ID.

`R3(config-rtr)#exit`	Returns to global configuration mode.
`R3(config)#exit`	Moves to privileged mode.
`R3#copy running-config startup-config`	Saves the configuration to NVRAM.

R2 Router

`Router>enable`	Moves to privileged mode.
`Router#configure terminal`	Moves to global configuration mode.
`Router(config)#hostname R2`	Assigns a hostname to the router.
`R2(config)#ipv6 unicast-routing`	Enables the forwarding of IPv6 unicast datagrams globally on the router. This command is required before any IPv6 routing protocol can be configured.
`R2(config)#interface fastethernet0/0`	Moves to interface configuration mode.
`R2(config-if)#ipv6 address 2001:db8:0:1::2/64`	Configures a global IPv6 address on the interface and enables IPv6 processing on the interface.
`R2(config-if)#ipv6 ospf 1 area 1`	Enables OSPFv3 on the interface and places this interface into area 1.
`R2(config-if)#no shutdown`	Enables the interface.
`R2(config-if)#interface loopback0`	Moves to interface configuration mode.
`R2(config-if)#ipv6 address 2001:db8:0:3::1/64`	Configures a global IPv6 address on the interface and enables IPv6 processing on the interface.
`R2(config-if)#ipv6 ospf 1 area 1`	Enables OSPFv3 on the interface and places this interface into area 1.
`R2(config-if)#no shutdown`	Enables the interface.
`R2(config-if)#exit`	Moves to global configuration mode.
`R2(config)#ipv6 router ospf 1`	Moves to OSPFv3 router config mode.
`R2(config-rtr)#router-id 2.2.2.2`	Sets a manually configured router ID.
`R2(config-rtr)#exit`	Returns to global configuration mode.
`R2(config)#exit`	Moves to privileged mode.
`R2#copy running-config startup-config`	Saves the configuration to NVRAM.

R1 Router

`Router>enable`	Moves to privileged mode.
`Router#configure terminal`	Moves to global configuration mode.
`Router(config)#hostname R1`	Assigns a hostname to the router.
`R1(config)#ipv6 unicast-routing`	Enables the forwarding of IPv6 unicast datagrams globally on the router. This command is required before any IPv6 routing protocol can be configured.
`R1(config)#interface fastethernet0/0`	Moves to interface configuration mode.
`R1(config-if)#ipv6 address 2001:db8:0:1::1/64`	Configures a global IPv6 address on the interface and enables IPv6 processing on the interface.
`R1(config-if)#ipv6 ospf 1 area 1`	Enables OSPFv3 on the interface and places this interface into area 1.
`R1(config-if)#no shutdown`	Enables the interface.
`R1(config-if)#interface serial0/0/0`	Moves to interface configuration mode.
`R1(config-if)#ipv6 address 2001:db8:0:7::1/64`	Configures a global IPv6 address on the interface and enables IPv6 processing on the interface.
`R1(config-if)#ipv6 ospf 1 area 0`	Enables OSPFv3 on the interface and places this interface into area 0.
`R1(config-if)#clock rate 56000`	Assigns a clock rate to this interface.
`R1(config-if)#no shutdown`	Enables the interface.
`R1(config-if)#exit`	Moves to global configuration mode.
`R1(config)#ipv6 router ospf 1`	Moves to OSPFv3 router config mode.
`R1(config-rtr)#router-id 1.1.1.1`	Sets a manually configured router ID.
`R1(config-rtr)#exit`	Returns to global configuration mode.
`R1(config)#exit`	Moves to privileged mode.
`R1#copy running-config startup-config`	Saves the configuration to NVRAM.

R4 Router

`Router>enable`	Moves to privileged mode.
`Router#configure terminal`	Moves to global configuration mode.
`Router(config)#hostname R4`	Assigns a hostname to the router.
`R4(config)#ipv6 unicast-routing`	Enables the forwarding of IPv6 unicast datagrams globally on the router. This command is required before any IPv6 routing protocol can be configured.
`R4(config)#interface serial0/0/0`	Moves to interface configuration mode.
`R4(config-if)#ipv6 address 2001:db8:0:7::2/64`	Configures a global IPv6 address on the interface and enables IPv6 processing on the interface.
`R4(config-if)#ipv6 ospf 1 area 0`	Enables OSPFv3 on the interface and places this interface into area 1.
`R4(config-if)#no shutdown`	Enables the interface.
`R4(config-if)#exit`	Moves to global configuration mode.
`R4(config)#ipv6 router ospf 1`	Moves to OSPFv3 router config mode.
`R4(config-rtr)#router-id 4.4.4.4`	Sets a manually configured router ID.
`R4(config-rtr)#exit`	Returns to global configuration mode.
`R4(config)#exit`	Moves to privileged mode.
`R4#copy running-config startup-config`	Saves the configuration to NVRAM.

Understanding Point-to-Point Protocols

This chapter provides information and commands concerning the following topics:

- Configuring High-Level Data Link Control encapsulation on a serial line
- Configuring Point-to-Point Protocol (PPP) on a serial line (mandatory commands)
- Configuring PPP on a serial line (optional commands): compression
- Configuring PPP on a serial line (optional commands): link quality monitoring
- Configuring PPP on a serial line (optional commands): authentication
- Verifying and troubleshooting a serial link/PPP encapsulation
- Configuration example: PPP with CHAP authentication
- Configuring Multilink Point-to-Point Protocol
- Verifying and troubleshooting MLPPP
- Configuring a DSL Connection using Point-to-Point Protocol over Ethernet

Configuring High-Level Data Link Control Encapsulation on a Serial Line

High-Level Data Link Control (HDLC) is the default encapsulation for synchronous serial links on Cisco routers. You would only use the **encapsulation hdlc** command to return the link to its default state.

Router#**configure terminal**	Moves to global configuration mode
Router(config)#**interface serial 0/0/0**	Moves to interface configuration mode
Router(config-if)#**encapsulation hdlc**	Sets the encapsulation mode for this interface to HDLC

CAUTION   Although HDLC is an open standard protocol, Cisco has modified HDLC as part of its implementation. This allows for multiprotocol support before PPP is specified. Therefore, you should only use HDLC between Cisco devices. If you are connecting to a non-Cisco device, use synchronous PPP.

Configuring Point-to-Point Protocol (PPP) on a Serial Line (Mandatory Commands)

Router#`configure terminal`	Moves to global configuration mode
Router(config)#`interface serial 0/0/0`	Moves to interface configuration mode
Router(config-if)#`encapsulation ppp`	Changes encapsulation from default HDLC to PPP

NOTE You must execute the **encapsulation ppp** command on both sides of the serial link for the link to become active.

Configuring PPP on a Serial Line (Optional Commands): Compression

Router(config-if)#`compress predictor`	Enables the predictor compression algorithm
Router(config-if)#`compress stac`	Enables the stac compression algorithm

Configuring PPP on a Serial Line (Optional Commands): Link Quality Monitoring

Router(config-if)#`ppp quality x`	Ensures the link has a quality of x percent. Otherwise, the link shuts down.

NOTE Link Quality Monitoring (LQM) monitors the link quality, and if the quality drops below a configured percentage, the router shuts down the link. The percentages are calculated for both the incoming and the outgoing directions. The outgoing quality is calculated by comparing the total number of packets and bytes sent with the total number of packets and bytes received by the destination node. The incoming quality is calculated by comparing the total number of packets and bytes received with the total number of packets and bytes sent by the destination peer.

NOTE When LQM is enabled, Link Quality Reports (LQRs) are sent, in place of keepalives, every keepalive period.

NOTE LQM is not compatible with Multilink PPP.

Configuring PPP on a Serial Line (Optional Commands): Authentication

`Router(config)#username routerb password cisco`	Sets a username of **routerb** and a password of *cisco* for authentication from the other side of the PPP serial link. This is used by the local router to authenticate the PPP peer.
`Router(config)#interface serial 0/0/0`	Moves to interface configuration mode.
`Router(config-if)#ppp authentication pap`	Turns on Password Authentication Protocol (PAP) authentication only.
`Router(config-if)#ppp authentication chap`	Turns on Challenge Handshake Authentication Protocol (CHAP) authentication only.
`Router(config-if)#ppp authentication pap chap`	Defines that the link will use PAP authentication but will try CHAP if PAP fails or is rejected by other side.
`Router(config-if)#ppp authentication chap pap`	Defines that the link will use CHAP authentication but will try PAP if CHAP fails or is rejected by other side.
`Router(config-if)#ppp pap sent-username user-name password password`	Reenables remote PAP support for an interface and uses the sent-username and password in the PAP authentication request packet to the peer.

TIP   When setting authentication, make sure that your usernames match the name of the router on the other side of the link and that the passwords on each router match the other. Passwords are case sensitive; usernames are not. Consider the following example.

`Edmonton(config)#username Calgarypassword cisco`	`Calgary(config)#username Edmonton password cisco`
`Edmonton(config)#interface serial 0/0/0`	`Calgary(config)#interface serial 0/0/0`
`Edmonton(config-if)#encapsulation ppp`	`Calgary(config-if)#encapsulation ppp`
`Edmonton(config-if)#ppp authentication chap`	`Calgary(config-if)#ppp authentication chap`

NOTE   Because PAP does not encrypt its password as it is sent across the link, recommended practice is that you use CHAP as your authentication method.

Verifying and Troubleshooting a Serial Link/PPP Encapsulation

Router#**show interfaces serial** *x/x/x*	Lists information for serial interface *x/x/x*
Router#**show controllers serial** *x/x/x*	Tells you what type of cable (DCE/DTE) is plugged into your interface and whether a clock rate has been set
Router#**debug serial interface**	Displays whether serial keepalive counters are incrementing
Router#**debug ppp**	Displays any traffic related to PPP
Router#**debug ppp packet**	Displays PPP packets that are being sent and received
Router#**debug ppp negotiation**	Displays PPP packets related to the negotiation of the PPP link
Router#**debug ppp error**	Displays PPP error packets
Router#**debug ppp authentication**	Displays PPP packets related to the authentication of the PPP link

TIP   With frequent lab use, serial cable pins often get bent, which might prevent the router from seeing the cable. The output from the command **show controllers interface serial** *x/x/x* shows no cable even though a cable is physically present.

Configuration Example: PPP with CHAP Authentication

Figure 16-1 illustrates the network topology for the configuration that follows, which shows how to configure PPP using the commands covered in this chapter.

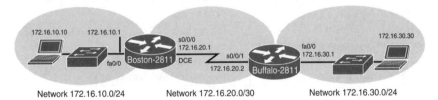

Network 172.16.10.0/24   Network 172.16.20.0/30   Network 172.16.30.0/24

Figure 16-1   Network Topology for PPP Configuration

NOTE   The hostname, password, and interfaces have been configured as per the configuration example in Chapter 11, "Configuring a Cisco Router."

Boston Router

`Boston>`**`enable`**	Moves to privileged mode
`Boston#`**`configure terminal`**	Moves to global configuration mode
`Boston(config)#`**`username Buffalo`** **`password academy`**	Sets the local username and password for PPP authentication of the PPP peer
`Boston(config-if)#`**`interface serial`** **`0/0/0`**	Moves to interface configuration mode
`Boston(config-if)#`**`description Link`** **`to Buffalo Router`**	Defines the locally significant link description
`Boston(config-if)#`**`ip address`** **`172.16.20.1 255.255.255.252`**	Assigns an IP address and netmask
`Boston(config-if)#`**`clock rate 56000`**	Sets the clock rate to the data communications equipment (DCE) side of the link
`Boston(config-if) #`**`encapsulation ppp`**	Turns on PPP encapsulation
`Boston(config-if)#`**`ppp authentication`** **`chap`**	Turns on CHAP authentication
`Boston(config-if)#`**`no shutdown`**	Turns on the interface
`Boston(config-if)#`**`exit`**	Returns to global configuration mode
`Boston(config)#`**`exit`**	Returns to privileged mode
`Boston#`**`copy running-config`** **`startup-config`**	Saves the configuration to NVRAM

Buffalo Router

`Buffalo>`**`enable`**	Moves to privileged mode
`Buffalo#`**`configure terminal`**	Moves to global configuration mode
`Buffalo(config)#`**`username Boston`** **`password academy`**	Sets the username and password for PPP authentication
`Buffalo(config-if)#`**`interface`** **`serial 0/0/1`**	Moves to interface configuration mode
`Buffalo(config-if)#`**`description`** **`Link to Boston Router`**	Defines the locally significant link description
`Buffalo(config-if)#`**`ip address`** **`172.16.20.2 255.255.255.252`**	Assigns an IP address and netmask
`Buffalo(config-if)` **`#encapsulation ppp`**	Turns on PPP encapsulation
`Buffalo(config-if)#`**`ppp`** **`authentication chap`**	Turns on CHAP authentication
`Buffalo(config-if)#`**`no shutdown`**	Turns on the interface
`Buffalo(config-if)#` `<Ctrl> <Z>`	Exits back to privileged mode
`Buffalo#`**`copy running-config`** **`startup-config`**	Saves the configuration to NVRAM

Configuring Multilink Point-to-Point Protocol

Multilink Point-to-Point Protocol (MLPPP) provides a method for spreading traffic across multiple physical WAN links that are bundled together into a single virtual link. Multilink PPP can also be referred to as MP, MPPP, MLP, and Multilink.

Figure 16-2 illustrates the network topology for the configuration that follows, which shows how to configure MLPPP.

Figure 16-2   MLPPP

Branch Router

Branch>**enable**	Moves to privileged mode
Branch#**configure terminal**	Moves to global configuration mode
Branch(config)#**interface Multilink 1**	Assigns a multilink interface number and enters interface configuration mode
Branch(config-if)#**ip address 192.168.10.1 255.255.255.0**	Assigns an IPv4 address to the multilink interface
Branch(config-if)#**ipv6 address 2001:db8:BA15:1::1/64**	Assigns an IPv6 address to the multilink interface
Branch(config-if)#**encapsulation ppp**	Turns on PPP encapsulation
Branch(config-if)#**ppp multilink**	Makes the interface multilink capable
Branch(config-if)#**exit**	Returns to global configuration mode
Branch(config)#**interface serial 0/0/0**	Moves to interface configuration mode
Branch(config-if)#**encapsulation ppp**	Turns on PPP encapsulation
Branch(config-if)#**ppp multilink**	Makes the interface multilink capable
Branch(config-if)#**ppp multilink group 1**	Puts the interface into multilink bundle group 1
Branch(config-if)#**no shutdown**	Turns the interface on
Branch(config-if)#**exit**	Returns to global configuration mode
Branch(config)#**interface serial 0/0/1**	Moves to interface configuration mode
Branch(config-if)#**encapsulation ppp**	Turns on PPP encapsulation
Branch(config-if)#**ppp multilink**	Makes the interface multilink capable

`Branch(config-if)#ppp multilink group 1`	Puts the interface into multilink bundle group 1
`Branch(config-if)#no shutdown`	Turns the interface on
`Branch(config-if)#exit`	Returns to global configuration mode
`Branch(config)#`	

NOTE   IP addresses are assigned to the multilink interface, not the physical interfaces. If necessary, remove any previously assigned addresses with the **no ip address** or **no ipv6 address** command.

HQ Router

`HQ>enable`	Moves to privileged mode
`HQ#configure terminal`	Moves to global configuration mode
`HQ(config)#interface Multilink 1`	Assigns a multilink interface number and enters interface configuration mode
`HQ(config-if)#ip address 192.168.10.2 255.255.255.0`	Assigns an IPv4 address to the multilink interface
`HQ(config-if)#ipv6 address 2001:db8:BA15:1::2/64`	Assigns an IPv6 address to the multilink interface
`HQ(config-if)#encapsulation ppp`	Turns on PPP encapsulation
`HQ(config-if)#ppp multilink`	Makes the interface multilink capable
`HQ(config-if)#exit`	Returns to global configuration mode
`HQ(config)#interface serial 0/0/0`	Moves to interface configuration mode
`HQ(config-if)#encapsulation ppp`	Turns on PPP encapsulation
`HQ(config-if)#ppp multilink`	Makes the interface multilink capable
`HQ(config-if)#ppp multilink group 1`	Puts the interface into multilink bundle group 1
`HQ(config-if)#no shutdown`	Turns the interface on
`HQ(config-if)#exit`	Returns to global configuration mode
`HQ(config)#interface serial 0/0/1`	Moves to interface configuration mode
`HQ(config-if)#encapsulation ppp`	Turns on PPP encapsulation
`HQ(config-if)#ppp multilink`	Makes the interface multilink capable
`HQ(config-if)#ppp multilink group 1`	Puts the interface into multilink bundle group 1
`HQ(config-if)#no shutdown`	Turns the interface on
`HQ(config-if)#exit`	Returns to global configuration mode
`HQ(config)#`	

Verifying and Troubleshooting MLPPP

`Router#show interfaces serial` x/x/x	Lists information for serial interface x/x/x
`Router#show controllers serial` x/x/x	Tells you what type of cable (DCE/DTE) is plugged into your interface and whether a clock rate has been set
`Router#show ppp multilink`	Displays information about a PPP multilink interface
`Router#debug ppp multilink data`	Debugs the first bytes of a multilink packet
`Router#debug ppp multilink events`	Debugs multilink events
`Router#debug ppp multilink fragments`	Debugs multilink fragments

Configuring a DSL Connection Using Point-to-Point Protocol over Ethernet

The Point-to-Point Protocol over Ethernet (PPPoE) protocol is used to encapsulate PPP frames inside Ethernet frames. It is most often used when working with broadband communications such as digital subscriber line (DSL), a family of technologies that provides Internet access over the wires of a local telephone network.

Figure 16-3 shows an asymmetric digital subscriber line (ADSL) connection to the ISP DSL address multiplexer.

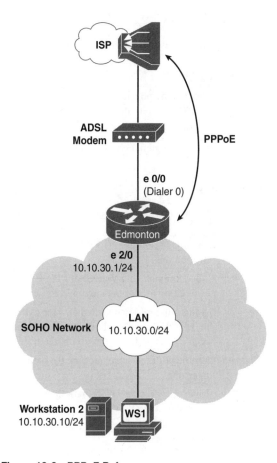

Figure 16-3   PPPoE Reference

The programming steps for configuring PPPoE on an Ethernet interface are as follows:

Step 1.   Configure PPPoE (external modem).

Step 2.   Configure the dialer interface.

Step 3.   Define interesting traffic and specify default routing.

Step 4.   Configure Network Address Translation (NAT). Choose one:

    4a. Using an access control list (ACL).

    4b. Using a route map.

Step 5.   Configure DHCP service.

Step 6.   Apply NAT programming.

Step 7.   Verify a PPPoE connection.

Step 1: Configure PPPoE (External Modem)

Edmonton(config)#**interface ethernet 0/0**	Enters interface configuration mode
Edmonton(config-if)#**pppoe enable**	Enables PPPoE on the interface
Edmonton(config-if)#**pppoe-client dial-pool-number 1**	Chooses the physical Ethernet interface for the PPPoE client dialer interface
Edmonton(config-if)#**no shutdown**	Enables the interface
Edmonton(config-if)#**exit**	Returns to global configuration mode

Step 2: Configure the Dialer Interface

Edmonton(config)#**interface dialer0**	Enters interface configuration mode.
Edmonton(config-if)#**ip address negotiated**	Obtains IP address via PPP/IPCP address negotiation.
Edmonton(config-if)#**ip mtu 1492**	Accommodates for the 6octet PPPoE header to eliminate fragmentation in the frame.
Edmonton(config-if)#**ip tcp adjust-mss 1452**	Adjusts the maximum segment size (MSS) of TCP SYN packets going through a router to eliminate fragmentation in the frame.
Edmonton(config-if)#**encapsulation ppp**	Enables PPP encapsulation on the dialer interface.
Edmonton(config-if)#**dialer pool 1**	Links the dialer interface with the physical interface Ethernet 0/1.
	NOTE The ISP defines the type of authentication to use.

For Password Authentication Protocol (PAP)

Edmonton(config-if)#**ppp authentication pap callin**	Uses PAP for authentication
Edmonton(config-if)#**ppp pap sent-username pieman password bananacream**	Enables outbound PAP user authentication with a username of *pieman* and a password of *bananacream*

For Challenge Handshake Authentication Protocol (CHAP)

Edmonton(config-if)#**ppp authentication chap callin**	Enables outbound CHAP user authentication
Edmonton(config-if)#**ppp chap hostname pieman**	Submits the CHAP username
Edmonton(config-if)#**ppp chap password bananacream**	Submits the CHAP password
Edmonton(config-if)#**exit**	Exits programming level

Step 3: Define Interesting Traffic and Specify Default Routing

Edmonton(config)#**dialer-list 2 protocol ip permit**	Declares which traffic invokes the dialing mechanism
Edmonton(config)#**interface dialer0**	Enters interface configuration mode
Edmonton(config-if)#**dialer-group 2**	Applies the "interesting traffic" rules in dialer-list 2
Edmonton(config)#**ip route 0.0.0.0 0.0.0.0 dialer0**	Specifies the dialer0 interface as the candidate default next-hop address

Step 4: Configure NAT (Choose 1 Method Only)

Step 4a: Configure NAT Using an ACL

Edmonton(config)#**access-list 1 permit 10.10.30.0 0.0.0.255**	Specifies an access control entry (ACE) for NAT.
Edmonton(config)#**ip nat pool NAT-POOL 192.31.7.1 192.31.7.2 netmask 255.255.255.0**	Defines the inside global (WAN side) NAT pool with subnet mask.
	NOTE When a range of public addresses is used for the NAT/port address translation (PAT) inside global (WAN) addresses, it is defined by an address pool and called in the NAT definition programming.
Edmonton(config)#**ip nat inside source list 1 pool NAT-POOL overload**	Specifies the NAT inside local addresses by ACL and the inside global addresses by address pool for the NAT process.
	NOTE When the ISP dynamically assigns the inside global (WAN) address, the outbound WAN interface is named in the NAT definition programming.
Edmonton(config)#**ip nat inside source list 1 interface dialer0 overload**	Specifies the NAT inside local addresses (LAN) and inside global addresses (WAN) for the NAT process.

Step 4b: Configure NAT Using a Route Map

NOTE   Using Route Maps to configure NAT is outside the scope of the CCNA Routing and Switching certification exam. It is shown here as a more advanced alternative.

`Edmonton(config)#access-list 3` `permit 10.10.30.0 0.0.0.255`	Specifies the ACE for NAT.
	NOTE The **route-map** command is typically used when redistributing routes from one routing protocol into another or to enable policy routing. The most commonly used method for defining the traffic to be translated in the NAT process is to use an ACL to choose traffic and call the ACL directly in the NAT programming. When used for NAT, a route map allows you to match any combination of ACL, next-hop IP address, and output interface to determine which pool to use. The Cisco Router and Security Device Manager (SDM) uses a route map to select traffic for NAT.
`Edmonton(config)#route-map` `ROUTEMAP permit 1`	Declares route-map name and enters route-map mode.
`Edmonton(config-route-` `map)#match ip address 3`	Specifies the ACL that defines the dialer "interesting traffic."
`Edmonton(config-route-map)#exit`	Exits route-map mode.

`Edmonton(config)#ip nat inside`
`source route-map ROUTEMAP`
`interface dialer0 overload`
	Specifies the NAT inside local (as defined by the route map) and inside global (interface dialer0) linkage for the address translation.

Step 5: Configure DHCP Service

`Edmonton(config)#ip dhcp`
`excluded-address 10.10.30.1`
`10.10.30.5`
	Excludes an IP address range from being offered by the router's DHCP service.

`Edmonton(config)#ip dhcp pool` `CLIENT-30`	Enters dhcp-config mode for the pool CLIENT-30.
`Edmonton(dhcp-config)#network` `10.10.30.0 255.255.255.0`	Defines the IP network address.

`Edmonton(dhcp-`
`config)#default-router`
`10.10.30.1`
	Declares the router's vlan10 interface address as a gateway address.

`Edmonton(dhcp-config)#import` `all`	Imports DHCP option parameters into the DHCP server database from external DHCP service.
	NOTE Any manually configured DHCP option parameters override the equivalent imported DHCP option parameters. Because they are obtained dynamically, these imported DHCP option parameters are not part of the router configuration and are not saved in NVRAM.
`Edmonton(dhcp-config)#dns-` `server 10.10.30.2`	Declares any required DNS server addresses.
`Edmonton(dhcp-config)#exit`	Exits dhcp-config mode.

Step 6: Apply NAT Programming

Edmonton(config)#**interface ethernet2/0**	Enters interface configuration mode
Edmonton(config-if)#**ip nat inside**	Specifies the interface as an inside local (LAN side) interface
Edmonton(config)#**interface dialer0**	Enters interface configuration mode
Edmonton(config-if)#**ip nat outside**	Specifies the interface as an inside global (WAN side) interface
Edmonton(config-if)#**end**	Returns to privileged EXEC mode

Step 7: Verify a PPPoE Connection

Edmonton#**debug pppoe events**	Displays PPPoE protocol messages about events that are part of normal session establishment or shutdown
Edmonton#**debug ppp authentication**	Displays authentication protocol messages such as CHAP and PAP
Edmonton#**show pppoe session**	Displays information about currently active PPPoE sessions
Edmonton#**show ip dhcp binding**	Displays address bindings on the Cisco IOS DHCP server
Edmonton#**show ip nat translations**	Displays active NAT translations

External Border Gateway Protocol (eBGP)

This chapter provides information and commands concerning the following topics:

- Configuring Border Gateway Protocol
- BGP and loopback addresses
- Configuration example: eBGP
- eBGP multihop
- Verifying BGP connections
- Troubleshooting BGP connections

Configuring Border Gateway Protocol

`Router(config)#router bgp 100`	Starts Border Gateway Protocol (BGP) routing process 100.
	NOTE Cisco IOS software permits only one BGP process to run at a time; therefore, a router cannot belong to more than one autonomous system (AS).
`Router(config-router) #neighbor 192.31.7.1 remote-as 200`	Identifies a peer router with which this router establishes a BGP session. The AS number determines whether the neighbor router is an external BGP (eBGP) or an internal BGP (iBGP) neighbor.
	TIP If the AS number configured in the **router bgp** command is identical to the AS number configured in the **neighbor** statement, BGP initiates an internal session (iBGP). If the field values differ, BGP builds an external session (eBGP).
	TIP **neighbor** statements must be symmetrical for a neighbor relationship to be established.
`Router(config-router) #network 192.135.250.0`	Tells the BGP process what locally learned networks to advertise.
	NOTE The networks can be connected routes, static routes, or routes learned via a dynamic routing protocol, such as Open Shortest Path First (OSPF) Protocol.
	NOTE Configuring just a **network** statement does not establish a BGP neighbor relationship.
	NOTE The networks must also exist in the local router's routing table; otherwise, they are not sent out in updates.

`Router(config-router)`
`#network 128.107.0.0`
`mask 255.255.255.0`
	Used to specify an individual subnet that must be present in the routing table to be advertised by BGP.

TIP   The CCNA Routing and Switching vendor certification exam focuses only on eBGP. iBGP is a topic in the Cisco ROUTE vendor certification exam.

TIP   Routes learned by the BGP process are propagated by default but are often filtered by a routing policy.

TIP   If you issue the command **network 192.168.0.0 mask 255.255.0.0** to advertise a classless interdomain routing (CIDR) block, BGP looks for 192.168.0.0/16 in the routing table. It may find 192.168.1.0/24 or 192.168.1.1/32; however, it may never find 192.168.0.0/16. Because there is no match to the network, BGP does not announce this network to neighbors. In this case, you can configure a static route toward a null interface so BGP can find an exact match in the routing table:

`ip route 192.168.0.0 255.255.0.0 null0`

After finding this exact match in the routing table, BGP announces the 192.168.0.0/16 network to any neighbors.

BGP and Loopback Addresses

`Router(config)#router` `bgp 100`	Starts the BGP routing process.

`Router(config-router)`
`#neighbor 172.16.1.2`
`update-source loopback0`
	Informs the router to use any operational interface as the source IP address for TCP connections (in this case, Loopback0). Because a loopback interface never goes down, this adds more stability to your configuration compared to using a physical interface.

	TIP Without the **neighbor update-source** command, BGP uses the closest IP interface to the peer. This command provides BGP with a more robust configuration because BGP still operates if the link to the closest interface fails and a redundant path is available to the peer address.
	NOTE You can use the **neighbor update-source** command with either eBGP or iBGP sessions. In the case of a point-to-point eBGP session, this command is not needed because there is only one path for BGP to use.

Configuration Example: eBGP

Figure 17-1 shows the network topology for the configuration that follows, which demonstrates how to configure eBGP. Assume that all basic configurations are accurate.

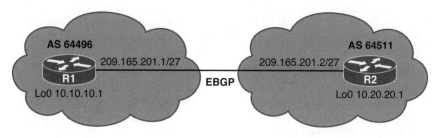

Figure 17-1   eBGP

R1(config)#**router bgp 64496**	Starts the BGP routing process
R1(config-router)#**neighbor 209.165.201.2 remote-as 64511**	Identifies a peer router at 10.20.20.1
R2(config)#**router bgp 64511**	Starts the BGP routing process
R2(config-router)#**neighbor 209.165.201.1 remote-as 64496**	Identifies a peer router at 10.10.10.1

eBGP Multihop

By default, eBGP neighbors exchange packets with a Time To Live (TTL) set to 1. If you attempt to establish an eBGP session between loopbacks, BGP packets will be dropped due to an expired TTL.

Figure 17-2 shows the network topology for the configuration that follows, which demonstrates how to configure eBGP multihop. Assume that all basic configurations are accurate.

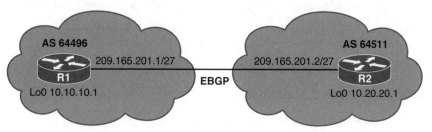

Figure 17-2   eBGP Multihop

R1(config)#**ip route 10.20.20.1 255.255.255.255 209.165.201.2**	Defines a static route to the Loopback 0 address on R2.
R1(config)#**router bgp 64496**	Starts the BGP routing process.
R1(config-router)#**neighbor 10.20.20.1 remote-as 64511**	Identifies a peer router at 10.20.20.1.

R1(config-router)#**neighbor** **10.20.20.1 update-source** **loopback0**	Informs R1 to use Loopback0 IP address as the source IP address for all BGP TCP packets sent to R2.
R1(config-router)#**neighbor** **10.20.20.1 EBGP-multihop 2**	Allows for two routers that are not using directly connected interfaces to establish an eBGP session. A TTL value of 2 is defined.
R2(config)#**ip route 10.10.10.1** **255.255.255.255 209.165.201.1**	Defines a static route to the Loopback 0 address on R1.
R2(config)#**router bgp 64511**	Starts the BGP routing process.
R2(config-router)#**neighbor** **10.10.10.1 remote-as 64496**	Identifies a peer router at 10.10.10.1
R2(config-router)#**neighbor** **10.10.10.1 update-source loop-** **back0**	Informs R2 to use the Loopback0 IP address as the source IP address for all BGP TCP packets sent to R1.
R2(config-router)#**neighbor** **10.10.10.1 EBGP-multihop 2**	Allows for two routers that are not using directly connected interfaces to establish an eBGP session. A TTL value of 2 is defined.

NOTE   The **EBGP-multihop** keyword is a Cisco IOS option that must be configured on each peer. The **EBGP-multihop** keyword is used only for eBGP sessions, not for iBGP.

eBGP neighbors are usually directly connected (over a WAN connection, for example) to establish an eBGP session. However, sometimes one of the directly connected routers is unable to run BGP. The **EBGP-multihop** keyword allows for a logical connection to be made between peer routers even if they are not using directly connected interfaces. The **EBGP-multihop** keyword allows for an eBGP peer to be up to 255 hops away and still create an eBGP session.

NOTE   If redundant links exist between two eBGP neighbors and loopback addresses are used, you must configure **EBGP-multihop** because of the default TTL of 1. Otherwise, the router decrements the TTL before giving the packet to the loopback interface, meaning that the normal IP forwarding logic discards the packet.

Verifying BGP Connections

Router#**show ip bgp**	Displays entries in the BGP table
Router#**show ip bgp** **neighbors**	Displays information about the BGP and TCP connections to neighbors
Router#**show ip bgp** **rib-failure**	Displays networks that are not installed in the Routing Information Base (RIB) and the reason that they were not installed
Router#**show ip bgp summary**	Displays the status of all BGP connections
Router#**show ip route bgp**	Displays the BGP entries from the routing table

Troubleshooting BGP Connections

Router#`clear ip bgp *`	Forces BGP to clear its table and resets all BGP sessions.
	CAUTION The **clear ip bgp *** command is both processor and memory intensive and should be used only in smaller environments.
Router#`clear ip bgp` `10.1.1.1`	Resets the specific BGP session with the neighbor at 10.1.1.1.
Router#`clear ip bgp` `10.1.1.2 soft`	Forces the routing table entry from this neighbor to be reconfigured and reactivated without clearing the BGP session.
	TIP The **clear ip bgp w.x.y.z soft out** command is highly recommended when you are changing an outbound policy on the router. The **soft out** option does not help if you are changing an inbound policy.
Router#`clear ip bgp` `10.1.1.2 soft in`	Forces the remote neighbor to resend all BGP information to the local router without resetting the connection. Routes from this neighbor are not lost.
Router#`clear ip bgp` `10.1.1.2 soft out`	Triggers an outbound soft reset.
	TIP If the **in** or **out** option is not specified, both inbound and outbound soft resets are triggered.

NOTE   Soft reset is recommended because it allows routing table policies to be reconfigured and activated without clearing the BGP session.

NOTE   When soft reset generates inbound updates from a neighbor, it is called *dynamic inbound soft reset*.

NOTE   When soft reset is used to send a new set of updates to a neighbor, it is called *outbound soft reset*.

NOTE   When a BGP session is reset and soft reconfiguration is used, several commands enable you to monitor BGP routes that are received, sent, or filtered:

Router#`show ip bgp`

Router#`show ip bgp neighbor` *address* `advertised-routes`

Router#`show ip bgp neighbor` *address* `received`

Router#`show ip bgp neighbor` *address* `received-routes`

Router#`show ip bgp neighbor` *address* `routes`

Router#`debug ip bgp`	Displays information related to processing BGP
Router#`debug ip bgp updates`	Displays information about the processing of BGP update

CAUTION   The **clear ip bgp *** command is both processor and memory intensive and should be used only in smaller environments. A more reasonable approach is to clear only a specific network or a specific session with a neighbor with the **clear ip bgp** *specific-network* command. However, you can use this command whenever the following occur:

- Additions or changes to the BGP-related access lists
- Changes to BGP-related weights
- Changes to BGP-related distribution lists
- Changes in the BGP timer's specifications
- Changes to the BGP administrative distance
- Changes to BGP-related route maps

Configuring Generic Routing Encapsulation (GRE) Tunnels

This chapter provides information and commands concerning the following topics:

- Configuring a GRE tunnel
- Verifying a GRE tunnel

Generic routing encapsulation (GRE) is a tunneling protocol that can encapsulate a variety of protocol packets inside IPv4 and IPv6 tunnels. GRE was developed by Cisco.

CAUTION GRE does not include strong security mechanisms to protect its payload. To ensure a secure tunnel, you should use IPsec in conjunction with a GRE tunnel.

Configuring a GRE Tunnel

Figure 18-1 illustrates the network topology for the configuration that follows, which shows how to configure a GRE tunnel between two remote sites. This example shows only the commands needed to set up the GRE tunnel. Other commands are necessary to complete the configuration: hostnames, physical interfaces, routing, and so on.

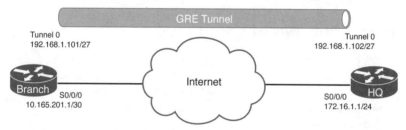

Figure 18-1 GRE Tunnel Configuration

Branch Router

`Branch(config)#interface tunnel0`	Moves to interface configuration mode
`Branch(config-if)#tunnel mode gre ip`	Sets tunnel encapsulation method to GRE over IP
`Branch(config-if)#ip address` `192.168.1.101 255.255.255.224`	Sets IP address and mask information for interface
`Branch(config-if)#tunnel source` `10.165.201.1`	Maps tunnel source to serial 0/0/0 interface
`Branch(config-if)#tunnel destination` `172.16.1.1`	Maps tunnel destination to HQ router

HQ Router

`HQ(config)#interface tunnel0`	Moves to interface configuration mode
`HQ(config-if)#tunnel mode gre ip`	Sets tunnel encapsulation method to GRE over IP
`HQ(config-if)#ip address` `192.168.1.102 255.255.255.224`	Sets IP address and mask information for interface
`HQ(config-if)#tunnel source` `172.16.1.1`	Maps tunnel source to serial 0/0/0 interface
`HQ(config-if)#tunnel destination` `10.165.201.1`	Maps tunnel destination to Branch router

Verifying a GRE Tunnel

`Router#show interface tunnel0`	Verifies GRE tunnel configuration.
`Router#show ip interface brief`	Shows brief summary of all interfaces, including tunnel interfaces.
`Router#show ip interface` `brief	include tunnel`	Shows summary of interfaces named *tunnel*.
`Router#show ip route`	Verifies a tunnel route between the Branch and HQ routers. The path will be seen as directly connected (C) in the route table.

Quality of Service (QoS)

This chapter provides information and commands concerning the following topics:

- High availability for voice and video
- Configuring basic QoS
- Verifying basic QoS
- Auto-QoS

NOTE The current version of the CCNA Routing and Switching vendor certification exam does not have commands for quality of service (QoS) as part of its blueprint. This chapter is for informational purposes and practice only.

High Availability for Voice and Video

Typical campus networks are designed with oversubscription because most campus links are underutilized. The rule-of-thumb recommendation for data oversubscription is 20:1 for access ports on the access-to-distribution uplink and 4:1 for the distribution-to-core links. QoS is needed when congestion occurs.

Configuring Basic QoS

`switch(config)#mls qos`	Enables QoS for the entire switch.
	NOTE The switch QoS is disabled by default.
	NOTE On a Layer 3 switch, entering this command may give you the following warning: QoS: ensure flow-control on all interfaces are OFF for proper operation. Refer to your platform's command reference.
`switch#show mls qos`	Displays the global QoS configuration.
`Switch(config)#interface fastethernet 0/10`	Moves to interface configuration mode.
`Switch(config-if)#switchport voice vlan 110`	Assigns this port to be a member port in the auxiliary voice VLAN 110.
`Switch(config-if)#mls qos trust`	Configures the switch port to trust the markings of a specified protocol or device as shown in the following rows.

	NOTE The **mls qos trust** *interface* configuration command configures the port trust state. Ingress traffic is trusted, and classification is performed by examining the packet Differentiated Services Code Point (DSCP), class of service (CoS), or IP-precedence field. It can also be configured to trust a Cisco IP phone.
`Switch(config-if)#`**`mls qos trust cos`**	Configures the interface to classify incoming traffic packets according to the CoS value. For untagged packets, the default CoS value is used. The default port CoS value is 0.
`Switch(config-if)#`**`mls qos trust dscp`**	Configures the interface to classify incoming traffic packets according to the DSCP value. For a non-IP packet, the packet CoS value is used if the packet is tagged. For an untagged packet, the default port CoS value is used.
`Switch(config-if)#`**`mls qos trust ip-precedence`**	Configures the interface to classify incoming packets according to the IP precedence value. For a non-IP packet, the packet CoS value is used if the packet is tagged. For an untagged packet, the default port CoS value is used.
`Switch(config-if)#`**`mls qos trust device cisco-phone`**	Configures the switch port to trust the QoS markings of a Cisco IP phone if detected.
`Switch (config-if)#`**`switchport priority extend cos 0`**	Configures the switch port to send Cisco Discovery Protocol (CDP) packets to the IP phone instructing the phone as to what CoS markings the phone should add to the data packets that it receives from the device attached to the access port on the Cisco IP Phone. In this case, the CoS value is set to 0.
	NOTE The CoS value is from 0 to 7, with 7 being the highest priority. The default value is CoS 0.
`Switch (config-if)#`**`switchport priority extend trust`**	Sets the priority of data traffic received from the IP Phone access port. The **trust** argument configures the IP Phone access port to trust the priority received from the PC or attached device.
	NOTE The **mls qos trust extend** command is only valid on the 6500 series switch. Although the 6500 series switch is not tested on the CCNA Routing and Switching certification exam, the **mls qos trust extend** command has been placed in this command guide because of the large number of network professionals working with the 6500 series switch.
	NOTE With the **mls qos trust extend** command enabled, if you set your phone to trusted mode, all the packets coming from the PC are sent untouched directly through the phone to the 6500 series switch. If you set the phone to untrusted mode, all traffic coming from the PC is re-marked with the configured CoS value before being sent to the 6500 series switch.

> **NOTE**   Each time that you enter the **mls qos trust extend** command, the mode is changed. If the mode was set to trusted, the result of this command would be to change the mode to untrusted.
>
> Use the **show queueing interface** command to display the current trust mode.

CAUTION   Although the QoS mechanisms for voice and video are the same, great care must be taken due to the high bandwidth requirements typical to video. This is true for both a one-way video session and an interactive two-way video session.

Verifying Basic QoS

`Switch#show interfaces`
`fastethernet 0/10`
`switchport`
	Displays the administrative and operational status of the switching port FastEthernet 0/10. This includes port blocking and port protection settings.

`Switch#show mls qos` `interface fastethernet 0/10`	Shows port level QoS information for FastEthernet 0/10. This includes trust state and default CoS value.

Auto-QoS

Auto-QoS automatically configures QoS for voice over IP within a QoS domain. It is disabled by default on all ports. When auto-QoS is enabled on a port, it uses the label on the incoming packet to categorize traffic, to assign other packet labels, and to configure input and output queues. When auto-QoS is used, configure all network devices in a QoS domain with auto-QoS to maintain consistent QoS next hop behavior.

> **NOTE**   The switch applies the auto-QoS-generated commands as if the commands were entered sequentially from the command-line interface (CLI). An existing user configuration can cause the application of the generated commands to fail or to be overridden by the generated commands.

> **TIP**   QoS is globally enabled when AutoQoS is enabled on the first interface.

Restrictions for Auto-QoS

The following are restrictions for Automatic QoS (Auto-QoS):

- Auto-QoS (and enhanced auto-QoS) is not supported on switches running the LAN Lite image.

- After auto-QoS is enabled, do not modify a policy map or aggregate policer that includes *AutoQoS* in its name. If you need to modify the policy map or aggregate policer, make a copy of it and change the copied policy map or policer. To use this new policy map instead of the generated one, remove the generated policy map from the interface and apply the new policy map to the interface.

- To take advantage of the auto-QoS defaults, you should enable auto-QoS before you configure other QoS commands. If necessary, you can fine-tune the QoS configuration, but it is recommended that you do so only after the auto-QoS configuration is completed.

- By default, CDP is enabled on all ports. For auto-QoS to function properly, do not disable CDP.

TIP You can enable auto-QoS on static, dynamic-access, voice VLAN access, and trunk ports.

Configuring Auto-QoS: 2960-X/3650/3750

Switch(config)#interface fastethernet 0/11	Moves to interface configuration mode.
Switch(config-if)#auto qos voip trust	Identifies this port as connected to a trusted switch or router and automatically configures QoS for VoIP. The port is configured to trust the CoS label or the DSCP value received on the packet.
Switch(config-if)#auto qos trust cos	Identifies this port as connected to a trusted switch or router and automatically configures QoS for VoIP. The port is configured to trust the CoS label.
Switch(config-if)#auto qos trust dscp	Identifies this port as connected to a trusted switch or router and automatically configures QoS for VoIP. The port is configured to trust the DSCP value.
Switch(config-if)#auto qos voip cisco-phone	Identifies this port as connected to a Cisco IP Phone and automatically configures QoS for VoIP.
	NOTE When using the **auto qos voip cisco-phone** command, if a phone is detected, the port is configured to trust the QoS label received in any packet. If a phone is not detected, the port is set not to trust the QoS label.
Switch(config-if)#auto qos voip cisco-softphone	Identifies this port as connected to a device with a Cisco IP Softphone installed on it and automatically configures QoS for VoIP.
Switch(config-if)#auto qos video cts	Identifies this port as connected to a Cisco Telepresence system.
Switch(config-if)#auto qos video ip-camera	Identifies this port as connected to a Cisco video surveillance camera.
Switch(config-if)#auto qos video media-player	Identifies this port as connected to a CDP-capable Cisco digital media player.
Switch(config-if)#auto qos classify	Enables auto QoS for classification.
Switch(config-if)#auto qos classify police	Enables policing. Policing is set up by defining the QoS policy maps and applying them to ports (port-based QoS)

Verifying Auto QoS: 2960-X/3650/3750

`Switch#show interface fastethernet 0/2 switchport`	Displays voice parameters configured on the interface
`Switch#show auto qos`	Displays the QoS commands entered on all interfaces
`Switch#show auto qos interface fastethernet 0/11`	Displays the QoS commands entered interface FastEthernet 0/11

The following commands generated the output shown in Example 19-1.

```
c3750(config)#interface fastethernet 0/2
c3750(config-if)#auto qos voip trust
c3750(config-if)#end
c3750#show running-config
```

Explanations for each of the mapping and queuing commands shown in Example 19-1 can be found in the IOS Command Reference for each specific switching platform.

EXAMPLE 19-1   Configuration Generated by the **auto qos** Command

```
mls qos map cos-dscp 0 8 16 24 32 46 48 56
!
mls qos srr-queue input bandwidth 90 10
mls qos srr-queue input threshold 1 8 16
mls qos srr-queue input threshold 2 34 66
mls qos srr-queue input buffers 67 33
!
mls qos srr-queue input cos-map queue 1 threshold 2 1
mls qos srr-queue input cos-map queue 1 threshold 3 0
mls qos srr-queue input cos-map queue 2 threshold 1 2
mls qos srr-queue input cos-map queue 2 threshold 2 4 6 7
mls qos srr-queue input cos-map queue 2 threshold 3 3 5
!
mls qos srr-queue input dscp-map queue 1 threshold 2 9 10 11 12 13 14 15
mls qos srr-queue input dscp-map queue 1 threshold 3 0 1 2 3 4 5 6 7
mls qos srr-queue input dscp-map queue 1 threshold 3 32
mls qos srr-queue input dscp-map queue 2 threshold 1 16 17 18 19 20 21 22 23
mls qos srr-queue input dscp-map queue 2 threshold 2 33 34 35 36 37 38 39 48
mls qos srr-queue input dscp-map queue 2 threshold 2 49 50 51 52 53 54 55 56
mls qos srr-queue input dscp-map queue 2 threshold 2 57 58 59 60 61 62 63
mls qos srr-queue input dscp-map queue 2 threshold 3 24 25 26 27 28 29 30 31
mls qos srr-queue input dscp-map queue 2 threshold 3 40 41 42 43 44 45 46 47
!
mls qos srr-queue output cos-map queue 1 threshold 3 5
mls qos srr-queue output cos-map queue 2 threshold 3 3 6 7
mls qos srr-queue output cos-map queue 3 threshold 3 2 4
```

```
mls qos srr-queue output cos-map queue 4 threshold 2 1
mls qos srr-queue output cos-map queue 4 threshold 3 0
!
mls qos srr-queue output dscp-map queue 1 threshold 3 40 41 42 43 44 45 46 47
mls qos srr-queue output dscp-map queue 2 threshold 3 24 25 26 27 28 29 30 31
mls qos srr-queue output dscp-map queue 2 threshold 3 48 49 50 51 52 53 54 55
mls qos srr-queue output dscp-map queue 2 threshold 3 56 57 58 59 60 61 62 63
mls qos srr-queue output dscp-map queue 3 threshold 3 16 17 18 19 20 21 22 23
mls qos srr-queue output dscp-map queue 3 threshold 3 32 33 34 35 36 37 38 39
mls qos srr-queue output dscp-map queue 4 threshold 1 8
mls qos srr-queue output dscp-map queue 4 threshold 2 9 10 11 12 13 14 15
mls qos srr-queue output dscp-map queue 4 threshold 3 0 1 2 3 4 5 6 7
!
mls qos queue-set output 1 threshold 1 138 138 92 138
mls qos queue-set output 1 threshold 2 138 138 92 400
mls qos queue-set output 1 threshold 3 36 77 100 318
mls qos queue-set output 1 threshold 4 20 50 67 400
mls qos queue-set output 2 threshold 1 149 149 100 149
mls qos queue-set output 2 threshold 2 118 118 100 235
mls qos queue-set output 2 threshold 3 41 68 100 272
mls qos queue-set output 2 threshold 4 42 72 100 242
!
mls qos queue-set output 1 buffers 10 10 26 54
mls qos queue-set output 2 buffers 16 6 17 61
mls qos
!
interface FastEthernet0/2
 no switchport
 ip address 172.19.20.2 255.255.255.0
 srr-queue bandwidth share 10 10 60 20
 priority-queue out
 mls qos trust cos
 auto qos voip trust
!
```

Configuring Auto-QoS: 6500

TIP Although the 6500 series switch is not tested on the CCNA Routing and Switching certification exam, these commands have been placed in this command guide because of the large number of network professionals working with the 6500 series switch. The 6500 series switch uses the Catalyst operating system as opposed to the Cisco IOS found on the 2960-x/3650/3750 series.

`Console> (enable) set qos autoqos`	Applies all global QoS settings to all ports on the switch
`Console> (enable) set port qos 3/1 - 48 autoqos trust cos`	Applies Auto-QoS to ports 3/1–48 and specifies that the ports should trust CoS markings
`Console> (enable) set port qos 3/1 - 48 autoqos trust dscp`	Applies Auto-QoS to ports 3/1–48 and specifies that the ports should trust DSCP markings
`Console> (enable) set port qos 4/1 autoqos voip ciscoipphone`	Applies Auto-QoS settings for any Cisco IP Phone on module 4, port 1
`Console> (enable) set port qos 4/1 autoqos voip ciscosoftphone`	Applies Auto-QoS settings for any Cisco IP SoftPhone on module 4, port 1

Verifying Auto-QoS Information: 6500

`Console> show port qos`	Displays all QoS-related information
`Console> show port qos 3/1`	Displays all QoS-related information for module 3, port 1

This chapter provides information and commands concerning the following topics:

- Configuring a DHCP server on an IOS router
- Using Cisco IP Phones with a DHCP server
- Verifying and troubleshooting DHCP configuration
- Configuring a DHCP helper address
- DHCP client on a Cisco IOS Software Ethernet interface
- Configuration example: DHCP

Configuring a DHCP Server on an IOS Router

`Router(config)#ip dhcp pool INTERNAL`	Creates a DHCP pool named INTERNAL. The name can be anything of your choosing.
`Router(dhcp-config)#network 172.16.10.0 255.255.255.0`	Defines the range of addresses to be leased.
`Router(dhcp-config) #default-router 172.16.10.1`	Defines the address of the default router for the client.
`Router(dhcp-config) #dns-server 172.16.10.10`	Defines the address of the Domain Name System (DNS) server for the client.
`Router(dhcp-config) #netbios-name-server 172.16.10.10`	Defines the address of the NetBIOS server for the client.
`Router(dhcp-config)#domain-name fakedomainname.com`	Defines the domain name for the client.
`Router(dhcp-config)# lease 14 12 23`	Defines the lease time to be 14 days, 12 hours, 23 minutes.
`Router(dhcp-config)#lease infinite`	Sets the lease time to infinity; the default time is 1 day.
`Router(dhcp-config)#exit`	Returns to global configuration mode.
`Router(config)#ip dhcp excluded-address 172.16.10.1 172.16.10.10`	Specifies the range of addresses not to be leased out to clients.
`Router(config)#service dhcp`	Enables the DHCP service and relay features on a Cisco IOS router.
`Router(config)#no service dhcp`	Turns the DHCP service off. The DHCP service is on by default in Cisco IOS Software.

Using Cisco IP Phones with a DHCP Server

Enterprises with small branch offices that implement a VoIP solution may choose to implement a Cisco CallManager at a central office to control Cisco IP Phones at small branch offices. This design allows for centralized call processing and reduces equipment and administration required (especially at the branch office).

Cisco IP Phones download their configuration from a TFTP server. When a Cisco IP Phone starts, if it does not have its IP address and TFTP server IP address preconfigured, it sends a request with option 150 or 66 to the DHCP server to obtain this information.

- DHCP option 150 provides the IP address of a list of TFTP servers.

- DHCP option 66 gives the IP address of a single TFTP server.

NOTE   Cisco IP Phones may also include DHCP option 3 in their requests, which sets a default route.

`Router(dhcp-config)#option 66` `ip 10.1.1.250`	Provides the IP address of a TFTP server for option 66
`Router(dhcp-config)#option 150` `ip 10.1.1.250`	Provides the name of a TFTP server for option 150
`Router(dhcp-config)#option 150` `ip 10.1.1.250 10.1.1.251`	Provides the names of two TFTP servers for option 150
`Router(dhcp-config)#option 3 ip` `10.1.1.1`	Sets the default route

Verifying and Troubleshooting DHCP Configuration

`Router#show ip dhcp binding`	Displays a list of all bindings created
`Router#show ip dhcp binding w.x.y.z`	Displays the bindings for a specific DHCP client with an IP address of *w.x.y.z*
`Router#clear ip dhcp binding` `a.b.c.d`	Clears an automatic address binding from the DHCP server database
`Router#clear ip dhcp binding *`	Clears all automatic DHCP bindings
`Router#show ip dhcp conflict`	Displays a list of all address conflicts that the DHCP server recorded
`Router#clear ip dhcp conflict` `a.b.c.d`	Clears address conflict from the database
`Router#clear ip dhcp conflict *`	Clears conflicts for all addresses
`Router#show ip dhcp database`	Displays recent activity on the DHCP database
`Router#show ip dhcp server` `statistics`	Displays a list of the number of messages sent and received by the DHCP server

Router#clear ip dhcp server statistics	Resets all DHCP server counters to 0
Router#debug ip dhcp server {events | packet | linkage | class}	Displays the DHCP process of addresses being leased and returned

Configuring a DHCP Helper Address

Router(config)#interface gigabitethernet 0/0	Moves to interface configuration mode.
Router(config-if)#ip helper-address 172.16.20.2	DHCP broadcasts will be forwarded as a unicast to this specific address rather than be dropped by the router.

NOTE The **ip helper-address** command forwards broadcast packets as a unicast to eight different UDP ports by default:

- TFTP (port 69)
- DNS (port 53)
- Time service (port 37)
- NetBIOS name server (port 137)
- NetBIOS datagram server (port 138)
- Boot Protocol (BOOTP) client and server datagrams (ports 67 and 68)
- TACACS service (port 49)

If you want to close some of these ports, use the **no ip forward-protocol udp** x command at the global configuration prompt, where x is the port number you want to close. The following command stops the forwarding of broadcasts to port 49:

Router(config)#no ip forward-protocol udp 49

If you want to open other UDP ports, use the **ip forward-helper udp** x command, where x is the port number you want to open:

Router(config)#ip forward-protocol udp 517

DHCP Client on a Cisco IOS Software Ethernet Interface

Router(config)#interface gigabitethernet 0/0	Moves to interface configuration mode
Router(config-if)#ip address dhcp	Specifies that the interface acquire an IP address through DHCP

Configuration Example: DHCP

Figure 20-1 illustrates the network topology for the configuration that follows, which shows how to configure DHCP services on a Cisco IOS router using the commands covered in this chapter.

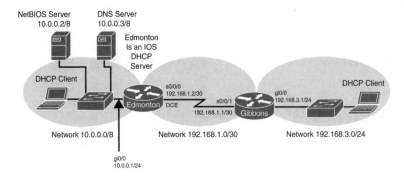

Figure 20-1 Network Topology for DHCP Configuration

Edmonton Router

`router>`**`enable`**	Moves to privileged mode
`router#`**`configure terminal`**	Moves to global configuration mode
`router(config)#`**`hostname Edmonton`**	Sets the hostname
`Edmonton(config)#`**`interface gigabitethernet 0/0`**	Moves to interface configuration mode
`Edmonton(config-if)#`**`description LAN Interface`**	Sets the local description of the interface
`Edmonton(config-if)#`**`ip address 10.0.0.1 255.0.0.0`**	Assigns an IP address and netmask
`Edmonton(config-if)#`**`no shutdown`**	Enables the interface
`Edmonton(config-if)#`**`interface serial 0/0/0`**	Moves to interface configuration mode
`Edmonton(config-if)#`**`description Link to Gibbons Router`**	Sets the local description of the interface
`Edmonton(config-if)#`**`ip address 192.168.1.2 255.255.255.252`**	Assigns an IP address and netmask
`Edmonton(config-if)#`**`clock rate 56000`**	Assigns the clock rate to the DCE cable on this side of link
`Edmonton(config-if)#`**`no shutdown`**	Enables the interface
`Edmonton(config-if)#`**`exit`**	Returns to global configuration mode
`Edmonton(config)#`**`router eigrp 10`**	Enables the EIGRP routing process for autonomous system 10
`Edmonton(config-router)#`**`network 10.0.0.0`**	Advertises the 10.0.0.0 network
`Edmonton(config-router)#`**`network 192.168.1.0`**	Advertises the 192.168.1.0 network
`Edmonton(config-router)#`**`exit`**	Returns to global configuration mode

Edmonton(config)#**service dhcp**	Verifies that the router can use DHCP services and that DHCP is enabled
Edmonton(config)#**ip dhcp pool 10NETWORK**	Creates a DHCP pool called 10NETWORK
Edmonton(dhcp-config)#**network 10.0.0.0 255.0.0.0**	Defines the range of addresses to be leased
Edmonton(dhcp-config)#**default-router 10.0.0.1**	Defines the address of the default router for clients
Edmonton(dhcp-config)#**netbios-name-server 10.0.0.2**	Defines the address of the NetBIOS server for clients
Edmonton(dhcp-config)#**dns-server 10.0.0.3**	Defines the address of the DNS server for clients
Edmonton(dhcp-config)#**domain-name fakedomainname.com**	Defines the domain name for clients
Edmonton(dhcp-config)#**lease 12 14 30**	Sets the lease time to be 12 days, 14 hours, 30 minutes
Edmonton(dhcp-config)#**exit**	Returns to global configuration mode
Edmonton(config)#**ip dhcp excluded-address 10.0.0.1 10.0.0.5**	Specifies the range of addresses not to be leased out to clients
Edmonton(config)#**ip dhcp pool 192.168.3NETWORK**	Creates a DHCP pool called the 192.168.3NETWORK
Edmonton(dhcp-config)#**network 192.168.3.0 255.255.255.0**	Defines the range of addresses to be leased
Edmonton(dhcp-config) #**default-router 192.168.3.1**	Defines the address of the default router for clients
Edmonton(dhcp-config) #**netbios-name-server 10.0.0.2**	Defines the address of the NetBIOS server for clients
Edmonton(dhcp-config)#**dns-server 10.0.0.3**	Defines the address of the DNS server for clients
Edmonton(dhcp-config)#**domain-name fakedomainname.com**	Defines the domain name for clients
Edmonton(dhcp-config)#**lease 12 14 30**	Sets the lease time to be 12 days, 14 hours, 30 minutes
Edmonton(dhcp-config)#**exit**	Returns to global configuration mode
Edmonton(config)#**exit**	Returns to privileged mode
Edmonton#**copy running-config startup-config**	Saves the configuration to NVRAM

Gibbons Router

`router>`**`enable`**	Moves to privileged mode.
`router#`**`configure terminal`**	Moves to global configuration mode.
`router(config)#`**`hostname Gibbons`**	Sets the hostname.
`Gibbons(config)#`**`interface giga-`** **`bitethernet 0/0`**	Moves to interface configuration mode.
`Gibbons(config-if)#`**`description`** **`LAN Interface`**	Sets the local description of the interface.
`Gibbons(config-if)#`**`ip address`** **`192.168.3.1 255.255.255.0`**	Assigns an IP address and netmask.
`Gibbons(config-if)#`**`ip`** **`helper-address 192.168.1.2`**	DHCP broadcasts will be forwarded as a unicast to this address rather than be dropped.
`Gibbons(config-if)#`**`no shutdown`**	Enables the interface.
`Gibbons(config-if)#`**`interface`** **`serial 0/0/1`**	Moves to interface configuration mode.
`Gibbons(config-if)#`**`description`** **`Link to Edmonton Router`**	Sets the local description of the interface.
`Gibbons(config-if)#`**`ip address`** **`192.168.1.1 255.255.255.252`**	Assigns an IP address and netmask.
`Gibbons(config-if)#`**`no shutdown`**	Enables the interface.
`Gibbons(config-if)#`**`exit`**	Returns to global configuration mode.
`Gibbons(config)#`**`router eigrp 10`**	Enables the EIGRP routing process for autonomous system 10.
`Gibbons(config-router)#`**`network`** **`192.168.3.0`**	Advertises the 192.168.3.0 network.
`Gibbons(config-router)#`**`network`** **`192.168.1.0`**	Advertises the 192.168.1.0 network.
`Gibbons(config-router)#`**`exit`**	Returns to global configuration mode.
`Gibbons(config)#`**`exit`**	Returns to privileged mode.
`Gibbons#`**`copy running-config`** **`startup-config`**	Saves the configuration to NVRAM.

First Hop Redundancy Protocols (FHRP): Hot Standby Router Protocol (HSRP)

This chapter provides information and commands concerning the following topics:

- First Hop Redundancy
- Hot Standby Router Protocol
- Configuring HSRP on a router
- Default HSRP configuration settings
- Verifying HSRP
- HSRP optimization options
  - Preempt
  - HSRP Message Timers
  - Interface tracking
- Debugging HSRP
- Configuration example: HSRP

First Hop Redundancy

A First Hop Redundancy Protocol (FHRP) is a networking protocol that is designed to transparently provide end users with at least one redundant default gateway by allowing two or more routers or Layer 3 switches to supply backup for the gateway address. If the active first-hop device fails, the backup router or Layer 3 switch assumes control of the address within a few seconds. First hop redundancy protocols are equally at home on routers as L3 switches. Although there are three different FHRPs used in networks today, only one is covered in this chapter: Hot Standby Router Protocol (HSRP). The other two protocols, Virtual Router Redundancy Protocol (VRRP) and Gateway Load Balancing Protocol (GLBP), are not part of the CCNA Routing and Switching vendor exam objectives.

HSRP

HSRP provides network redundancy for IP networks, ensuring that user traffic immediately and transparently recovers from first-hop failures in network edge devices or access circuits.

Configuring HSRP on a Router

`Router(config)#interface fastethernet 0/0`	Moves to interface configuration mode.
`Router(config-if)#ip address 172.16.0.10 255.255.255.0`	Assigns an IP address and netmask.
`Router(config-if)#standby version x`	Assigns version of HSRP to be used. There are two versions of HSRP—1 and 2. HSRP versions must match for communication to occur. The default version is 1.
`Router(config-if)#standby 1 ip 172.16.0.1`	Activates HSRP group 1 on the interface and creates a virtual IP address of 172.16.0.1 for use in HSRP.
	NOTE The group number can be from 0 to 255. The default is 0.
`Router(config-if)#standby 1 priority 120`	Assigns a priority value of 120 to standby group 1.
	NOTE The priority value can be from 0 to 255. The default is 100. A higher priority results in that router being elected the active router. If the priorities of all routers in the group are equal, the router with the highest IP address becomes the active router.

Default HSRP Configuration Settings

Feature	Default Setting
HSRP version	Version 1.
	NOTE HSRPv1 and HSRPv2 have a different packet structure. The same HSRP version must be configured on all devices to properly communicate.
HSRP groups	None configured.
Standby group number	0.
Standby MAC address	System assigned as 0000.0c07.ac*XX*, where *XX* is the HSRP group number.
Standby priority	100.
Standby delay	0 (no delay).
Standby track interface priority	10.
Standby hello time	3 seconds.
Standby holdtime	10 seconds.

Verifying HSRP

Router#**show running-config**	Displays what is currently running on the router.
Router#**show standby**	Displays HSRP information.
Router#**show standby brief**	Displays a single-line output summary of each standby group.
Switch#**show standby vlan 1**	Displays HSRP information on the VLAN 1 group.
	NOTE HSRP can be run on an L3 switch; therefore, it is possible to have HSRP run inside different VLANs.

HSRP Optimization Options

Options are available that make it possible to optimize HSRP operation in the campus network. The next three sections explain three of these options: standby preempt, message timers, and interface tracking.

Preempt

Router(config)#**interface gigabitethernet 0/0**	Moves to interface configuration mode.
Router(config-if)#**standby 1 preempt**	This router preempts, or takes control of, the active router if the local priority is higher than the active router.
Router(config-if)#**standby 1 preempt delay minimum 180**	Causes the local router to postpone taking over as the active router for 180 seconds once the router priority is identified as greater than the current HSRP active device.
Router(config-if)#**standby 1 preempt delay reload** *x*	Allows for preemption to occur only after a router reloads. *x* is the number of seconds between 0 and 3600 for the reload delay.
Router(config-if)#**no standby 1 preempt delay reload**	Disables the preemption delay, but preemption itself is still enabled. Use **the no standby** *x* **preempt** command to eliminate preemption.
	NOTE If the **preempt** argument is not configured, the local router assumes control as the active router only if the local router receives information indicating that no router is currently in the active state.

HSRP Message Timers

Router(config)#**interface gigabitethernet 0/0**	Moves to interface configuration mode.
Router(config-if)#**standby 1 timers 5 15**	Sets the hello timer to 5 seconds and sets the hold timer to 15 seconds.
	NOTE The hold timer is normally set to be greater than or equal to 3 times the hello timer.

	NOTE The hello timer can be from 1 to 254; the default is 3. The hold timer can be from one second greater than the hello timer to 255; the default is 10. The default unit of time is seconds.
`Router(config-if)#standby 1 timers msec 200 msec 600`	Sets the hello timer to 200 milliseconds and sets the hold timer to 600 milliseconds.
	NOTE If the **msec** argument is used, the hello timers can be an integer from 15 to 999, and the hold timer can be an integer from 50 to 3000.

Interface Tracking

`Router(config)#interface gigabitethernet 0/0`	Moves to interface configuration mode.
`Router(config-if)#standby 1 track serial 0/0/0 25`	HSRP tracks the availability of interface serial 0/0/0. If serial 0/0/0 goes down, the priority of the router in group 1 is decremented by 25.
	NOTE The default value of the **track** argument is 10.
	TIP The **track** argument does not assign a new priority if the tracked interface goes down. The **track** argument assigns a value that the priority decreases if the tracked interface goes down. Therefore, if you are tracking serial 0/0/0 with a track value of 25 (**standby 1 track serial 0/0/0 25**) and serial 0/0/0 goes down, the priority is decreased by 25; assuming a default priority of 100, the new priority becomes 75.

Debugging HSRP

`Router#debug standby`	Displays all HSRP debugging information, including state changes and transmission/reception of HSRP packets
`Router#debug standby errors`	Displays HSRP error messages
`Router#debug standby events`	Displays HSRP event messages
`Router#debug standby events terse`	Displays all HSRP events except for hellos and advertisements
`Router#debug standby events track`	Displays all HSRP tracking events
`Router#debug standby packets`	Displays HSRP packet messages
`Router#debug standby terse`	Displays all HSRP errors, events, and packets, except for hellos and advertisements

Configuration Example: HSRP

Figure 21-1 shows the network topology for the configuration that follows, which shows how to configure HSRP using the commands covered in this chapter. Note that only the commands specific to HSRP are shown in this example.

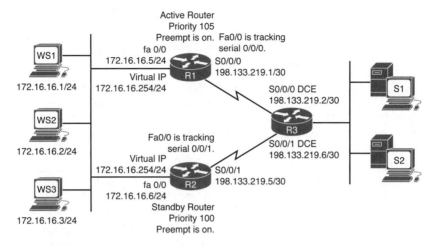

Figure 21-1   Network Topology for HSRP Configuration Example

Router 1

`Router>`**`enable`**	Moves to privileged mode.
`Router#`**`configure terminal`**	Moves to global configuration mode.
`Router(config)#`**`hostname R1`**	Sets router name to R1.
`R1(config)#`**`interface fastethernet 0/0`**	Moves to interface configuration mode.
`R1(config-if)#`**`ip address 172.16.16.5 255.255.255.0`**	Assigns IP address and netmask.
`R1(config-if)#`**`standby 1 ip 172.16.16.254`**	Activates HSRP group 1 on the interface and creates a virtual IP address of 172.16.6.254.
`R1(config-if)#`**`standby 1 priority 105`**	Assigns a priority value of 105 to standby group 1.
`R1(config-if)#`**`standby 1 preempt`**	This router preempts, or takes control of, the active router if the local priority is higher than the active router.
`R1(config-if)#`**`standby 1 track serial 0/0/0`**	HSRP tracks the availability of interface serial 0/0/0. If serial 0/0/0 goes down, the router priority is decremented by the default 10.
`R1(config-if)#`**`no shutdown`**	Enables the interface.
`R1(config-if)#`**`interface serial 0/0/0`**	Moves to interface configuration mode.
`R1(config-if)#`**`ip address 198.133.219.1 255.255.255.252`**	Assigns IP address and netmask.
`R1(config-if)#`**`no shutdown`**	Enables the interface.
`R1(config-if)#`**`exit`**	Returns to global configuration mode.
`R1(config)#`**`exit`**	Returns to privileged mode.
`R1#`**`copy running-config startup-config`**	Saves configuration to NVRAM.

Router 2

`Router>enable`	Moves to privileged mode.
`Router#configure terminal`	Moves to global configuration mode.
`Router(config)#hostname R2`	Sets router name to R2.
`R2(config)#interface fastethernet 0/0`	Moves to interface configuration mode.
`R2(config-if)#ip address 172.16.16.6 255.255.255.0`	Assigns IP address and netmask.
`R2(config-if)#standby 1 ip 171.16.16.254`	Activates HSRP group 1 on the interface and creates a virtual IP address of 172.16.6.254. Note that this is the same virtual IP address as was assigned on router R1.
`R2(config-if)#standby 1 priority 100`	Assigns a priority value of 100 to standby group 1.
	NOTE Even though the default is 100, the command is added here as a visual reminder that the priority on this device is lower than on the other device.
`R2(config-if)#standby 1 preempt`	This router preempts, or takes control of, the active router if the local priority is higher than the active router.
`R2(config-if)#standby 1 track serial 0/0/1`	HSRP tracks the availability of interface serial 0/0/1. If S0/0/1 goes down, the router priority is decremented by the default 10.
`R2(config-if)#no shutdown`	Enables the interface.
`R2(config-if)#interface serial 0/0/1`	Moves to interface configuration mode.
`R2(config-if)#ip address 198.133.219.5 255.255.255.252`	Assigns the IP address and netmask.
`R2(config-if)#no shutdown`	Enables the interface.
`R2(config-if)#exit`	Returns to global configuration mode.
`R2(config)#exit`	Returns to privileged mode.
`R2#copy running-config startup-config`	Saves configuration to NVRAM.

Network Address Translation (NAT)

This chapter provides information and commands concerning the following topics:

- Private IP addresses: RFC 1918
- Configuring dynamic Network Address Translation: One private to one public address translation
- Configuring PAT: Many private to one public address translation
- Configuring static NAT: One private to one permanent public address translation
- Verifying NAT and PAT configurations
- Troubleshooting NAT and PAT configurations
- Configuration example: PAT

Private IP Addresses: RFC 1918

The following table lists the address ranges as specified in RFC 1918 that anyone can use as internal private addresses. These will be your "inside-the-LAN" addresses that will have to be translated into public addresses that can be routed across the Internet. Any network is allowed to use these addresses; however, these addresses are not allowed to be routed onto the public Internet.

Private Addresses		
Class	RFC 1918 Internal Address Range	CIDR Prefix
A	10.0.0.0–10.255.255.255	10.0.0.0/8
B	172.16.0.0–172.31.255.255	172.16.0.0/12
C	192.168.0.0–192.168.255.255	192.168.0.0/16

Configuring Dynamic Network Address Translation: One Private to One Public Address Translation

NOTE For a complete configuration of Network Address Translation (NAT)/Port Address Translation/(PAT) with a diagram for visual assistance, see the sample configuration at the end of this chapter.

Dynamic Address Translation (Dynamic NAT) maps unregistered (private) IP addresses to registered (public) IP addresses from a pool of registered IP addresses.

Step 1: Define a static route on the remote router stating where the public addresses should be routed.	`ISP(config)#ip` `route 64.64.64.64` `255.255.255.192 s0/0/0`	Informs the ISP router where to send packets with addresses destined for 64.64.64.64 255.255.255.192.
Step 2: Define a pool of usable public IP addresses on your local router that will perform NAT.		The private address will receive the first available public address in the pool.
	`Corp(config)#ip nat` `pool scott 64.64.64.65` `64.64.64.126 netmask` `255.255.255.192`	Defines the following: The name of the pool is *scott*. (The name of the pool can be anything.) The start of the pool is 64.64.64.65. The end of the pool is 64.64.64.126. The subnet mask is 255.255.255.192.
Step 3: Create an access control list (ACL) that will identify which private IP addresses will be translated.	`Corp(config)#access-list` `1 permit 172.16.10.0` `0.0.0.255`	
Step 4: Link the ACL to the pool of addresses (create the translation).	`Corp(config)#ip nat` `inside source list 1` `pool scott`	Defines the following: The source of the private addresses is from ACL 1. The pool of available public addresses is named *scott*.
Step 5: Define which interfaces are inside (contain the private addresses).	`Router(config)#interface` `gigabitethernet 0/0`	Moves to interface configuration mode.
	`Router(config-if)#ip nat` `inside`	You can have more than one inside interface on a router. Addresses from each inside interface are then allowed to be translated into a public address.
Step 6: Define the outside interface (the interface leading to the public network).	`Router(config-if)#exit`	Returns to global configuration mode.
	`Router(config)#interface` `serial 0/0/0`	Moves to interface configuration mode.
	`Router(config-if)#ip nat` `outside`	Defines which interface is the outside interface for NAT.

Configuring PAT: Many Private to One Public Address Translation

PAT maps multiple unregistered (private) IP addresses to a single registered (public) IP address (many to one) using different ports. This is also known as overloading or over-load translations. By using PAT or overloading, thousands of users can be connected to the Internet by using only one real registered public IP address.

Step 1: Define a static route on the remote router stating where public addresses should be routed.	`ISP(config)#ip` `route 64.64.64.64` `255.255.255.192 s0/0/0`	Informs the Internet service provider (ISP) router where to send packets with addresses destined for 64.64.64.64 255.255.255.192.
Step 2: Define a pool of usable public IP addresses on your local router that will perform NAT (optional).		Use this step if you have many private addresses to translate. A single public IP address can handle thousands of private addresses. Without using a pool of addresses, you can translate all private addresses into the IP address of the exit interface (the serial link to the ISP, for example).
	`Corp(config)#ip nat` `pool scott 64.64.64.65` `64.64.64.70 netmask` `255.255.255.192`	Defines the following: The name of the pool is *scott*. (The name of the pool can be anything.) The start of the pool is 64.64.64.65. The end of the pool is 64.64.64.70. The subnet mask is 255.255.255.192.
Step 3: Create an ACL that will identify which private IP addresses will be translated.	`Corp(config)` `#access-list 1 permit` `172.16.10.0 0.0.0.255`	

Step 4 (Option 1): Link the ACL to the outside public interface (create the translation).	`Corp(config)#ip nat inside source list 1 interface serial 0/0/0 overload`	The source of the private addresses is from ACL 1. The public address to be translated into is the one assigned to serial 0/0/0. The **overload** keyword states that port numbers will be used to handle many translations.
Step 4 (Option 2): Link the ACL to the pool of addresses (create the translation).		If using the pool created in Step 2 . . .
	`Corp(config)#ip nat inside source list 1 pool scott overload`	The source of the private addresses is from ACL 1. The pool of the available addresses is named *scott*. The **overload** keyword states that port numbers will be used to handle many translations.
Step 5: Define which interfaces are inside (contain the private addresses).	`Corp(config)#interface gigabitethernet 0/0`	Moves to interface configuration mode.
	`Corp(config-if)#ip nat inside`	You can have more than one inside interface on a router.
Step 6: Define the outside interface (the interface leading to the public network).	`Corp(config-if)#exit`	Returns to global configuration mode.
	`Corp(config)#interface serial 0/0/0`	Moves to interface configuration mode.
	`Corp(config-if)#ip nat outside`	Defines which interface is the outside interface for NAT.

NOTE You can have an IP NAT pool of more than one address, if needed. The syntax for this is as follows:

```
Corp(config)#ip nat pool scott 64.64.64.70 64.64.64.75 netmask
  255.255.255.128
```

You would then have a pool of six addresses (and all their ports) available for translation.

NOTE The theoretical maximum number of translations between internal addresses and a single outside address using PAT is 65,536. Port numbers are encoded in a 16-bit field, so $2^{16} = 65,536$.

Configuring Static NAT: One Private to One Permanent Public Address Translation

Static Address Translation (Static NAT) allows one-to-one mapping between local (private) and global (public) IP addresses.

Step 1: Define a static route on the remote router stating where the public addresses should be routed.	`ISP(config)#ip route 64.64.64.64 255.255.255.192 s0/0`	Informs the ISP router where to send packets with addresses destined for 64.64.64.64 255.255.255.192.
Step 2: Create a static mapping on your local router that will perform NAT.	`Corp(config)#ip nat inside source static 172.16.10.5 64.64.64.65`	Permanently translates the inside address of 172.16.10.5 to a public address of 64.64.64.65. Use the command for each of the private IP addresses you want to statically map to a public address.
Step 3: Define which interfaces are inside (contain the private addresses).	`Corp(config)#interface gigabitethernet 0/0`	Moves to interface configuration mode.
	`Corp(config-if)#ip nat inside`	You can have more than one inside interface on a router.
Step 4: Define the outside interface (the interface leading to the public network).	`Corp(config-if) #interface serial 0/0/0`	Moves to interface configuration mode.
	`Corp(config-if)#ip nat outside`	Defines which interface is the outside interface for NAT.

CAUTION Make sure that you have in your router configurations a way for packets to travel back to your NAT router. Include a static route on the ISP router defining a path to your NAT addresses/networks and how to travel back to your internal network. Without this in place, a packet can leave your network with a public address, but it cannot return if your ISP router does not know where the public addresses exist in the network. You should be advertising the public addresses, not your private addresses.

Verifying NAT and PAT Configurations

`Router#show access-list`	Displays access lists
`Router#show ip nat translations`	Displays the translation table
`Router#show ip nat statistics`	Displays NAT statistics
`Router#clear ip nat translation inside 1.1.1.1 2.2.2.2 outside 3.3.3.3 4.4.4.4`	Clears a specific translation from the table before it times out 1.1.1.1 = Global IP address 2.2.2.2 = Local IP address 3.3.3.3 = Local IP address 4.4.4.4 = Global IP address
`Router#clear ip nat translation*`	Clears the entire translation table before entries time out

NOTE The default timeout for a translation entry in a NAT table is 24 hours.

Troubleshooting NAT and PAT Configurations

`Router#debug ip nat`	Displays information about every packet that is translated. Be careful with this command. The router's CPU might not be able to handle this amount of output and might therefore hang the system.
`Router#debug ip nat detailed`	Displays greater detail about packets being translated.

Configuration Example: PAT

Figure 22-1 shows the network topology for the PAT configuration that follows using the commands covered in this chapter.

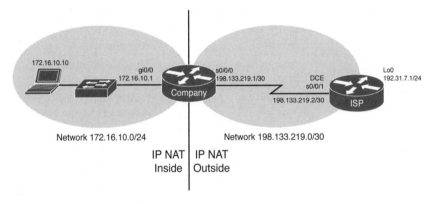

Figure 22-1   Port Address Translation Configuration

ISP Router

`router>enable`	Moves to privileged mode.
`router#configure terminal`	Moves to global configuration mode.
`router(config)#hostname ISP`	Sets the hostname.
`ISP(config)#no ip domain-lookup`	Turns off Domain Name System (DNS) resolution to avoid wait time due to DNS lookup of spelling errors.
`ISP(config)#enable secret cisco`	Sets the encrypted password to *cisco*.
`ISP(config)#line console 0`	Moves to line console mode.
`ISP(config-line)#login`	User must log in to be able to access the console port.
`ISP(config-line)#password class`	Sets the console line password to *class*.
`ISP(config-line)#logging synchronous`	Commands will be appended to a new line.

ISP(config-line)#**exit**	Returns to global configuration mode.
ISP(config)#**interface serial 0/0/1**	Moves to interface configuration mode.
ISP(config-if)#**ip address 198.133.219.2 255.255.255.252**	Assigns an IP address and netmask.
ISP(config-if)#**clock rate 56000**	Assigns the clock rate to the DCE cable on this side of the link.
ISP(config-if)#**no shutdown**	Enables the interface.
ISP(config-if)#**interface loopback 0**	Creates loopback interface 0 and moves to interface configuration mode.
ISP(config-if)#**ip address 192.31.7.1 255.255.255.255**	Assigns an IP address and netmask.
ISP(config-if)#**exit**	Returns to global configuration mode.
ISP(config)#**exit**	Returns to privileged mode.
ISP#**copy running-config startup-config**	Saves the configuration to NVRAM.

Company Router

router>**enable**	Moves to privileged mode.
router#**configure terminal**	Moves to global configuration mode.
router(config)#**hostname Company**	Sets the hostname.
Company(config)#**no ip domain-lookup**	Turns off DNS resolution to avoid wait time due to DNS lookup of spelling errors.
Company(config)#**enable secret cisco**	Sets the secret password to *cisco*.
Company(config)#**line console 0**	Moves to line console mode.
Company(config-line)#**login**	User must log in to be able to access the console port.
Company(config-line)#**password class**	Sets the console line password to *class*.
Company(config-line)#**logging synchronous**	Commands will be appended to a new line.
Company(config-line)#**exit**	Returns to global configuration mode.
Company(config)#**interface gigabitethernet 0/0**	Moves to interface configuration mode.
Company(config-if)#**ip address 172.16.10.1 255.255.255.0**	Assigns an IP address and netmask.
Company(config-if)#**no shutdown**	Enables the interface.
Company(config-if)#**interface serial 0/0/0**	Moves to interface configuration mode.
Company(config-if)#**ip address 198.133.219.1 255.255.255.252**	Assigns an IP address and netmask.
Company(config-if)#**no shutdown**	Enables the interface.

Company(config-if)#**exit**	Returns to global configuration mode.
Company(config)#**ip route 0.0.0.0 0.0.0.0 198.133.219.2**	Sends all packets not defined in the routing table to the ISP router.
Company(config)#**access-list 1 permit 172.16.10.0 0.0.0.255**	Defines which addresses are permitted through; these addresses are those that will be allowed to be translated with NAT.
Company(config)#**ip nat inside source list 1 interface serial 0/0/0 overload**	Creates NAT by combining list 1 with the interface serial 0/0/0. Overloading will take place.
Company(config)#**interface gigabitethernet 0/0**	Moves to interface configuration mode.
Company(config-if)#**ip nat inside**	Location of private inside addresses.
Company(config-if)#**interface serial 0/0/0**	Moves to interface configuration mode.
Company(config-if)#**ip nat outside**	Location of public outside addresses.
Company(config-if)#**Ctrl-z**	Returns to privileged mode.
Company#**copy running-config startup-config**	Saves the configuration to NVRAM.

Switch Port Security

This chapter provides information and commands concerning the following topics:

- Setting passwords on a switch
- Configuring static MAC addresses
- Switch port security
- Verifying switch port security
- Sticky MAC addresses
- Recovering Automatically from error-disabled ports
- Verifying autorecovery of error-disabled ports
- Configuration example

Setting Passwords on a Switch

Setting passwords for the 2960 series switches is the same method as used for a router.

`Switch2960(config)#enable password cisco`	Sets the enable password to *cisco*
`Switch2960(config)#enable secret class`	Sets the encrypted secret password to *class*
`Switch2960(config)#line console 0`	Enters line console mode
`Switch2960(config-line)#login`	Enables password checking
`Switch2960(config-line)#password cisco`	Sets the password to *cisco*
`Switch2960(config-line)#exit`	Exits line console mode
`Switch2960(config)#line vty 0 15`	Enters line vty mode for all 16 virtual ports
`Switch2960(config-line)#login`	Enables password checking
`Switch2960(config-line)#password cisco`	Sets the password to *cisco*
`Switch2960(config-line)#exit`	Exits line vty mode
`Switch2960(config)#`	

Configuring Static MAC Addresses

`Switch2960(config)#mac address-table`
`static aaaa.aaaa.aaaa vlan 1 interface`
`fastethernet 0/1`
	Sets a permanent address to port fastethernet 0/1 in VLAN 1

`Switch2960(config)#no mac address-table`
`static aaaa.aaaa.aaaa vlan 1 interface`
`fastethernet 0/1`
	Removes the permanent address to port fastethernet 0/1 in VLAN 1

Switch Port Security

`Switch(config)#interface` `fastethernet 0/1`	Moves to interface configuration mode.
`Switch(config-if)#switchport` `mode access`	Sets the interface to access mode (as opposed to trunk mode).
	NOTE A port cannot be in Dynamic Trunking Protocol (DTP) dynamic mode for port security to be enabled. It must be in either access or trunk mode.
`Switch(config-if)#switchport` `port-security`	Enables port security on the interface.
`Switch(config-if)#switchport` `port-security maximum 4`	Sets a maximum limit of four MAC addresses that will be allowed on this port.
	NOTE The maximum number of secure MAC addresses that you can configure on a switch is set by the maximum number of available MAC addresses allowed in the system.

`Switch(config-if)#switchport`
`port-security mac-address`
`1234.5678.90ab`
	Sets a specific secure MAC address 1234.5678.90ab. You can add additional secure MAC addresses up to the maximum value configured.

`Switch(config-if)#switchport` `port-security violation shutdown`	Configures port security to shut down the interface if a security violation occurs.
	NOTE In shutdown mode, the port is errdisabled, a log entry is made, and manual intervention or errdisable recovery must be used to reenable the interface.
`Switch(config-if)#switchport` `port-security violation restrict`	Configures port security to restrict mode if a security violation occurs.
	NOTE In restrict mode, frames from a nonallowed address are dropped, and a log entry is made. The interface remains operational.
`Switch(config-if)#switchport` `port-security violation protect`	Configures port security to protect mode if a security violation occurs.
	NOTE In protect mode, frames from a nonallowed address are dropped, but no log entry is made. The interface remains operational.

Verifying Switch Port Security

Switch#show port-security	Displays security information for all interfaces
Switch#show port-security interface fastethernet 0/5	Displays security information for interface fastethernet 0/5
Switch#show port-security address	Displays all secure MAC addresses configured on all switch interfaces
Switch#show mac address-table [dynamic]	Displays the entire MAC address table or simply the dynamic addresses learned
Switch#clear mac address-table dynamic	Deletes all dynamic MAC addresses
Switch#clear mac address-table dynamic address aaaa.bbbb.cccc	Deletes the specified dynamic MAC address
Switch#clear mac address-table dynamic interface fastethernet 0/5	Deletes all dynamic MAC addresses on interface fastethernet 0/5
Switch#clear mac address-table dynamic vlan 10	Deletes all dynamic MAC addresses on VLAN 10
Switch#clear mac address-table notification	Clears MAC notification global counters
	NOTE Beginning with Cisco IOS Software Release 12.1(11)EA1, the **clear mac address-table** command (no hyphen in mac address) replaces the **clear mac-address-table** command (with the hyphen in mac-address).

Sticky MAC Addresses

Sticky MAC addresses are a feature of port security. Sticky MAC addresses limit switch port access to a specific MAC address that can be dynamically learned, as opposed to a network administrator manually associating a MAC address with a specific switch port. These addresses are stored in the running configuration file. If this file is saved, the sticky MAC addresses do not have to be relearned when the switch is rebooted and thus provide a high level of switch port security.

Switch(config)#interface fastethernet 0/5	Moves to interface configuration mode.
Switch(config-if)#switchport port-security mac-address sticky	Converts all dynamic port security learned MAC addresses to sticky secure MAC addresses.
Switch(config-if)#switchport port-security mac-address sticky vlan 10 voice	Converts all dynamic port security learned MAC addresses to sticky secure MAC addresses on voice VLAN 10.
	NOTE The **voice** keyword is available only if a voice VLAN is first configured on a port and if that port is not the access VLAN.

Recovering Automatically from Error-Disabled Ports

You can also configure a switch to autorecover error-disabled ports after a specified amount of time. By default, the autorecover feature is disabled.

Switch(config)#errdisable recovery cause psecure-violation	Enables the timer to recover from a port security violation disable state.
Switch(config)#errdisable recovery interval *seconds*	Specifies the time to recover from the err-disable state. The range is 30 to 86,400 seconds. The default is 300 seconds
	TIP Disconnect the offending host; otherwise, the port remains disabled, and the violation counter is incremented.

Verifying Autorecovery of Error-Disabled Ports

Switch#show errdisable recovery	Displays error-disabled recovery timer information associated with each possible reason the switch could error-disable a port
Switch#show interfaces status err-disabled	Displays Interface status or a list of interfaces in error-disabled state
Switch#clear errdisable interface *interface-id* vlan *[vlan-list]*	Reenables all or specified VLANs that were error-disabled on an interface

Configuration Example

Figure 23-1 shows the network topology for the secure configuration of a 2960 series switch using commands covered in this chapter. Commands from other chapters are used as well.

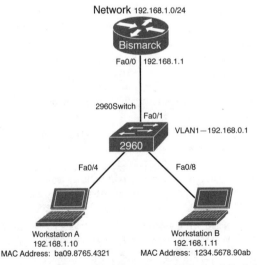

Figure 23-1 Network Topology for 2960 Series Switch Secure Configuration

`Switch>`**`enable`**	Enters privileged mode.
`Switch#`**`configure terminal`**	Enters global configuration mode.
`Switch(config)#`**`no ip domain-lookup`**	Turns off Domain Name System (DNS) queries so that spelling mistakes do not slow you down.
`switch(config)#`**`hostname Switch2960`**	Sets the hostname.
`Switch2960(config)#`**`enable secret cisco`**	Sets the encrypted secret password to *cisco*.
`Switch2960(config)#`**`line console 0`**	Enters line console mode.
`Switch2960(config-line)#`**`logging synchronous`**	Appends commands to a new line; router information will not interrupt.
`Switch2960(config-line)#`**`login`**	User must log in to console before use.
`Switch2960(config-line)#`**`password switch`**	Sets the password to *switch*.
`Switch2960(config-line)` **`#exec-timeout 0 0`**	Console will never log out from not entering input.
`Switch2960(config-line)#`**`exit`**	Moves back to global configuration mode.
`Switch2960(config)#`**`line vty 0 15`**	Moves to configure all 16 vty ports at the same time.
`Switch2960(config-line)#`**`login`**	User must log in to vty port before use.
`Switch2960(config-line)#`**`password class`**	Sets the password to *class*.
`Switch2960(config-line)#`**`exit`**	Moves back to global configuration mode.
`Switch2960(config)#`**`ip default-gateway 192.168.1.1`**	Sets default gateway.
`Switch2960(config)#`**`interface vlan 1`**	Moves to virtual interface VLAN 1 configuration mode.
`Switch2960(config-if)#`**`ip address 192.168.1.2 255.255.255.0`**	Sets the IP address and netmask for switch.
`Switch2960(config-if)#`**`no shutdown`**	Turns the virtual interface on.
`Switch2960(config-if)#`**`interface fastethernet 0/1`**	Moves to interface configuration mode for fastethernet 0/1.
`Switch2960(config-if)#`**`description Link to Bismarck Router`**	Sets a local description.
`Switch2960(config-if)#`**`interface fastethernet 0/4`**	Moves to interface configuration mode for fastethernet 0/4.
`Switch2960(config-if)#`**`description Link to Workstation A`**	Sets a local description.
`Switch2960(config-if)#`**`switchport mode access`**	Sets the interface to access mode.
`Switch2960(config-if)#`**`switchport port-security`**	Activates port security.

`Switch2960(config-if)#`**`switchport port-security maximum 1`**	Only one MAC address is allowed in the MAC table. This is the default number and not a required command, shown here for a visual reminder.
`Switch2960(config-if)#`**`switchport port-security violation shutdown`**	Port will be turned off if more than one MAC address is reported. This is the default action and not a required command, shown here for a visual reminder.
`Switch2960(config-if)#`**`interface fastethernet 0/8`**	Moves to interface configuration mode for fastethernet 0/8.
`Switch2960(config-if)#`**`description Link to Workstation B`**	Sets a local description.
`Switch2960(config-if)#`**`switchport mode access`**	Sets the interface to access mode.
`Switch2960(config-if)#`**`switchport port-security mac-address 1234.5678.90ab`**	Sets a specific secure MAC address 1234.5678.90ab. You can add additional secure MAC addresses up to the maximum value configured.
`Switch2960(config-if)#`**`switchport port-security maximum 1`**	Only one MAC address is allowed in the MAC table. This is the default number and not a required command, shown here for a visual reminder.
`Switch2960(config-if)#`**`switchport port-security violation shutdown`**	Port will be turned off if more than one MAC address is reported. This is the default action and not a required command, shown here for a visual reminder.
`Switch2960(config-if)#`**`exit`**	Returns to global configuration mode.
`Switch2960(config)#`**`exit`**	Returns to privileged mode.
`Switch2960#`**`copy running-config startup-config`**	Saves the configuration to NVRAM.
`Switch2960#`	

Managing Traffic Using Access Control Lists (ACL)

This chapter provides information and commands concerning the following topics:

- Access list numbers
- Using wildcard masks
- ACL keywords
- Creating standard ACLs
- Applying standard ACLs to an interface
- Verifying ACLs
- Removing ACLs
- Creating extended ACLs
- Applying extended ACLs to an interface
- The **established** keyword
- The **log** keyword
- Creating named ACLs
- Using sequence numbers in named ACLs
- Removing specific lines in named ACLs using sequence numbers
- Sequence number tips
- Including comments about entries in ACLs
- Restricting virtual terminal access
- Tips for configuring ACLs
- IPv6 ACLs
- Verifying IPv6 ACLs
- Configuration examples: IPv4 ACLs
- Configuration examples: IPv6 ACLs

Access List Numbers

Although many different protocols can use access control lists (ACL), the CCNA Routing and Switching vendor certification exams are concerned only with IPv4 ACLs. The following chart shows some of the other protocols that can use ACLs.

| 1–99 or 1300–1999 | Standard IPv4 |
| 100–199 or 2000–2699 | Extended IPv4 |

NOTE IPv6 ACLs do not use numbers; IPv6 ACLs are configured using names only.

Using Wildcard Masks

When applied to an IP address, a wildcard mask identifies which addresses get matched to be applied to the **permit** or **deny** argument in an ACL statement. A wildcard mask can identify a single host, a range of hosts, a complete network or subnetwork, or even all possible addresses.

There are two rules when working with wildcard masks:

- A 0 (zero) in a wildcard mask means to check the corresponding bit in the address for an exact match.

- A 1 (one) in a wildcard mask means to ignore the corresponding bit in the address—can be either 1 or 0. In the examples, this is shown as x.

Example 1: 172.16.0.0 0.0.255.255

$$172.16.0.0 = 10101100.00010000.00000000.00000000$$
$$0.0.255.255 = 00000000.00000000.11111111.11111111$$
$$result = 10101100.00010000.xxxxxxxx.xxxxxxxx$$

172.16.x.x (Anything between 172.16.0.0 and 172.16.255.255 matches the example statement.)

TIP   An octet of all 0s means that the octet has to match exactly to the address. An octet of all 1s means that the octet can be ignored.

Example 2: 172.16.8.0 0.0.7.255

$$172.16.8.0 = 10101100.00010000.00001000.00000000$$
$$0.0.7.255 = 00000000.00000000.00000111.11111111$$
$$result = 10101100.00010000.00001xxx.xxxxxxxx$$
$$00001xxx = 00001000 \text{ to } 00001111 = 8–15$$
$$xxxxxxxx = 00000000 \text{ to } 11111111 = 0–255$$

Anything between 172.16.8.0 and 172.16.15.255 matches the example statement.

ACL Keywords

`any`	Used in place of 0.0.0.0 255.255.255.255, matches any address that it is compared against
`host`	Used in place of 0.0.0.0 in the wildcard mask, matches only one specific address

Creating Standard ACLs

NOTE Standard ACLs are the oldest type of ACL. They date back as early as Cisco IOS Release 8.3. Standard ACLs control traffic by comparing the source of the IP packets to the addresses configured in the ACL.

NOTE Each line in an ACL is called an access control entry (ACE). Many ACEs grouped form a single ACL.

`Router(config)#access-list`
`10 permit 172.16.0.0`
`0.0.255.255`
	Read this line to say, "All packets with a source IP address of 172.16.*x.x* will be matched by the statement, and the packet will be exited from processing the rest of the ACL."

`access-list`	ACL command.
`10`	Arbitrary number between 1 and 99, or 1300 and 1999, designating this as a standard IP ACL.
`permit`	Packets that match this statement will be allowed to continue.
`172.16.0.0`	Source IP address to be compared to.
`0.0.255.255`	Wildcard mask.
`Router(config)#access-list` `10 deny host 172.17.0.1`	Read this line to say, "All packets with a source IP address of 172.17.0.1 will be dropped and discarded."
`access-list`	ACL command.
`10`	Number between 1 and 99, or 1300 and 1999, designating this as a standard IP ACL.
`deny`	Packets that match this statement will be dropped and discarded.
`host`	Keyword.
`172.17.0.1`	Specific host address.
`Router(config)#access-list` `10 permit any`	Read this line to say, "All packets with any source IP address will be matched by the statement, and the packet will be exited from processing the rest of the ACL."
`access-list`	ACL command.
`10`	Number between 1 and 99, or 1300 and 1999, designating this as a standard IP ACL.
`permit`	Packets that match this statement will be allowed to continue.
`any`	Keyword to mean all IP addresses.

TIP An implicit **deny** statement is assumed into every ACL. You cannot see it, but it states "deny everything not already matched by an ACE in the list." This is always the last line of any ACL. If you want to defeat this implicit **deny**, put a **permit any** statement in your standard ACLs or a **permit ip any any** in your extended ACLs as the last line.

Applying Standard ACLs to an Interface

`Router(config)#interface gigabitethernet 0/0`	Moves to interface configuration mode.
`Router(config-if)#ip access-group 10 out`	Takes all ACEs that are defined as being part of group 10 and applies them in an outbound manner. Packets leaving the router through interface gigabitethernet 0/0 will be checked.

TIP   Access lists can be applied in either an inbound direction (keyword **in**) or an outbound direction (keyword **out**). Best practice is to have ACLs applied in an outbound direction.

TIP   Not sure in which direction to apply an ACL? Look at the flow of packets. Do you want to filter packets as they are going *in* a router's interface from an external source? Use the keyword **in** for this ACL. Do you want to filter packets before they go *out* of the router's interface toward another device? Use the keyword **out** for this ACL.

TIP   Apply a standard ACL as close as possible to the destination network or device. You do not want packets with the same source IP address to be filtered out early and prevented from reaching a legitimate destination.

Verifying ACLs

`Router#show ip interface`	Displays any ACLs applied to that interface
`Router#show access-lists`	Displays the contents of all ACLs on the router
`Router#show access-list access-list-number`	Displays the contents of the ACL by the number specified
`Router#show access-list name`	Displays the contents of the ACL by the *name* specified
`Router#show run`	Displays all ACLs and interface assignments

Removing ACLs

`Router(config)#no access-list 10`	Removes *all* ACEs in ACL number 10

Creating Extended ACLs

NOTE   Extended ACLs were also introduced in Cisco IOS Release 8.3. Extended ACLs control traffic by comparing the source and destination of the IP packets to the addresses configured in the ACL. Extended ACLs can also filter packets using protocol/port numbers for a more granular filter.

Router(config)#**access-list 110 permit tcp 172.16.0.0 0.0.0.255 192.168.100.0 0.0.0.255 eq 80**	Read this line to say, "HTTP packets with a source IP address of 172.16.0.*x* will be matched by the statement, and the packet will be exited from processing the rest of the ACL."
access-list	ACL command.
110	Number is between 100 and 199, or 2000 and 2699, designating this as an extended IP ACL.
permit	Packets that match this statement will be allowed to continue.
tcp	Protocol must be TCP.
172.16.0.0	Source IP address to be compared to.
0.0.0.255	Wildcard mask for the source IP address.
192.168.100.0	Destination IP address to be compared to.
0.0.0.255	Wildcard mask for the destination IP address.
eq	Operand; means "equal to."
80	Port 80, indicating HTTP traffic.
Router(config)#**access-list 110 deny tcp any 192.168.100.7 0.0.0.0 eq 23**	Read this line to say, "Telnet packets with any source IP address will be dropped if they are addressed to specific host 192.168.100.7."
access-list	ACL command.
110	Number is between 100 and 199, or 2000 and 2699, designating this as an extended IP ACL.
deny	Packets that match this statement will be dropped and discarded.
tcp	Protocol must be TCP protocol.
any	Any source IP address.
192.168.100.7	Destination IP address to be compared to.
0.0.0.0	Wildcard mask; address must match exactly.
eq	Operand, means "equal to."
23	Port 23, indicating Telnet traffic.

Applying Extended ACLs to an Interface

Router(config)#**interface gigabitethernet 0/0** Router(config-if)#**ip access-group 110 in**	Moves to interface configuration mode and takes all access list lines that are defined as being part of group 110 and applies them in an inbound manner. Packets going in gigabitethernet 0/0 will be checked.

TIP   Access lists can be applied in either an inbound direction (keyword **in**) or an outbound direction (keyword **out**). Best practice for extended ACLs is to apply them in an inbound manner.

TIP   Only one access list can be applied per interface, per direction.

TIP   Apply an extended ACL as close as possible to the source network or device. This ensures that packets that are intended to be dropped are not allowed to travel.

The established Keyword

The **established** keyword is an optional keyword that is used with the TCP protocol only. It indicates an established connection. A match occurs only if the TCP segment has the ACK or RST control bits set.

`Router(config)#`**`access-list 110 permit tcp`** **`172.16.0.0 0.0.0.255 eq 80 192.168.100.0`** **`0.0.0.255 established`**	Indicates an established connection

TIP   The **established** keyword works only for TCP, not User Datagram Protocol (UDP).

TIP   Consider the following situation: You do not want hackers exploiting destination port 80 to access your network. Because you do not host a local web server (destination port 80), it is possible to block incoming (to your network) traffic on destination port 80, except that your internal users need web access. When they request a web page from the Internet, return traffic inbound on source port 80 must be allowed. The solution to this problem is to use the **established** command. The ACL allows the response to enter your network because it has the ACK bit set as a result of the initial request from inside your network. Requests from the outside world are blocked because the ACK bit is not set, but responses are allowed through.

The log Keyword

Logging is an optional keyword that causes an informational logging message about the packet matching the entry to be sent to the console. The log message includes the access list number, whether the packet was permitted or denied, the source address, the number of packets, and if appropriate, the user-defined cookie or router-generated hash value. The message is generated for the first packet that matches and then at 5-minute intervals, including the number of packets permitted or denied in the prior 5-minute interval.

CAUTION   ACL logging can be CPU intensive and can negatively affect other functions of the network device.

`Router(config)#`**`access-list 1`** **`permit 172.16.10.0 0.0.0.255`** **`log`**	Indicates that logging will be enabled on this ACE.
`Router(config)#`**`access-list 1`** **`permit 172.16.10.0 0.0.0.255`** **`log SampleUserValue`**	Indicates that logging will be enabled on this ACE. The word *SampleUserValue* will be appended to each syslog entry.

`Router(config)#access-list 110 permit tcp 172.16.0.0 0.0.0.255 192.168.100.0 0.0.0.255 eq 80 log`	Indicates that logging will be enabled on this ACE.
`Router(config)#access-list 110 permit tcp 172.16.0.0 0.0.0.255 192.168.100.0 0.0.0.255 eq 80 log-input`	Logging will be enabled on this input and will include the input interface and source MAC address or virtual circuit in the logging output.
`Router(config)#access-list 110 permit tcp 172.16.0.0 0.0.0.255 192.168.100.0 0.0.0.255 eq 80 log-input SampleUserValue`	Indicates that logging will be enabled on this ACE and will include the input interface and source MAC address or virtual circuit in the logging output. The word *SampleUserValue* will be appended to each syslog entry.

TIP The level of messages logged to the console is controlled by the **logging console** command.

TIP After you specify the **log** keyword (and the associated word argument) or the **log-input** keyword (and the associated word argument), you cannot specify any other keywords or settings for this command.

TIP The **log-input** keyword (and the associated word argument) is only available in extended ACLs for IPv4 or IPv6 ACLs.

Creating Named ACLs

`Router(config)#ip access-list extended serveraccess`	Creates an extended named ACL called *serveraccess* and moves to named ACL configuration mode.
`Router(config-ext-nacl)#permit tcp any host 131.108.101.99 eq smtp`	Permits mail packets from any source to reach host 131.108.101.99.
`Router(config-ext-nacl)#permit udp any host 131.108.101.99 eq domain`	Permits Domain Name System (DNS) packets from any source to reach host 131.108.101.99.
`Router(config-ext-nacl)#deny ip any any log`	Denies all other packets from going anywhere. If any packets do get denied, this logs the results for you to look at later.
`Router(config-ext-nacl)#exit`	Returns to global configuration mode.
`Router(config)#interface gigabitethernet 0/0` `Router(config-if)#ip access-group serveraccess out`	Moves to interface configuration mode and applies this ACL to the gigabitethernet interface 0/0 in an outbound direction.

Router(config)#**ip access-list standard teststandardacl**	Creates a standard-named ACL called *teststandardacl* and moves to named ACL configuration mode.
Router(config-std-nacl)#**permit host 192.168.1.11**	Permits packets from source address 192.168.1.11.
Router(config-std-nacl)#**exit**	Returns to global configuration mode.
Router(config)#**interface gigabitethernet 0/1** Router(config-if)#**ip access-group teststandardacl out**	Moves to interface configuration mode and applies this ACL to the gigabitethernet interface 0/1 in an outbound direction.

TIP   The prompt of the device changes according to whether the named ACL is standard (config-std-nacl) or extended (config-ext-nacl).

Using Sequence Numbers in Named ACLs

Router(config)#**ip access-list extended serveraccess2**	Creates an extended-named ACL called *serveraccess2*.
Router(config-ext-nacl)#**10 permit tcp any host 131.108.101.99 eq smtp**	Uses a sequence number 10 for this line.
Router(config-ext-nacl)#**20 permit udp any host 131.108.101.99 eq domain**	Sequence number 20 will be applied after line 10.
Router(config-ext-nacl)#**30 deny ip any any log**	Sequence number 30 will be applied after line 20.
Router(config-ext-nacl)#**exit**	Returns to global configuration mode.
Router(config)#**interface gigabitethernet 0/0**	Moves to interface configuration mode.
Router(config-if)#**ip access-group serveraccess2 out**	Applies this ACL in an outbound direction.
Router(config-if)#**exit**	Returns to global configuration mode.
Router(config)#**ip access-list extended serveraccess2**	Moves to named ACL configuration mode for the ACL *serveraccess2*.
Router(config-ext-nacl)#**25 permit tcp any host 131.108.101.99 eq ftp**	Sequence number 25 places this line after line 20 and before line 30.
Router(config-ext-nacl)#**exit**	Returns to global configuration mode.

TIP   Sequence numbers are used to allow for easier editing of your ACLs. The preceding example used numbers 10, 20, and 30 in the ACL lines. If you had needed to add another line to this ACL, it would have previously been added after the last line—line 30. If you had needed a line to go closer to the top, you would have had to remove the entire ACL and then reapply it with the lines in the correct order. Now you can enter a new line with a sequence number, placing it in the correct location.

NOTE   The *sequence-number* argument was added in Cisco IOS Software Release 12.2(14)S. It was integrated into Cisco IOS Software Release 12.2(15)T.

Removing Specific Lines in Named ACLs Using Sequence Numbers

`Router(config)#ip access-list extended serveraccess2`	Moves to named ACL configuration mode for the ACL *serveraccess2*
`Router(config-ext-nacl)#no 20`	Removes line 20 from the list
`Router(config-ext-nacl)#exit`	Returns to global configuration mode

Sequence Number Tips

- Sequence numbers start at 10 and increment by 10 for each line.
- The maximum sequence number is 2147483647.
  - If you have an ACL that is so complex that it needs a number this big, I'd ask your boss for a raise.
- If you forget to add a sequence number, the line is added to the end of the list and assigned a number that is 10 greater than the last sequence number.
- If you enter an entry that matches an existing entry (except for the sequence number), no changes are made.
- If the user enters a sequence number that is already present, an error message of "Duplicate sequence number" displays. You have to reenter the line with a new sequence number.
- Sequence numbers are changed on a router reload to reflect the increment by 10 policy (see first tip in this section). If your ACL has numbers 10, 20, 30, 32, 40, 50, and 60 in it, on reload these numbers become 10, 20, 30, 40, 50, 60, 70.
- If you want to change the numbering sequence of your ACLs to something other than incrementing by 10, use the global configuration command **ip access-list resequence** *name/number start# increment#*:

  `Router(config)#ip access-list resequence serveracces 1 2`

  - This resets the ACL named *serveraccess* to start at 1 and increment by steps of 2 (1, 3, 5, 7, 9, and so on). The range for using this command is 1 to 2147483647.
- Sequence numbers cannot be seen when using the Router#**show running-config** or Router#**show startup-config** command. To see sequence numbers, use one of the following commands:

  `Router#show access-lists`

  `Router#show access-lists` *list_name*

  `Router#show ip access-list`

  `Router#show ip access-list` *list_name*

Including Comments About Entries in ACLs

Router(config)#access-list 10 remark only Jones has access	The **remark** command allows you to include a comment (limited to 100 characters).
Router(config)#access-list 10 permit host 172.16.100.119	Read this line to say, "Host 172.16.100.119 will be permitted through the internetwork."
Router(config)#ip access-list extended telnetaccess	Creates a named ACL called *telnetaccess* and moves to named ACL configuration mode.
Router(config-ext-nacl)#remark do not let Smith have telnet	The **remark** command allows you to include a comment (limited to 100 characters).
Router(config-ext-nacl)#deny tcp host 172.16.100.153 any eq telnet	Read this line to say, "Deny this specific host Telnet access to anywhere in the internetwork."

TIP   You can use the **remark** command in any of the IP numbered standard, IP numbered extended, or named IP ACLs.

TIP   You can use the **remark** command either before or after a **permit** or **deny** statement. Therefore, be consistent in your placement to avoid confusion about which line the **remark** statement is referring to.

Restricting Virtual Terminal Access

Router(config)#access-list 2 permit host 172.16.10.2	Permits host from source address of 172.16.10.2 to telnet/SSH into this router based on where this ACL is applied.
Router(config)#access-list 2 permit 172.16.20.0 0.0.0.255	Permits anyone from the 172.16.20.*x* address range to telnet/SSH into this router based on where this ACL is applied.
	The implicit **deny** statement restricts anyone else from being permitted to telnet/SSH.
Router(config)#line vty 0 4	Moves to vty line configuration mode.
Router(config-line)#access-class 2 in	Applies this ACL to all five vty virtual interfaces in an inbound direction.

TIP   When restricting access through Telnet, use the **access-class** command rather than the **access-group** command, which is used when applying an ACL to a physical interface.

CAUTION   Do not apply an ACL intending to restrict Telnet traffic on a physical interface. If you apply to a physical interface, *all* packets are compared to the ACL before it can continue on its path to its destination. This scenario can lead to a large reduction in router performance.

Tips for Configuring ACLs

- Each statement in an ACL is known as an ACE.

- Conversely, ACEs are commonly called ACL statements.

- The type of ACL determines what is filtered.

- Standard filters only on source IP

    - Extended filters on source IP, destination IP, protocol number, and port number

- Use only one ACL per interface, per protocol (IPv4 or IPv6), per direction.

- Place your most specific statements at the top of the ACL. The most general statements should be at the bottom of the ACL.

- The last test in any ACL is the implicit **deny** statement. You cannot see it, but it is there.

- Every ACL must have at least one **permit** statement. Otherwise, you will deny everything.

- Place extended ACLs as close as possible to the source network or device when applying ACLs to an interface.

- Place standard ACLs as close as possible to the destination network or device when applying ACLs to an interface.

- You can use numbers when creating a named ACL. The name you choose is the number: For example, **ip access-list extended 150** creates an extended ACL named 150.

- An ACL can filter traffic going through a router, depending on how the ACL is applied.

    - Think of yourself as standing in the middle of the router. Are you filtering traffic that is coming into the router toward you? Make the ACL an inbound one using the keyword **in**.

    - Are you filtering traffic that is going away from you and the router and toward another device? Make the ACL an outbound one using the keyword **out**.

- Access lists that are applied to interfaces do not filter traffic that originates from that router.

- When restricting access through Telnet, use the **access-class** command rather than the **access-group** command, which is used when applying an ACL to a physical interface.

IPv6 ACLs

ACLs can also be created in IPv6. The syntax for creating an IPv6 ACL is limited to named ACLs.

`Router(config)#ipv6 access-list v6example`	Creates an IPv6 ACL called *v6example* and moves to IPv6 ACL configuration mode.
`Router(config-ipv6-acl)#permit tcp 2001:db8:300:201::/32 eq telnet any`	Permits the specified IPv6 address to telnet to any destination.
`Router(config-ipv6-acl)#deny tcp host 2001:db8:1::1 any log-input`	Denies a specific IPv6 host. Attempts will be logged.
`Router(config-ipv6-acl)#exit`	Returns to global configuration mode.
`Router(config)#interface gigabitethernet 0/0`	Moves to interface configuration mode.
`Router(config-if)#ipv6 traffic-filter v6example out`	Applies the IPv6 ACL named *v6example* to the interface in an outbound direction.

TIP   You use the **traffic-filter** keyword rather than the **access-group** keyword when assigning IPv6 ACLs to an interface.

TIP   Wildcard masks are not used in IPv6 ACLs. Instead, the prefix-length is used.

TIP   You still use the **access-class** keyword to assign an IPv6 ACL to virtual terminal (vty) lines for restricting Telnet/SSH access.

Verifying IPv6 ACLs

`R1#show ipv6 access-list`	Displays the configured statements, their matches, and the sequence number of all access lists

Configuration Examples: IPv4 ACLs

Figure 24-1 illustrates the network topology for the configuration that follows, which shows five ACL examples using the commands covered in this chapter.

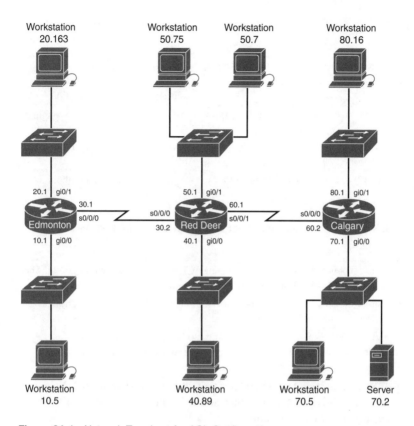

Figure 24-1   Network Topology for ACL Configuration

Example 1: Write an ACL that prevents the 10.0 network from accessing the 40.0 network but allows everyone else to.

RedDeer(config)#**access-list 10 deny 172.16.10.0 0.0.0.255**	The standard ACL denies the complete network for the complete TCP/IP suite of protocols.
RedDeer(config)#**access-list 10 permit any**	Defeats the implicit **deny**.
RedDeer(config)#**interface gigabitethernet 0/0**	Moves to interface configuration mode.
RedDeer(config)#**ip access-group 10 out**	Applies ACL in an outbound direction.

Example 2: Write an ACL that states that 10.5 cannot access 50.7. Everyone else can.

`Edmonton(config)#access list 115 deny ip host 172.16.10.5 host 172.16.50.7`	The extended ACL denies a specific host for the entire TCP/IP suite to a specific destination.
`Edmonton(config)#access list 115 permit ip any any`	All others are permitted through.
`Edmonton(config)#interface gigabitethernet 0/0`	Moves to interface configuration mode.
`Edmonton(config)#ip access-group 115 in`	Applies the ACL in an inbound direction.

Example 3: Write an ACL that states that 10.5 can telnet to the Red Deer router. No one else can.

`RedDeer(config)#access-list 20 permit host 172.16.10.5`	The standard ACL allows a specific host access. The implicit deny statement filters everyone else out.
`RedDeer(config)#line vty 0 4`	Moves to virtual terminal lines configuration mode.
`RedDeer(config-line) #access-class 20 in`	Applies ACL 20 in an inbound direction. Remember to use **access-class**, not **access-group**.

Example 4: Write a named ACL that states that 20.163 can telnet to 70.2. No one else from 20.0 can telnet to 70.2. Any other host from any other subnet can connect to 70.2 using anything that is available.

`Edmonton(config)#ip access-list extended serveraccess`	Creates a named ACL and moves to named ACL configuration mode.
`Edmonton(config-ext-nacl)#10 permit tcp host 172.16.20.163 host 172.16.70.2 eq telnet`	The specific host is permitted Telnet access to a specific destination.
`Edmonton(config-ext-nacl)#20 deny tcp 172.16.20.0 0.0.0.255 host 172.16.70.2 eq telnet`	No other hosts are allowed to telnet to the specified destination.
`Edmonton(config-ext-nacl)#30 permit ip any any`	Defeats the implicit **deny** statement and allows all other traffic to pass through.
`Edmonton(config-ext-nacl)#exit`	Returns to global configuration mode.
`Edmonton(config)#interface gigabitethernet 0/0`	Moves to interface configuration mode.
`Edmonton(config)#ip access-group serveraccess in`	Sets the ACL named *serveraccess* in an outbound direction on the interface.

Example 5: Write an ACL that states that hosts 50.1 to 50.63 are not allowed web access to 80.16. Hosts 50.64 to 50.254 are. Everyone can do everything else.

RedDeer(config)#**access-list 101 deny tcp 172.16.50.0 0.0.0.63 host 172.16.80.16 eq 80**	Creates an ACL that denies HTTP traffic from a range of hosts to a specific destination
RedDeer(config)#**access-list 101 permit ip any any**	Defeats the implicit **deny** statement and allows all other traffic to pass through
RedDeer(config)#**interface gigabitethernet 0/1**	Moves to interface configuration mode
RedDeer(config)#**ip access-group 101 in**	Applies the ACL in an inbound direction

Configuration Examples: IPv6 ACLs

Figure 24-2 shows the network topology for the configuration that follows, which demonstrates how to configure IPv6 ACLs. Assume that all basic configurations are accurate. The objective here is to create an ACL that acts as a firewall allowing HTTP, HTTPS, DNS, and Internet Control Message Protocol (ICMP) traffic to return from the Internet.

Figure 24-2 Configure IPv6 ACLs

R1(config)#**ipv6 access-list FIREWALL**	Creates a named extended IPv6 access list called FIREWALL and moves to IPv6 access list configuration mode.
R1(config-ipv6-acl)#**permit tcp any eq www any established**	Permits HTTP traffic to return to the corporate LAN from the Internet if that traffic was originally sourced from the corporate LAN.
R1(config-ipv6-acl)#**permit tcp any eq 443 any established**	Permits HTTPS traffic to return to the corporate LAN from the Internet if that traffic was originally sourced from the corporate LAN.
R1(config-ipv6-acl)#**permit udp any eq domain any**	Permits DNS responses to return to the corporate LAN from the Internet.
R1(config-ipv6-acl)#**permit icmp any any echo-reply**	Permits ICMP ping responses to return to the corporate LAN from the Internet.
R1(config-ipv6-acl)#**permit icmp any any packet-too-big**	Permits ICMP Packet Too Big messages to return to the corporate LAN from the Internet.

	NOTE In IPv6, maximum transmission unit (MTU) discovery has moved from the router to the hosts. It is important to allow Packet Too Big messages to flow through the router to allow hosts to detect whether fragmentation is required.
`R1(config-ipv6-acl)#exit`	Returns to global configuration mode.
`R1(config)#interface gigabitethernet0/0`	Enters GigabitEthernet0/0 interface configuration mode.
`R1(config-if)#ipv6 traffic-filter FIREWALL in`	Applies the IPv6 access list names FIREWALL to the interface in the inbound direction.

NOTE   The "implicit deny" rule has changed for IPv6 access lists to take into account the importance of the Neighbor Discovery Protocol (NDP). NDP is to IPv6 what Address Resolution Protocol (ARP) is to IPv4, so naturally the protocol should not be disrupted. That is the reason two additional implicit statements have been added before the "implicit deny" statement at the end of each IPv6 ACL.

These implicit rules are as follows:

```
permit icmp any any nd-na
permit icmp any any nd-ns
deny ipv6 any any
```

It is important to understand that any explicit **deny ipv6 any any** statement overrides all three implicit statements, which can lead to problems because NDP traffic is blocked.

Device Hardening

This chapter provides information about the following topics:

- Securing Cisco device according to recommended practices
- Securing Cisco IOS routers checklist
- Components of a router security policy
- Configuring passwords
- Password encryption
- Configuring SSH
- Verifying SSH
- Restricting virtual terminal access
- Disabling unused services

Securing Cisco Device According to Recommended Practices

Device security is critical to network security. A compromised device can cause the network to be compromised on a larger scale. The following sections deal with different ways to secure your Cisco IOS devices.

Securing Cisco IOS Routers Checklist

Table 25-1 shows the checklist that you should use when securing Cisco IOS routers.

TABLE 25-1   Securing Cisco IOS Routers Checklist

Recommended Practice	Y/N
Set up and follow security policy	
Use encrypted passwords	
Secure access to the router using access control lists (ACL)	
Use secure management protocols	
Periodically back up configurations	
Implement logging	
Disable unused services	

Components of a Router Security Policy

Table 25-2 shows the items that should be part of any router security policy.

TABLE 25-2 Router Security Policy

Password Encryption and Complexity Settings
Authentication settings
Management access settings
Unneeded services settings
Ingress/egress filtering settings
Routing protocol security settings
Configuration maintenance
Change management
Router redundancy
Monitoring and incident handling
Security updates

Configuring Passwords

These commands work on both routers and switches.

Edmonton(config)#**enable password cisco**	Sets the **enable** password. This password is stored as clear text.
Edmonton(config)#**enable secret class**	Sets the **enable secret** password. This password is stored using a cryptographic hash function (SHA-256).
Edmonton(config)#**line console 0**	Enters console line mode.
Edmonton(config-line)#**password console**	Sets the console line mode password to *console*.
Edmonton(config-line)#**login**	Enables password checking at login.
Edmonton(config)#**line vty 0 4**	Enters the vty line mode for all five vty lines.
Edmonton(config-line)#**password telnet**	Sets the vty password to *telnet*.
Edmonton(config-line)#**login**	Enables password checking at login.
Edmonton(config)#**line aux 0**	Enters auxiliary line mode.
Edmonton(config-line)#**password backdoor**	Sets auxiliary line mode password to *backdoor*.
Edmonton(config-line)#**login**	Enables password checking at login.

CAUTION   As of release 15.0(1)S, the **enable secret** *password* is encrypted by default using the SHA-256 cryptographic hash function. Prior to this, the MD5 hash was used. The **enable password** is not encrypted; it is stored as clear text. For this reason, recommended practice is that you *never* use the **enable password** command. Use only the **enable secret** *password* command in a router or switch configuration.

TIP   You can set both **enable secret** *password* and **enable** *password* to the same password. However, doing so defeats the use of encryption.

CAUTION   Line passwords are stored as clear text. They should be encrypted using the **service password-encryption** command at a bare minimum. However, this encryption method is weak and easily reversible. It is therefore recommended to enable authentication by the **username** command with the **secret** option because the **password** option to the **username** command still stores information using clear text.

TIP   The best place to store passwords is on an external authentication, authorization, and accounting (AAA) server.

Password Encryption

Edmonton(config)#**service password-encryption**	Applies a Vigenere cipher (type 7) weak encryption to passwords
Edmonton(config)#**enable password cisco**	Sets the enable password to *cisco*
Edmonton(config)#**line console 0**	Moves to console line mode
Edmonton(config-line)#**password cisco**	Continue setting passwords as above
	...
Edmonton(config)#**no service password-encryption**	Turns off password encryption

CAUTION   If you have turned on service password encryption, used it, and then turned it off, any passwords that you have encrypted stay encrypted. New passwords remain unencrypted.

TIP   If you want to enter in a password that is already encrypted with the SHA-256 hash (for example, if you are copying an existing configuration into the router), you have to instruct the router that the password is already encrypted. To do this, use the **enable secret 4** command:

Edmonton(config)#**enable secret 4 Rv4kArhts7yA2xd8BD2YTVbts**

To specify the message digest 5 (MD5) authentication hash of the password, use the **enable secret 5** command, followed by the MD5 hash of the password:

Edmonton(config)#**enable secret 5 00271A5307542A02D22842**

TIP The **service password-encryption** command works on the following passwords:

Username

Authentication key

Privileged command

Console

Virtual terminal line access

BGP neighbors

Passwords using this encryption are shown as type 7 passwords in the router configuration:

```
Edmonton#show running-config
                  <output omitted>
enable secret 4 Rv4kArhts7yA2xd8BD2YTVbts (4 signifies SHA-256 hash)
<output omitted>
line con 0
 password 7 00271A5307542A02D22842 (7 signifies Vigenere cipher)
line vty 0 4
 password 7 00271A5307542A02D22842 (7 signifies Vigenere cipher)
<output omitted>
R1#
```

Configuring SSH

Although Telnet is the default way of accessing a router, it is the most unsecure. Secure Shell (SSH) provides an encrypted alternative for accessing a router.

CAUTION SSH Version 1 implementations have known security issues. It is recommended to use SSH Version 2 whenever possible.

NOTE The device name cannot be the default *Switch* (on a switch) or *Router* (on a router). Use the **hostname** command to configure a new hostname of the device.

NOTE The Cisco implementation of SSH requires Cisco IOS Software to support Rivest, Shamir, Adleman (RSA) authentication and minimum Data Encryption Standard (DES) encryption (a cryptographic software image).

`Edmonton(config)#`**`username`** `Roland password tower`	Creates a locally significant username/password combination. These are the credentials you must enter when connecting to the router with SSH client software.
`Edmonton(config)#`**`username`** `Roland privilege 15 secret tower`	Creates a locally significant username of *Roland* with privilege level 15. Assigns a secret password of *tower*.
`Edmonton(config)#`**`ip domain-name test.lab`**	Creates a host domain for the router.

Edmonton(config)#**crypto key generate rsa modulus 2048**	Enables the SSH server for local and remote authentication on the router and generates an RSA key pair. The number of modulus bits on the command line is 2048. The size of the key modulus is 360 to 4096 bits.
Edmonton(config)#**ip ssh version 2**	Enables SSH version 2 on the device.
	NOTE To work, SSH requires a local username database, a local IP domain, and an RSA key to be generated.
Edmonton(config)#**line vty 0 4**	Moves to vty configuration mode for all five vty lines of the router.
	NOTE Depending on the IOS and platform, there may be more than five vty lines.
Edmonton(config-line)#**login local**	Enables password checking on a per-user basis. The username and password will be checked against the data entered with the **username** global configuration command.
Edmonton(config-line)#**transport input ssh**	Limits remote connectivity to ssh connections only—disables Telnet.

Verifying SSH

Edmonton#**show ip ssh**	Verifies that SSH is enabled
Edmonton#**show ssh**	Checks the SSH connection to the device

Restricting Virtual Terminal Access

Edmonton(config)#**access-list 2 permit host 172.16.10.2**	Permits host from source address of 172.16.10.2 to telnet/SSH into this router based on where this ACL is applied.
Edmonton(config)#**access-list 2 permit 172.16.20.0 0.0.0.255**	Permits anyone from the 172.16.20.*x* address range to telnet/SSH into this router based on where this ACL is applied.
	The implicit deny statement restricts anyone else from being permitted to telnet/SSH.
Edmonton(config)#**access-list 2 deny any log**	Any packets that are denied by this ACL are logged for review at a later time. This line is used instead of the implicit deny line.
Edmonton(config)#**line vty 0 4**	Moves to vty line configuration mode.
	NOTE Depending on the IOS and platform, there may be more than five vty lines.
Edmonton(config-line)#**access-class 2 in**	Applies this ACL to all vty virtual interfaces in an inbound direction.

TIP When restricting access on vty lines, use the **access-class** command rather than the **access-group** command, which is used when applying an ACL to a physical interface.

CAUTION Do not apply an ACL intending to restrict vty traffic on a physical interface. If you apply to a physical interface, *all* packets are compared to the ACL before it can continue on its path to its destination. This can lead to a large reduction in router performance. An ACL on a physical interface has to specify the SSH or Telnet port number that you are trying to deny, in addition to identifying all the router's addresses that you could potentially SSH/telnet to.

Disabling Unneeded Services

Services that are not being used on a router can represent a potential security risk. If you do not need a specific service, you should disable it.

TIP If a service is off by default, disabling it does not appear in the running configuration.

TIP Do not assume that a service is disabled by default; you should explicitly disable all unneeded services, even if you think they are already disabled.

TIP Depending on the IOS Software release, some services are on by default; some are off. Be sure to check the IOS configuration guide for your specific software release to determine the default state of the service.

Table 25-3 lists the services that you should disable if you are not using them.

TABLE 25-3 Disabling Unneeded Services

Service	Commands Used to Disable Service
DNS name resolution	Edmonton(config)#no ip domain-lookup
Cisco Discovery Protocol (CDP) (globally)	Edmonton(config)#no cdp run
CDP (on a specific interface)	Edmonton(config-if)#no cdp enable
Network Time Protocol (NTP)	Edmonton(config-if)#ntp disable
BOOTP server	Edmonton(config)#no ip bootp server
DHCP	Edmonton(config)#no service dhcp
Proxy Address Resolution Protocol (ARP)	Edmonton(config-if)no ip proxy-arp
IP source routing	Edmonton(config)#no ip source-route
IP redirects	Edmonton(config-if)#no ip redirects
HTTP service	Edmonton(config)#no ip http server

Backing Up and Restoring Cisco IOS Software and Configurations

This chapter provides information and commands concerning the following topics:

- Boot system commands
- The Cisco IOS File System
- Viewing the Cisco IOS File System
- Commonly used URL prefixes for Cisco network devices
- Deciphering IOS image filenames
- Backing up configurations to a TFTP server
- Restoring configurations from a TFTP server
- Backing up the Cisco IOS Software to a TFTP server
- Restoring/upgrading the Cisco IOS Software from a TFTP server
- Restoring the Cisco IOS Software from ROM Monitor mode using Xmodem
- Restoring the Cisco IOS Software using the ROM Monitor environmental variables and **tftpdnld** command
- Secure Copy
- Configuring a Secure Copy Server
- Verifying and Troubleshooting Secure Copy
- Configuration Example: Using Secure Copy

Boot System Commands

Router(config)#**boot system flash:** *image-name*	Loads the Cisco IOS Software with *image-name*.
Router(config)#**boot system tftp://172.16.10.3/***image-name*	Loads the Cisco IOS Software with *image-name* from a TFTP server.
Router(config)#**boot system rom**	Loads the Cisco IOS Software from ROM.
Router(config)#**exit**	Returns to Privileged EXEC mode.
Router#**copy running-config startup-config**	Saves the running configuration to NVRAM. The router executes commands in their order on the next reload.

TIP If you enter **boot system flash** first, that is the first place the router goes to look for the Cisco IOS Software. If you want to go to a TFTP server first, make sure that the **boot system tftp** command is the first command you enter.

TIP   If the configuration has no **boot system** commands, the router defaults to loading the first valid Cisco IOS image in flash memory and running it. If no valid Cisco IOS image is found in flash memory, the router attempts to boot from a network TFTP server. After six unsuccessful attempts of locating a network TFTP server, the router loads into ROMmon mode.

The Cisco IOS File System

NOTE   The Cisco IOS File System (IFS) provides a single interface to all the file systems available on a routing device, including the flash memory file system; network file systems such as TFTP, Remote Copy Protocol (RCP), and FTP; and any other endpoint for reading and writing data, such as NVRAM, or the running configuration. The Cisco IFS minimizes the required prompting for many commands. Instead of entering in an EXEC-level **copy** command and then having the system prompt you for more information, you can enter a single command on one line with all necessary information.

Cisco IOS Software Commands	IFS Commands
`copy tftp running-config`	`copy tftp: system:running-config`
`copy tftp startup-config`	`copy tftp: nvram:startup-config`
`show startup-config`	`more nvram:startup-config`
`erase startup-config`	`erase nvram:`
`copy running-config startup-config`	`copy system:running-config` `nvram:startup-config`
`copy running-config tftp`	`copy system:running-config tftp:`
`show running-config`	`more system:running-config`

Viewing the Cisco IOS File System

`Router#show file systems`	Displays all the available file systems on the device

NOTE   The Cisco IOS File System uses a URL convention to specify files on network devices and the network. Many of the most commonly used URL prefixes are also available in the Cisco IOS File System.

Commonly Used URL Prefixes for Cisco Network Devices

`flash:`	Flash memory. Available on all platforms. An alias for the flash: prefix is slot0.
`ftp:`	FTP network server.
`http:`	HTTP network server.
`nvram:`	NVRAM.
`rcp:`	RCP network server.

`scp:`	Secure Copy.
`system:`	Contains system memory, including the current running configuration.
`tftp:`	TFTP network server.
`usbflash0,` `usbflash1`	Universal Serial Bus (USB) flash.

Deciphering IOS Image Filenames

Although it looks long and complex, there is a reason that Cisco names its IOS images the way that it does. It is important to understand the meaning behind an IOS image name so that you can correctly choose which file to work with.

There are different parts to the image filename, as follows:

c2900-universalk9-mz.SPA.152-4.M1.bin

c2900	The platform on which the image runs. In this case, it is a Cisco 2900 router.
universal	Specifies the feature set. Universal on a 2900 would include IP Base, Security, Unified Communication, and Data feature sets. Each router is activated for IP Base; the others need software activation.
	NOTE k9 in an image name means that strong encryption, such as 3DES/AES, is included.
mz	Indicates where the image runs and if it is compressed. m means the file runs from RAM. z means the file is compressed.
SPA	This software is digitally signed. There are two file extensions possible: SPA and SSA. The first character *S* stands for digitally signed software. The second character *P* in SPA means that this release is meant for production. A second character *S* in SSA means it is a special image and has limited use or special conditions. The third character *A* indicates the key version used to digitally sign the image.
152-4.M1	The version number of the software. In this case, it is major release 15, minor release 2, new feature release 4. *M* means Extended Maintenance Release, and *1* is the Maintenance Rebuild Number.
.bin	This is the file extension. .bin shows that this file is a binary executable file.

NOTE   The Cisco IOS naming conventions, meanings, content, and other details are subject to change.

Backing Up Configurations to a TFTP Server

Denver#**copy running-config startup-config**	Saves the running configuration from DRAM to NVRAM (locally).
Denver#**copy running-config tftp**	Copies the running configuration to the remote TFTP server.
Address or name of remote host [ ]? 192.168.119.20	The IP address of the TFTP server.
Destination Filename [Denver-confg]?⏎Enter	The name to use for the file saved on the TFTP server.
!!!!!!!!!!!!!!!	Each bang symbol (!) = 1 datagram of data.
624 bytes copied in 7.05 secs	
Denver#	File has been transferred successfully.

NOTE   You can also use the preceding sequence for a **copy startup-config tftp** command sequence.

Restoring Configurations from a TFTP Server

Denver#**copy tftp running-config**	Merges the configuration file from the TFTP server with the running-config file in DRAM.
Address or name of remote host [ ]? 192.168.119.20	The IP address of the TFTP server.
Source filename [ ]?Denver-confg	Enter the name of the file you want to retrieve.
Destination filename [running-config]? ⏎Enter	Pressing the Enter key will begin the copy process.
Accessing tftp://192.168.119.20/ Denver-confg...	
Loading Denver-confg from 192.168.119.02 (via Gigabit Ethernet 0/0):	
!!!!!!!!!!!!!!!	
[OK-624 bytes]	
624 bytes copied in 9.45 secs	
Denver#	File has been transferred successfully.

NOTE   You can also use the preceding sequence for a **copy tftp startup-config** command sequence.

NOTE   When copying a file into a configuration file, the **no shutdown** command does not carry over into the configuration file. You must enable the interfaces with the **no shutdown** command.

Backing Up the Cisco IOS Software to a TFTP Server

Denver#**copy flash0: tftp:**	
Source filename [ ]? **c2900-universalk9-mz.SPA.152-4.M1.bin**	Name of the Cisco IOS Software image.
Address or name of remote host [ ]? 192.168.119.20	Address of the TFTP server.
Destination filename [**c2900-universalk9-mz.SPA.152-4.M1.bin**]? ⏎Enter	The destination filename is the same as the source filename, so just press ⏎Enter.
!! !!	
8906589 bytes copied in 263.68 seconds	
Denver#	

Restoring/Upgrading the Cisco IOS Software from a TFTP Server

Denver#**copy tftp: flash:**	
Address or name of remote host [ ]? **192.168.119.20**	
Source filename [ ]? **c2900-universalk9-mz.SPA.152-4.M1.bin**	
Destination filename [**c2900-universalk9-mz.SPA.152-4.M1.bin**]? ⏎Enter	
Accessing tftp://192.168.119.20/ **c2900-universalk9-mz.SPA.152-4.M1.bin**	
Erase flash: before copying? [confirm] ⏎Enter	If flash memory is full, erase it first.
Erasing the flash file system will remove all files	
Continue? [confirm] ⏎Enter	Press Ctrl-C if you want to cancel.
Erasing device eeeeeeeeeeeeeeeeee...erased	Each *e* represents data being erased.
Loading **c2900-universalk9-mz.SPA.152-4.M1.bin** **from 192.168.119.20**	
(via) GigabitEthernet 0/0): !!!!!!!!!!!!!!!!!! !! !!!!!!!!!!!!!!!!!!!!!!!!!!!	Each bang symbol (!) = 1 datagram of data.
Verifying Check sum .... OK	
[OK - 8906589 Bytes]	
8906589 bytes copied in 277.45 secs	
Denver#	Success.

Restoring the Cisco IOS Software from ROM Monitor Mode Using Xmodem

The output that follows was taken from a 1720 router. Some of this output might vary from yours, depending on the router model you are using.

```rommon 1 >confreg```	Shows the configuration summary. Step through the questions, answering defaults until you can change the console baud rate. Change it to **115200**; it makes transfer go faster.

```Configuration Summary```
 ```enabled are:```
 ```load rom after netboot fails```
 ```console baud: 9600```
 ```boot: image specified by the boot system```
 ```commands```
 ```or default to: cisco2-c1700```	

```do you wish to change the configuration? y/n```
 ```[n]: y```
 ```enable "diagnostic mode"? y/n [n]: n```
 ```enable "use net in IP bcast address"? y/n```
 ```[n]: n```
 ```disable "load rom after netboot fails"? y/n```
 ```[n]: n```
 ```enable "use all zero broadcast"? y/n [n]: n```
 ```enable "break/abort has effect"? y/n [n]: n```
 ```enable "ignore system config info"? y/n```
 ```[n]: n```
 ```change console baud rate? y/n [n]: y```
 ```enter rate: 0=9600, 1=4800, 2=1200, 3=2400```
 ```4=19200, 5=38400, 6=57600, 7=115200 [0]: 7```
 ```change the boot characteristics? y/n [n]: n```
	Prompts begin to ask a series of questions that allow you to change the configuration register. Answer **n** to all questions except the one that asks you to change the console baud rate. For the enter rate, choose **7** because that is the number that represents a baud rate of 115200.

```Configuration Summary```
 ```enabled are:```
 ```load rom after netboot fails```
 ```console baud: 115200```
 ```boot: image specified by the boot system```
 ```commands```
 ```or default to: cisco2-c1700```
 ```do you wish to change the configuration? y/n```
 ```[n]: n```
 ```rommon2>```
	After the summary is shown again, choose **n** to not change the configuration and go to the rommon> prompt again.

`rommon 2>reset`	Reloads the router at the new com speed. Change the terminal emulator software setting to **115200** to match the router's new console setting.
`Rommon 1>xmodem c1700-js-1_121-3.bin`	Asking to transfer this image using Xmodem.
`...<output cut>...`	
`Do you wish to continue? y/n [n ]:y`	Choose **y** to continue.
	In HyperTerminal, go to Transfer, then Send File (see Figure 26-1). Locate the Cisco IOS Software file on the hard drive and click Send (see Figure 26-2).
`Router will reload when transfer is completed.`	
`Reset baud rate on router.`	
`Router(config)#line con 0`	
`Router(config-line)#speed 9600`	
`Router(config-line)#exit`	HyperTerminal will stop responding. Reconnect to the router using 9600 baud, 8-N-1.

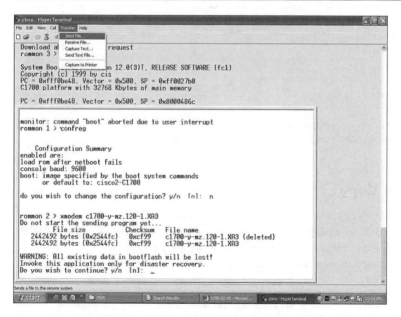

Figure 26-1   Finding the Cisco IOS Software Image File

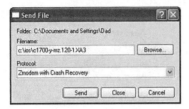

Figure 26-2 Sending the Cisco IOS Software Image File to the Router

Restoring the Cisco IOS Software Using the ROM Monitor Environmental Variables and tftpdnld Command

rommon 1>IP_ ADDRESS=192.168.100.1	Indicates the IP address for this unit.
rommon 2>IP_SUBNET_ MASK=255.255.255.0	Indicates the subnet mask for this unit.
rommon 3>DEFAULT_ GATEWAY=192.168.100.1	Indicates the default gateway for this unit.
rommon 4>TFTP_ SERVER=192.168.100.2	Indicates the IP address of the TFTP server.
rommon 5>TFTP_FILE= c2900 -universalk9-mz.SPA.152-4. M1.bin	Indicates the filename to fetch from the TFTP server.
rommon 6>tftpdnld	Starts the process.
...<output cut>...	
Do you wish to continue? y/n: [n]:y	
...<output cut>...	
Rommon 7>i	Resets the router. The *i* stands for initialize.

CAUTION Commands and environmental variables are case sensitive, so be sure that you have not accidentally added spaces between variables and answers.

Secure Copy

The Secure Copy (SCP) feature provides a secure and authenticated method for copying device configurations or device image files. SCP relies on Secure Shell (SSH). SCP allows a user with appropriate authorization to copy any file that exists in the Cisco IOS File System (IFS) to and from a device by using the **copy** command.

NOTE Before enabling SCP, you must correctly configure SSH, authentication, and authorization on the device and replace Telnet with SSH on the vty ports. See Chapter 25, "Device Hardening," for the commands needed to configure SSH.

NOTE   Because SCP relies on SSH for its secure transport, the device must have a Rivest, Shamir, and Adelman (RSA) key pair.

Configuring a Secure Copy Server

Denver#**configure terminal**	Moves to global configuration mode.
Denver(config)#**aaa new-model**	Sets AAA authentication at login.
Denver(config)#**aaa authentication login default local**	Enables the AAA access control system. In this example, authentication comes from a local username.
Denver(config)#**aaa authorization exec default local**	Sets parameters that restrict user access to a network. In this example, authorization comes from a local database.
Denver(config)#**username superuser privilege 15 password 0 superpassword**	Creates a local username/password combination. In this example, the username is *superuser*. There is a privilege level of 15, and the password is unencrypted (denoted by the *0*) and is *superpassword*.
Denver(config)#**ip scp server enable**	Enables SCP server-side functionality.

Verifying and Troubleshooting Secure Copy

Denver#**show running-config**	Shows current configuration in DRAM. The IP SCP server is enabled and visible in the running config.
Denver#**debug ip scp**	Displays output related to SCP authentication problems.

Configuration Example: Using Secure Copy

The following example shows the commands for using SCP to transfer an IOS image from flash to a remote host that supports SSH.

NOTE   Your router does not need to be set up as an SCP server for this transfer to work. You need only to have SSH configured.

Denver#**copy flash: scp:**	Initiates secure copy from flash: to a remote host.
Source filename [ ]? **c1900-universalk9-mz.SPA.151-1.T.bin**	Enter the name of the file you want to transfer.
Address or name of remote host[ ]? **192.168.119.20**	The IP address of the remote host.

`Source username [Router]?superuser`	The username needed for the connection.
`Destination filename [c1900-universalk9-mz.SPA.151-1.T.bin]?`	Press [Enter] as the filename is already prompted.
`Writing c1900-universalk9-mz.SPA.151-1.T.bin`	Connection is being created and verified.
`Password:`	Enter the password when prompted.
`!!!!!!!!!!!!!!!!!!!!!!!!!!!!!!!!!!!!!!!! !!!!!!`	Each bang is a datagram being copied.
`Denver#`	File has been transferred successfully.

NOTE As with any use of the **copy** command, you can enter some of the specific details into the command itself:

```
Denver#copy flash:c1900-universalk9-mz.SPA.151-1.T.bin
scp://superuser@10.10.10.2/
```

NOTE When using SCP, you cannot enter the password into the **copy** command; you must enter it when prompted.

Password Recovery Procedures and the Configuration Register

This chapter provides information and commands concerning the following topics:

- The configuration register
- A visual representation of the configuration register
- What the bits mean
- The boot field
- Console terminal baud rate settings
- Changing the console line speed: CLI
- Changing the console line speed: ROM Monitor mode
- Password-recovery procedures for Cisco routers
- Password-recovery procedures for 2960 series switches

The Configuration Register

router#**show version**	The last line of output tells you what the configuration register is set to.
router#**configure terminal**	This moves to global configuration mode.
router(config)#**config-register 0x2142**	This changes the configuration register to 2142.

A Visual Representation of the Configuration Register

The configuration register is a 16-bit field stored in NVRAM. The bits are numbered from 15 to 0 looking at the bit stream from left to right. Bits are split up into groups of 4, and each group is represented by a hexadecimal digit.

15 14 13 12	11 10 9 8	7 6 5 4	3 2 1 0	Bit places
0 0 1 0	0 0 0 1	0 1 0 0	0 0 1 0	Register bits
2	1	4	2	Bits represented in hex
In this example, bits 13, 8 , 6, and 1 are turned on. Converting these groups of four binary nibbles gives you the hexadecimal number of 0x2142.				
A nibble is half of a byte, or 4 bits.				

TIP   To distinguish between a number in decimal and a number in hexadecimal, use the prefix **0x** to represent a hexadecimal number; 0x2102 is not the same as 2102.

TIP   See Appendix A, "Binary/Hex/Decimal Chart," for a list of numbers written down in both decimal and hexadecimal (as well as binary).

TIP   The two most important configuration register values for you to remember are

0x2102: This is the default register setting. Your router should always be set to this value during normal operation of the device.

0x2142: This is the setting used during the password recovery procedure. It causes the router to boot while ignoring the contents of the NVRAM. It does not erase or modify the contents of the NVRAM; it just tells the router to ignore the contents of NVRAM (which includes the Startup-Config file) during bootup. Once you complete the password recovery procedure, reset the configuration register back to 0x2102.

What the Bits Mean

Bit Number	Hexadecimal	Meaning
00–03	0x0000–0x000F	Boot field.
06	0x0040	Ignore NVRAM contents.
07	0x0080	OEM bit enabled.
08	0x0100	Break disabled.
09	0x0200	Causes system to use secondary bootstrap (typically not used).
10	0x0400	IP broadcast with all 0s.
5, 11, 12	0x0020, 0x0800, 0x1000	Console line speed.
13	0x2000	Boots default ROM software if network boot fails.
14	0x4000	IP broadcasts do not have net numbers.
15	0x8000	Enables diagnostic messages and ignores NVRAM contents.

The Boot Field

NOTE   Even though there are 16 possible combinations in the boot field, only 3 are used.

Boot Field	Meaning
00	Stays at the ROM Monitor on a reload or power cycle
01	Boots the first image in onboard flash memory as a system image
02–F	Enables default booting from flash memory Enables **boot system** commands that override default booting from flash memory

TIP   Because the default boot field has 14 different ways to represent it, a configuration register setting of 0x2102 is the same as 0x2109 or 0x210F. The **boot system** command is described in Chapter 26, "Backing Up and Restoring Cisco IOS Software and Configurations."

Console Terminal Baud Rate Settings

Baud	Bit 5	Bit 12	Bit 11
115200	1	1	1
57600	1	1	0
38400	1	0	1
19200	1	0	0
9600	0	0	0
4800	0	0	1
2400	0	1	1
1200	0	1	0

Changing the Console Line Speed: CLI

router#**configure terminal**	
router(config)#**line console 0**	Enters console line mode
router(config-line)#**speed 19200**	Changes the speed to 19200 baud

TIP   Cisco IOS Software does not allow you to change the console speed bits directly with the **config-register** command.

CAUTION   Changing the speed of the console port from the command-line interface (CLI) can lead to disastrous results when booting a router. If the configuration register has the default speed of 9600 baud, and your terminal program is also set to 9600 baud, you will see normal output on the screen upon startup of the router. However, because the startup-config file is loaded into RAM, the **speed** command then changes the console port baud setting to a different number, and your terminal program no longer displays the correct output on the screen; you may get garbage characters or nothing at all.

Changing the Console Line Speed: ROM Monitor Mode

| ```
rommon1>confreg
``` | Shows configuration summary. Step through the questions, answering with the defaults until you can change the console baud rate. |
| ```
Configuration Summary
enabled are:
load rom after netboot fails
console baud: 9600
boot: image specified by the boot system commands
or default to: x (name of system image)
``` | |
| ```
do you wish to change the configuration? y/n
[n]: y
enable "diagnostic mode"? y/n.[n]: n
enable "use net in IP bcast address"? y/n [n]: n
disable "load rom after netboot fails"? y/n
[n]: n
enable "use all zero broadcast"? y/n [n]: n
enable "break/abort has effect"? y/n [n]: n
enable "ignore system config info"? y/n [n]: n
change console baud rate? y/n [n]: y
enter rate: 0=9600, 1=4800, 2=1200, 3=2400
4=19200, 5=38400, 6=57600, 7=115200 [0]: 7
``` | |
| ```
Configuration Summary
enabled are:
load rom after netboot fails
console baud: 115200
boot: image specified by the boot system commands
or default to: x (name of system image)
``` | |
| ```
change the boot characteristics? y/n [n]: n
``` | After the summary is shown again, choose **n** to indicate you do not want change the configuration, and go to the rommon> prompt again. |
| ```
rommon2>
``` | |

TIP　Make sure that after you change the console baud rate, you change your terminal program to match the same rate.

Password-Recovery Procedures for Cisco Routers

Step	2500 Series Commands	1700/2600/ISR/ISR2 Series Commands
Step 1: Boot the router and interrupt the boot sequence as soon as text appears on the screen. The Break sequence differs depending on the terminal program you are using. In HyperTerminal and PuTTY, the command is Ctrl - Break. In TeraTerm, the command is Alt -B. Make sure you know the correct sequence.	Press Ctrl - Break	Press Ctrl - Break rommon 1>

Step 2: Change the configuration register to ignore contents of NVRAM.	`>o/r 0x2142`
	
	`>`
		`rommon 1>confreg 0x2142`
		
		`rommon 2>`

Step 3: Reload the router.	`>i`	`rommon 2>reset`
Step 4: Enter privileged EXEC mode. (Do not enter setup mode.)	`Router>enable` `Router#`	`Router>enable` `Router#`

Step 5: Merge the startup configuration into the running configuration.	`Router#copy startup-`
	`config running-config`
	`...<output cut>...`
	
	`Denver#`
	
	Note that the name of the router changes to whatever was saved in the startup-config file.
		`Router#copy startup-`
		`config running-config`
		`...<output cut>...`
		
		`Denver#`
		
		Note that the name of the router changes to whatever was saved in the startup-config file.

	NOTE When you merge the **startup-config** into the **running-config**, your interfaces will be in shutdown mode because the **no shutdown** command is not part of the startup-config file. You must issue the **no shutdown** command to enable the interfaces.	**NOTE** When you merge the **startup-config** into the **running-config**, your interfaces will be in shutdown mode because the **no shutdown** command is not part of the startup-config file. You must issue the **no shutdown** command to enable the interfaces.

Step 6: Change the password.	Denver#**configure terminal**	Denver#**configure terminal**
	Denver(config)#**enable secret** *newpassword*	Denver(config)#**enable secret** *newpassword*
	Denver(config)#	Denver(config)#
Step 7: Reset the configuration register to its default value.	Denver(config)#**config-register 0x2102**	Denver(config)#**config-register 0x2102**
	Denver(config)#	Denver(config)#
Step 8: Save the configuration.	Denver(config)#**exit**	Denver(config)#**exit**
	Denver#**copy running-config startup-config**	Denver#**copy running-config startup-config**
	Denver#	Denver#
Step 9: Verify the configuration register.	Denver#**show version**	Denver#**show version**
	...<output cut>...	...<output cut>...
	Configuration register is 0x2142 (will be 0x2102 at next reload).	Configuration register is 0x2142 (will be 0x2102 at next reload).
	Denver#	Denver#
Step 10: Reload the router.	Denver#**reload**	Denver#**reload**

Password Recovery for 2960 Series Switches

Unplug the power supply from the back of the switch.	
Press and hold the Mode button on the front of the switch.	
Plug the switch back in.	
Release the Mode button when the SYST LED blinks amber and then turns solid green. When you release the Mode button, the SYST LED blinks green.	
Issue the following commands:	
switch: **flash_init**	Initializes the flash memory.
switch: **load_helper**	
switch: **dir flash:**	Do not forget the colon. This displays which files are in flash memory.
switch: **rename flash:config.text flash:config.old**	You are renaming the configuration file. The config.text file contains the password.
switch: **boot**	Boots the switch.

When asked whether you want to enter the configuration dialog, enter **n** to exit out to the switch prompt.	Takes you to user mode.
`switch>`**`enable`**	Enters privileged mode.
`switch#`**`rename flash:config.old`** **`flash:config.text`**	Renames the configuration file to the original name.
`Destination filename [config.text]`	Press ⏎Enter.
`switch#`**`copy flash:config.text`** **`system:running-config`**	Copies the configuration file into memory.
`768 bytes copied in 0.624 seconds`	
`2960Switch#`	The configuration file is now reloaded. Notice the new prompt.
`2960Switch#`**`configure terminal`**	Enters global configuration mode.
`2960Switch(config)#`	
`Proceed to change the passwords as needed`	
`2960Switch(config)#`**`exit`**	
`2960Switch#`**`copy running-config`** **`startup-config`**	Saves the configuration into NVRAM with new passwords.

Cisco Discovery Protocol (CDP) and Link Layer Discovery Protocol (LLDP)

This chapter provides information and commands concerning the following topic:

- Cisco Discovery Protocol
- Configuring CDP
- Verifying and Troubleshooting CDP
- CDP Design Tips
- Link Layer Discovery Protocol (802.1AB)
- Configuring LLDP (802.1AB)
- Verifying and troubleshooting LLDP

Cisco Discovery Protocol

Cisco Discovery Protocol (CDP) is a Cisco proprietary Layer 2 protocol. It is media and protocol independent and runs on all Cisco-manufactured equipment including routers, bridges, access servers, and switches. CDP is primarily used to obtain protocol addresses of neighboring devices and discover the platform of those devices. CDP can also be used to display information about the interfaces that your device uses.

Configuring CDP

NOTE CDP is enabled on all Cisco devices by default.

`Router(config)#cdp holdtime x`	Changes the length of time to keep CDP packets
`Router(config)#cdp timer x`	Changes how often CDP updates are sent
`Router(config)#cdp run`	Enables CDP globally (on by default)
`Router(config)#no cdp run`	Turns off CDP globally
`Router(config-if)#cdp enable`	Enables CDP on a specific interface
`Router(config-if)#no cdp enable`	Turns off CDP on a specific interface

Verifying and Troubleshooting CDP

`Router#show cdp`	Displays global CDP information (such as timers)
`Router#show cdp neighbors`	Displays information about neighbors
`Router#show cdp neighbors detail`	Displays more detail about the neighbor device
`Router#show cdp entry word`	Displays information about the device named *word*
`Router#show cdp entry *`	Displays information about all devices
`Router#show cdp interface`	Displays information about interfaces that have CDP running
`Router#show cdp interface x`	Displays information about specific interface *x* running CDP
`Router#show cdp traffic`	Displays traffic information—packets in/out/version
`Router#clear cdp counters`	Resets traffic counters to 0
`Router#clear cdp table`	Deletes the CDP table
`Router#debug cdp adjacency`	Monitors CDP neighbor information
`Router#debug cdp events`	Monitors all CDP events
`Router#debug cdp ip`	Monitors CDP events specifically for IP
`Router#debug cdp packets`	Monitors CDP packet-related information

CDP Design Tips

CAUTION   Although CDP is necessary for some management applications, CDP should still be disabled in some instances.

Disable CDP globally if

- CDP is not required at all.
- The device is located in an insecure environment.

Use the command **no cdp run** to disable CDP globally:

```
RouterOrSwitch(config)#no cdp run
```

Disable CDP on any interface if

- Management is not being performed.
- The switch interface is a nontrunk interface.
- The interface is connected to a nontrusted network.

Use the interface configuration command **no cdp enable** to disable CDP on a specific interface:

```
RouterOrSwitch(config)#interface fastethernet 0/1
RouterOrSwitch(config-if)#no cdp enable
```

Link Layer Discovery Protocol (802.1AB)

Link Layer Discovery Protocol (LLDP) is an industry standard alternative to CDP.

NOTE   LLDP works on Ethernet type interfaces only.

Configuring LLDP (802.1AB)

`Switch(config)#lldp run`	Enables LLDP globally on the switch.
`Switch(config)#no lldp run`	Disables LLDP globally on the switch.
`Switch(config)#lldp holdtime 180`	Specifies the amount of time a receiving device should hold the information sent by another device before discarding it. The default value is 120 seconds. The range is 0 to 65,535 seconds.
`Switch(config)#lldp timer 60`	Sets the transmission frequency of LLDP updates in seconds. The default value is 30 seconds. The range is 5 to 65,534 seconds.
`Switch(config)#interface fastethernet0/1`	Specifies the interface on which you are enabling or disabling LLDP and enters interface configuration mode.
`Switch(config-if)#lldp transmit`	Enables the interface to send LLDP.
`Switch(config-if)#lldp receive`	Enables the interface to receive LLDP.
`Switch(config-if)#no lldp transmit`	No LLDP packets are sent on the interface.
`Switch(config-if)#no lldp receive`	No LLDP packets are received on the interface.

Verifying and Troubleshooting LLDP

Switch#`clear lldp counters`	Resets the traffic counters to 0.
Switch#`clear lldp table`	Deletes the LLDP table of information about neighbors.
Switch#`debug lldp packets`	Enables debugging of LLDP packets. Use the **no** form of this command to disable debugging.
Switch#`show lldp`	Displays global information, such as frequency of transmissions, the holdtime for packets being sent, and the delay time for LLDP to initialize on an interface.
Switch#`show ldp entry` *entry-name*	Displays information about a specific neighbor. You can enter an asterisk (*) to display all neighbors, or you can enter the name of the neighbor about which you want information.
Switch#`show lldp interface` [*interface-id*]	Displays information about interfaces where LLDP is enabled. You can limit the display to the interface about which you want information.
Switch#`show lldp neighbors` [*interface-id*] [*detail*]	Displays information about neighbors, including device type, interface type and number, holdtime settings, capabilities, and port ID.
Switch#`show lldp traffic`	Displays LLDP counters, including the number of packets sent and received, number of packets discarded, and number of unrecognized Type Length Value (TLV) fields.

IOS Tools

This chapter provides information and commands concerning the following topics:

- Configuring a device to accept a remote Telnet connection
- Using Telnet to remotely connect to other devices
- Verifying Telnet
- Internet Control Message Protocol redirect messages
- The **ping** command
- Examples of using the **ping** and the extended **ping** commands
- The **traceroute** command

Configuring a Device to Accept a Remote Telnet Connection

NOTE The ability to telnet into a Cisco device is part of every Cisco IOS. You only need to assign passwords to allow a remote connection into a device.

`Router(config)#line vty 0 4`	Enters vty line mode for 5 vty lines numbered 0 through 4.
	NOTE An ISR2 router has 5 vty lines numbered 0 through 4. A 2960/3560 switch has 16 vty lines numbered 0 through 15. Make sure that you assign a password to all vty lines of your devices.
`Router(config-line)#password letmein`	Sets vty password to *letmein*.
`Router(config-line)#login`	Enables password checking at login.

NOTE A device must have two passwords for a remote user to be able to make changes to the configuration:

- Line vty password
- **enable** or **enable secret** password

Without the **enable** or **enable secret** password, a remote user will only be able to get to user mode, not to privileged EXEC mode. Remember that without an **enable** or **enable secret** password set, a user logged in through the console will still access privileged EXEC mode. But a remote user needs one of these passwords to gain access. This is extra security.

Using Telnet to Remotely Connect to Other Devices

The following five commands all achieve the same result: the attempt to connect remotely to the router named Paris at IP address 172.16.20.1.

`Denver>`**`telnet paris`**	Enter if **ip host** command was used previously to create a mapping of an IP address to the word *paris*.
	NOTE The **ip host** command is covered in Chapter 11, "Configuring a Cisco Router," in the "Assigning a Local Hostname to an IP Address" section.
`Denver>`**`telnet`** **`172.16.20.1`**	
`Denver>`**`paris`**	Enter if **ip host** command is using a default port number.
`Denver>`**`connect paris`**	
`Denver>`**`172.16.20.1`**	

Any of the preceding commands lead to the following configuration sequence:

`Paris>`	As long as a vty password is set.
`Paris>`**`exit`**	Terminates the Telnet session and returns you to the Denver prompt.
`Denver>`	
OR	
`Paris>`**`logout`**	Terminates the Telnet session and returns you to the Denver prompt.
`Denver>`	
`Paris>`, Ctrl - ⬆Shift - 6 `release, then press` x	Suspends the Telnet session but does not terminate it, and returns you to the Denver prompt.
`Denver>`	
`Denver>`↵Enter	Resumes the connection to Paris.
`Paris>`	
`Denver>`**`resume`**	Resumes the connection to Paris.
`Paris>`	
`Denver>`**`disconnect`** **`paris`**	Terminates the session to Paris.
`Denver>`	

Verifying Telnet

`Denver#`**`show sessions`**	Displays connections you opened to other sites.
`Denver#`**`show users`**	Displays who is connected remotely to you.
`Denver#`**`clear line`** *x*	Disconnects the remote user connected to you on line *x*. The line number is listed in the output gained from the **show users** command.

Denver(config)#**line vty 0 4**	Moves to line configuration mode for vty lines 0 to 4.
Denver(config-line) **session-limit** x	Limits the number of simultaneous sessions per vty line to x number.

CAUTION   The following configuration creates a big security hole. Never use it in a live production environment. Use it in the lab only!

Denver(config)#**line vty 0 4**	Moves you to line configuration mode for vty lines 0 to 4.
Denver(config-line)#**no password**	The remote user is not challenged when telnetting to this device.
Denver(config-line)#**no login**	The remote user moves straight to user mode.

NOTE   A device must have two passwords for a remote user to be able to make changes to the configuration:

- Line vty password (or have it explicitly turned off; see the preceding Caution)
- **Enable** or **enable secret** password

Without the **enable** or **enable secret** password, a remote user will only be able to get to user mode, not to privileged mode. This is extra security.

Internet Control Message Protocol Redirect Messages

Internet Control Message Protocol (ICMP) is used to communicate to the original source the errors encountered while routing packets and to exercise control on the traffic. Routers use ICMP redirect messages to notify the hosts on the data link that a better route is available for a particular destination.

Router(config-if)#**no ip redirects**	Disables ICMP redirects from this specific interface
Router(config-if)#**ip redirects**	Reenables ICMP redirects from this specific interface

The ping Command

Router#**ping** w.x.y.z	Checks for Layer 3 connectivity with device at IPv4 address w.x.y.z
Router#**ping aaaa:aaaa:a aaa:aaaa:aaaa:aaaa:aaaa :aaaa**	Checks for Layer 3 connectivity with device at IPv6 address aaaa:aaaa:aaaa:aaaa:aaaa:aaaa:aaaa:aaaa
Router#**ping 172.16.20.1 source loopback1**	Checks for Layer 3 connectivity with device at IPv4 address 172.16.20.1 with the packets originating from source interface loopback1

`Router#`**`ping 2001::1`** **`source loopback1`**	Checks for Layer 3 connectivity with device at IPv6 address 2001::1 with the packets originating from source interface loopback1
`Router#`**`ping`**	Enters extended ping mode, which provides more options

The following table describes the possible ping output characters.

Character	Description
!	Each exclamation point indicates receipt of a reply.
.	Each period indicates that the network server timed out while waiting for a reply.
?	Unknown error.
@	Unreachable for unknown reason.
A	Administratively unreachable. Usually means that an access control list (ACL) is blocking traffic.
B	Packet too big.
H	Host unreachable.
N	Network unreachable (beyond scope).
P	Port unreachable.
R	Parameter problem.
T	Time exceeded.
U	No route to host.

Examples of Using the ping and the Extended ping Commands

`Router#`**`ping 172.16.20.1`**	Performs a basic Layer 3 test to IPv4 address 172.16.20.1.
`Router#`**`ping paris`**	Same as above but through the IP hostname.
`Router#`**`ping 2001:db8:D1A5:C900::2`**	Checks for Layer 3 connectivity with device at IPv6 address 2001:db8:D1A5:C900::2.
`Router#`**`ping`**	Enters extended ping mode; can now change parameters of ping test.
`Protocol [ip]:` `⏎Return`	Press `⏎Return` to use ping for IP.
`Target IP address:` **`172.16.20.1`**	Enter the target IP address.
`Repeat count [5]:` **`100`**	Enter the number of echo requests you want to send. The default is 5.
`Datagram size [100]:` `⏎Return`	Enter the size of datagrams being sent. The default is 100.

`Timeout in Seconds [2]: `⟨↵Return⟩	Enter the timeout delay between sending echo requests.
`Extended commands [n]: `**yes**	Allows you to configure extended commands.
`Source address or interface:` **`10.0.10.1`**	Allows you to explicitly set where the pings are originating from. An interface name may also be used here.
`Type of Service [0]`	Allows you to set the TOS field in the IP header.
`Set DF bit in IP header [no]`	Allows you to set the DF bit in the IP header.
`Validate reply data? [no]`	Allows you to set whether you want validation.
`Data Pattern [0xABCD]`	Allows you to change the data pattern in the data field of the ICMP echo request packet.

`Loose, Strict, Record, Timestamp,`
`Verbose[none]:`
`Sweep range of sizes [no]:`
`Type escape sequence to abort`
`Sending 100, 100-byte ICMP Echos`
`to 172.16.20.1, timeout is 2 sec-`
`onds:`
`Packet sent with a source address`
`of 10.0.10.1`
`!!!!!!!!!!!!!!!!!!!!!!!!!!!!!!!!!!!`
`!!!!!!!!!!!!!!!!!!!!!!!!!!!!!!!!!!!`
`!!!!!!!!!!!!!!!!!!!!!!!!!!!!!!!!!!!`
`!!!!!!!!!!!!!!!!!!!!!!!!`
`Success rate is 100 percent`
`(100/100) round-trip min/avg/max`
`= 1/1/4 ms`	

TIP   If you want to interrupt the ping operation, use the ⟨Ctrl⟩-⟨↑Shift⟩-⟨6⟩ keystroke combination. This ends the operation and returns you to the prompt.

The traceroute Command

The **traceroute** command (or **tracert** in Windows) is a utility that allows observation of the path between two hosts.

Router#**traceroute** 172.16.20.1	Discovers the route taken to travel to the IPv4 destination of 172.16.20.1
Router#**traceroute** paris	Command with IP hostname rather than IP address
Router#**traceroute** 2001:**db8**:**D1A5**:**C900**::**2**	Discovers the route taken to travel to the IPv6 destination of 2001:db8:D1A5:C900::2
Router#**trace** 172.16.20.1	Common shortcut spelling of the **traceroute** command

NOTE   In Windows operating systems, the command to allow observation between two hosts is **tracert**:

C:\Windows\system32>**tracert 172.16.20.1**

C:\Windows\system32>**tracert 2001:DB8:c:18:2::1**

Device Monitoring

This chapter provides information about the following topics:

- Device Monitoring
- Simple Network Management Protocol
- Configuring SNMP
- Securing SNMPv1 or SNMPv2
- Securing SNMPv3
- Verifying SNMP
- Configuration backups
- Implementing logging
- Configuring syslog
- Syslog message format
- Syslog severity levels
- Syslog message example
- Configuring NetFlow
- Verifying NetFlow
- Network Time Protocol
- Network Time Protocol configuration
- Verifying NTP
- Setting the clock on a router
- Using time stamps

Device Monitoring

Network administrators need to be able to perform more than just the configuration of network devices. They need to be able to monitor network devices to ensure that the network is operating as efficiently as possible and to identify potential bottlenecks or trouble spots. The following sections deal with protocols that can help monitor a network.

Simple Network Management Protocol

Simple Network Management Protocol (SNMP) is the most commonly used network management protocol.

TIP If SNMP is not required on a router, you should turn it off by using the **no snmp-server** command at the global configuration mode prompt.

```
Edmonton(config)#no snmp-server
```

NOTE Cisco IOS software supports three different versions of SNMP:

1. SNMPv1—Defined originally in RFC 1157. Security is based upon community strings.

2. SNMPv2c—An experimental protocol originally defined in RFCs 1901, 1905, and 1906. It uses the same community-based security model of SNMPv1.

3. SNMPv3—Version 3 of SNMP. An interoperable standards-based protocol originally defined in RFCs 2273 to 2275. SNMPv3 provides secure access to devices by a combination of authenticating and encrypting packets over the network.

NOTE You must configure the SNMP agent (your Cisco device) to use the version of SNMP supported by the management station. An agent can communicate with multiple managers; you can configure Cisco IOS software to support communications with one management station using SNMPv1, one using SNMPv2c and another using SNMPv3.

NOTE Beginning with SNMPv3, methods to ensure the secure transmission of data between manager and agent were added. You can now define a security policy per group or limit IP addresses to which its members can belong. You will now have to define encryption, hashing algorithms, and passwords for each user.

Table 30-1 shows the different SNMP security models.

TABLE 30-1 SNMP Security Models

SNMP Version	Access Mode	Authentication	Encryption
SNMPv1	noAuthNoPriv	Community string	No
SNMPv2	noAuthNoPriv	Community string	No
SNMPv3	noAuthNoPriv	Username	No
	authNoPriv	MD5 or SHA-1	No
	authPriv	MD5 or SHA-1	Data Encryption Standard (DES), 3DES, or AES

TIP The SNMP security levels are as follows:

- **noAuthNoPriv**—Authenticates SNMP messages using a community string. No encryption is provided.

- **authNoPriv**—Authenticates SNMP messages using either HMAC with MD5 or SHA-1. No encryption is provided.

- **authPriv**—Authenticates SNMP messages by using either HMAC-MD5 or SHA. It encrypts SNMP messages using DES, 3DES, or AES.

- **priv**—Does not authenticate SNMP messages. Encrypts only DES or AES.

TIP   SNMPv3 provides all three security level options. It should be used wherever possible.

TIP   If SNMPv3 cannot be used, secure SNMPv1 or SNMPv2 by using uncommon, complex community strings and by enabling read-only access.

TIP   If community strings are also used for SNMP traps, they must be different from community strings for get and set methods. This is considered best practice.

Configuring SNMP

NOTE   There is no specific command used to enable SNMP. The first **snmp-server** command that you enter enables the supported versions of SNMP.

Router(config)#**snmp-server community academy ro**	Sets a read-only (**ro**) community string called academy
Router(config)#**snmp-server community academy rw**	Sets a read-write (**rw**) community string called academy
Router(config)#**snmp-server location 2nd Floor IDF**	Defines an SNMP string that describes the physical location of the SNMP server
Router(config)#**snmp-server contact Scott Empson 555-5243**	Defines an SNMP string that describes the sysContact information

NOTE   A community string is like a password. In the case of the first command, the community string grants you access to SNMP.

Securing SNMPv1 or SNMPv2

Edmonton(config)#**snmp-server community C0mpl3xAdmin ro 98**	Sets a community string named *C0mpl3xAdmin*. It is read-only and refers to access control list (ACL) 98 to limit SNMP access to the authorized hosts.
	NOTE A named ACL can also be used.
Edmonton(config)#**access-list 98 permit host 192.168.10.3**	Creates an ACL that limits the SNMP access to the specific host of 192.168.10.3.
Edmonton(config) #**snmp-server host 192.168.10.3 AdminC0mpl3x**	Sets the Network Management System (NMS) IP address of 192.168.10.3 and the community string of *AdminC0mpl3x*, which protects the sending of the SNMP traps. The community string is also used to connect to the host.

Securing SNMPv3

Edmonton(config)#**access-list 99 permit 10.1.1.0 0.0.0.255**	Creates an ACL that limits SNMP access to the local device from SNMP managers within the 10.1.1.0/24 subnet.
Edmonton(config)#**snmp-server view MGMT SysUpTime included**	Defines an SNMP view named *MGMT* and an object identifier (OID) name of *SysUpTime*. This OID is included in the view.
Edmonton(config)#**snmp-server view MGMT ifDescr included**	Defines an SNMP view named *MGMT* and an OID name of *ifDescr*. This OID is included in the view.
Edmonton(config)#**snmp-server view MGMT ifAdminStatus included**	Defines an SNMP view named *MGMT* and an OID name of *ifAdminStatus*. This OID is included in the view.
Edmonton(config)#**snmp-server view MGMT ifOperStatus included**	Defines an SNMP view named *MGMT* and an OID name of *ifOperStatus*. This OID is included in the view.
Edmonton(config)#**snmp-server group groupAAA v3 priv read MGMT write MGMT access 99**	Defines SNMPv3 group. The group is configured with the following: "authPriv" security level = **groupAAA v3 priv** SNMP read and write access limited to devices defined in access list 99 = **read MGMT write MGMT access 99**
Edmonton(config)#**snmp-server user userAAA groupAAA v3 auth sha itsa5ecret priv aes 256 another5ecret**	Configures a new user to the SNMP group with authentication and encryption: User and group = **snmp-server user userAAA groupAAA** Password for authentication = **auth sha itsa5ecret** Password for encryption = **priv aes 256 another5ecret**
Edmonton(config)#**snmp-server enable traps**	Enables SNMP traps.
	NOTE A common message may occur after this command is entered. It is a warning that, depending on your design, you may need to address or choose to ignore: % NHRP MIB is not enabled: Trap generation suppressed. However, configuration changes effective

`Edmonton(config)#snmp-server host 10.1.1.50 traps version 3 priv userAAA cpu port-security`	Defines a receiving manager for traps at IP address 10.1.1.50. UserAAA will have authPriv security level (**priv** events limited to CPU and port security-related events) = **cpu port-security**
`Edmonton(config)#snmp-server ifindex persist`	Prevents index shuffle.
	NOTE SNMP does not identify object instances by names but by numeric indexes. The index number may change due to instance changes, such as a new interface being configured. This command guarantees index persistence when changes occur.

Verifying SNMP

`Edmonton#show snmp`	Provides basic information about SNMP configuration
`Edmonton#show snmp view`	Provides information about SNMP views
`Edmonton#show snmp group`	Provides information about configured SNMP groups
`Edmonton#show snmp user`	Provides information about configured SNMP users

Configuration Backups

It is important to keep a copy of a router's configuration in a location other than NVRAM. Automated jobs can be set up to copy configurations from the router at regular intervals to local or remote file systems.

`Edmonton(config)#archive`	Enters archive configuration mode.
`Edmonton(config-archive) #path ftp:// admin:cisco123@192.168.10.3/ $h.cfg`	Sets the base file path for the remote location of the archived configuration. The FTP server is located at 192.168.10.3. The username to access the FTP Server is *admin*. The password is *cisco123*. The path can be a local or a remote path. Path options include **flash**, **ftp**, **http**, **https**, **rcp**, **scp**, or **tftp**. Two variables can be used with the **path** command: **$h** will be replaced with the device hostname. **$t** will be replaced with the date and time of the archive. If you do not use **$t**, the names of the new files will be appended with a version number to differentiate from the previous configurations from the same device.

Edmonton(config-archive) #**time-period 1440**	Sets the period of time (in minutes) in which to automatically archive the running-config. This number can range from 1 to 525,600 minutes. 1440 minutes = 1 day. 525,600 minutes = 1 year.
Edmonton(config-archive) #**write-memory**	Enables automatic backup generation during write memory.
Edmonton#**show archive**	Displays the list of archives. This command also has a pointer to the most recent archive.

TIP To create an archive copy manually, use the **archive config** command from EXEC mode:

```
Edmonton#archive config
```

TIP When the **write-memory** command is enabled, the **copy running-config startup-config** command triggers an archive to occur.

Implementing Logging

Network administrators should implement logging to get the insight into what is occurring in their network. When a router reloads, all local logs are lost, so it is important to implement logging to an external destination. These next sections deal with the different mechanisms that you can use to configure logging to a remote location.

Configuring Syslog

Edmonton(config)#**logging on**	Enables logging to all supported destinations.
Edmonton(config)#**logging 192.168.10.53**	Logging messages are sent to a syslog server host at address 192.168.10.53.
Edmonton(config)#**logging sysadmin**	Logging messages are sent to a syslog server host named *sysadmin*.
Edmonton(config)#**logging trap x**	Sets the syslog server logging level to value *x*, where *x* is a number between 0 and 7 or a word defining the level. Table 30-2 provides more details.
Edmonton(config)#**service sequence-numbers**	Stamps syslog messages with a sequence number.
Edmonton(config)#**service timestamps log datetime**	Syslog messages now have a time stamp included.
Edmonton(config)#**service timestamps log datetime msec**	Syslog messages now have a time stamp in milliseconds included.

Syslog Message Format

The general format of syslog messages generated on Cisco IOS Software is as follows:

```
seq no:timestamp: %facility-severity-MNEMONIC:description
```

Item in Syslog Message	Definition
seq no	Sequence number. Stamped only if the **service sequence-numbers** global configuration command is configured.
timestamp	Date and time of the message. Appears only if the **service timestamps log datetime** global configuration command is configured.
facility	The facility to which the message refers (SNMP, SYS, and so on).
severity	Single-digit code from 0 to 7 that defines the severity of the message. See Table 30-2 for descriptions of the levels.
MNEMONIC	String of text that uniquely defines the message.
description	String of text that contains detailed information about the event being reported.

Syslog Severity Levels

Table 30-2 shows the eight levels of severity in logging messages.

TABLE 30-2   Syslog Severity Levels

Level #	Level Name	Description
0	Emergencies	System unusable
1	Alerts	Immediate action needed
2	Critical	Critical conditions
3	Errors	Error conditions
4	Warnings	Warning conditions
5	Notifications	Normal but significant conditions
6	Informational	Informational messages (default level)
7	Debugging	Debugging messages

Setting a level means you will get that level and everything numerically below it. Level 6 means you will receive messages for levels 0 through 6.

Syslog Message Example

The easiest syslog message to use as an example is the one that shows up every time you exit from global configuration back to privileged EXEC mode. You have just finished entering a command, and you want to save your work, but after you type **exit** you see something like this:

```
Edmonton(config)#exit
Edmonton#
*Jun 23:22:45:20.878: %SYS-5-CONFIG_I: Configured from console by console
Edmonton#
```

(Your output will differ depending on whether you have sequence numbers or time/date stamps configured).

So what does this all mean?

- No sequence number is part of this message.

- The message occurred at June 23, at 22:45:20.878 (or 10:45 PM, and 20.878 seconds).

- It is a sys message, and it is level 5 (a notification).

- It is a config message; specifically, the configuration occurred from the console.

Configuring NetFlow

NetFlow is an application for collecting IP traffic information. It is used for network accounting and security auditing.

CAUTION NetFlow consumes additional memory. If you have limited memory, you might want to preset the size of the NetFlow cache to contain a smaller number of entries. The default cache size depends on the platform of the device.

`Edmonton(config)#interface` `gigabitethernet0/0`	Moves to interface configuration mode.
`Edmonton(config-if)#ip flow` `ingress`	Enables NetFlow on the interface. Captures traffic that is being received by the interface.
`Edmonton(config-if)#ip flow` `egress`	Enables NetFlow on the interface. Captures traffic that is being transmitted by the interface.
`Edmonton(config-if)#exit`	Returns to global configuration mode.
`Edmonton(config)#ip` `flow-export destination` `ip_address udp_port`	Defines the IP address of the workstation to which you want to send the NetFlow information as well as the User Datagram Protocol (UDP) port on which the workstation is listening for the information.
`Edmonton(config)#ip` `flow-export version x`	Specifies the version format that the export packets used.

NOTE NetFlow exports data in UDP in one of five formats: 1, 5, 7, 8, 9. Version 9 is the most versatile, but it is not backward compatible with Versions 5 or 8.

Verifying NetFlow

Edmonton#`show ip interface gigabitethernet0/0`	Displays information about the interface, including NetFlow as being either ingress or egress enabled
Edmonton#`show ip flow export`	Verifies status and statistics for NetFlow accounting data export
Edmonton#`show ip cache flow`	Displays a summary of NetFlow statistics on a Cisco IOS router

NOTE The **show ip cache flow** command is useful for seeing which protocols use the highest volume of traffic and between which hosts this traffic flows.

Network Time Protocol

Most networks today are being designed with high performance and reliability in mind. Delivery of content is, in many cases, guaranteed by service-level agreements (SLA). Having your network display an accurate time is vital to ensuring that you have the best information possible when reading logging messages or troubleshooting issues.

Network Time Protocol Configuration

Edmonton(config)#`ntp server 209.165.200.254`	Configures the Edmonton router to synchronize its clock to a public Network Time Protocol (NTP) server at address 209.165.200.254.
	NOTE This command makes the Edmonton router an NTP client to the external NTP server.
	NOTE A Cisco IOS router can be both a client to an external NTP server and an NTP server to client devices inside its own internal network.
	NOTE When NTP is enabled on a Cisco IOS router, it is enabled on all interfaces.
Edmonton(config)#`ntp server 209.165.200.234 prefer`	Specifies a preferred NTP server if multiple ones are configured.
	TIP It is recommended that you configure more than one NTP server.
Edmonton(config)#`ntp server 2001:DB8:0:0:8:800:200c:417A version 4`	Configures the Edmonton router to synchronize its clock to a public NTP server at address 2001:DB8:0:0:8:800:200c:417A.
	NOTE Version 4 of NTP is also selected because it is the only NTP version with support for IPv6.
Edmonton(config-if)#`ntp disable`	Prevents an interface from receiving NTP packets.

	TIP Use this command on interfaces connected to external networks.
`Edmonton(config)#ntp master` *`stratum`*	Configures the router to be an NTP master clock to which peers synchronize when no external NTP source is available. The *stratum* is an optional number between 1 and 15. When enabled, the default stratum is 8.
	NOTE A reference clock (for example, an atomic clock) is said to be a stratum-0 device. A stratum-1 server is directly connected to a stratum-0 device. A stratum-2 server is connected across a network path to a stratum-1 server. The larger the stratum number (moving toward 15), the less authoritative and accurate that server is.
`Edmonton(config)#ntp` `max-associations 200`	Configures the maximum number of NTP peer-and-client associations that the router serves. The range is 0 to 4,294,967,295. The default is 100.
`Edmonton(config)` `#access-list 101 permit udp` `any host a.b.c.d eq ntp`	Creates an access list statement that allows NTP communication for the NTP server at address *a.b.c.d*. This ACL should be placed in an inbound direction.
`Edmonton(config)#ntp` `access-group peer 101`	Controls access to the NTP services on the system. In this example, the keyword **peer** allows time requests and NTP control queries and allows the system to synchronize to the remote system. **101** refers to the previously configured ACL 101.

NOTE When a local device is configured with the **ntp master** command, it can be identified by a syntactically correct but invalid IP address. This address is in the form of 127.127.x.x. The master synchronizes with itself and uses the 127.127.x.x address to identify itself. This address is displayed with the **show ntp associations** command and must be permitted via an access list if you are authenticating your NTP servers.

Verifying NTP

`Edmonton#show ntp` `associations`	Displays the status of NTP associations.
`Edmonton#show ntp` `associations detail`	Displays detailed information about each NTP association.
`Edmonton#show ntp status`	Displays the status of the NTP. This command shows whether the router's clock has synchronized with the external NTP server.
`Edmonton#debug ip packets`	Checks to see whether NTP packets are received and sent.
`Edmonton#debug ip packet 1`	Limits debug output to ACL 1.
`Edmonton#debug ntp adjust`	Displays debug output for NTP clock adjustments.

Edmonton#**debug ntp all**	Displays all NTP debugging output.
Edmonton#**debug ntp events**	Displays all NTP debugging events.
Edmonton#**debug ntp packet**	Displays NTP packet debugging; lets you see the time that the peer/server gives you in a received packet.
Edmonton#**debug ntp packet detail**	Displays detailed NTP packet dump.
Edmonton#**debug ntp packet peer A.B.C.D** or Edmonton#**debug ntp packet peer X:X:X:X::X**	Displays debugging from NTP peer at address A.B.C.D. or Displays debugging from NTP peer at address X:X:X:X::X.

Setting the Clock on a Router

NOTE   It is important to have your routers display the correct time for use with time stamps and other logging features.

If the system is synchronized by a valid outside timing mechanism, such as an NTP, or if you have a router with a hardware clock, you do not need to set the software clock. Use the software clock if no other time sources are available.

Edmonton#**calendar set 16:30:00 22 March 2016**	Manually sets the system hardware clock. The time is set using military (24-hour) format. The hardware clock runs continuously, even if the router is powered off or rebooted.
Edmonton#**show calendar**	Displays the hardware calendar.
Edmonton(config)#**clock calendar-valid**	Configures the system as an authoritative time source for a network based on its hardware clock.
	NOTE Because the hardware clock is not as accurate as other time sources (it runs off of a battery), you should use this only when a more accurate time source (such as NTP) is not available.
Edmonton#**clock read-calendar**	Manually reads the hardware clock settings into the software clock.
Edmonton#**clock set 16:30:00 22 March 2016**	Manually sets the system software clock. The time is set using military (24-hour) format.

Edmonton(config)#**clock summer-time** *zone* **recurring** [*week day month hh:mm week day month hh:mm [offset]*] Edmonton(config)#**clock summer-time** *zone* **date** *date month year hh:mm date month year hh:mm [offset]* Edmonton(config)#**clock summer-time** *zone* **date** *month date year hh:mm month date year hh:mm [offset]*	Configures the system to automatically switch to summer time (daylight saving time). **NOTE** Summer time is disabled by default. Arguments for the command are as follows: *zone*—Name of the time zone. **recurring**—Summer time should start and end on the corresponding specified days every year. **date**—Indicates that summer time should start on the first specific date listed in the command and end on the second specific date in the command. *week*—(Optional) Week of the month (1 to 5 or **last**). *day*—(Optional) Day of the week (Sunday, Monday, and so on). *date*—Date of the month (1 to 31). *month*—(Optional) Month (January, February, and so on). *year*: Year (1993 to 2035). *hh:mm*—(Optional) Time (military format) in hours and minutes. *offset*—(Optional) Number of minutes to add during summer time (default is 60).
Edmonton(config)#**clock timezone** *zone hours-offset* [*minutes-offset*]	Configures the time zone for display purposes. To set the time to coordinated universal time (UTC), use the **no** form of this command.
Edmonton(config)#**clock timezone MST -7**	Configures the time zone to mountain standard time, which is 7 hours behind UTC.
Edmonton(config)#**clock timezone NL -3 30**	Configures the time zone to Newfoundland time for Newfoundland, Canada, which is 3.5 hours behind UTC. *zone*: Name of the time zone to be displayed when standard time is in effect. See Tables 30-3 and 30-4 for common time zone acronyms. *hours-offset*: Hours difference from UTC. *minutes-offset*: (Optional) Minutes difference from UTC.
Edmonton#**clock update-calendar**	Updates the hardware clock from the software clock.

Edmonton#**show clock**	Displays the time and date from the system software clock.
Edmonton#**show clock detail**	Displays the clock source (NTP, hardware) and the current summer-time setting (if any).

Table 30-3 shows the common acronyms used for setting the time zone on a router.

TABLE 30-3   Common Time Zone Acronyms

Region/Acronym	Time Zone Name and UTC Offset
Europe	
GMT	Greenwich mean time, as UTC
BST	British summer time, as UTC + 1 hour
IST	Irish summer time, as UTC + 1 hour
WET	Western Europe time, as UTC
WEST	Western Europe summer time, as UTC + 1 hour
CET	Central Europe time, as UTC + 1
CEST	Central Europe summer time, as UTC + 2
EET	Eastern Europe time, as UTC + 2
EEST	Eastern Europe summer time, as UTC + 3
MSK	Moscow time, as UTC + 3
MSD	Moscow summer time, as UTC + 4
United States and Canada	
AST	Atlantic standard time, as UTC − 4 hours
ADT	Atlantic daylight time, as UTC − 3 hours
ET	Eastern time, either as EST or EDT, depending on place and time of year
EST	Eastern standard time, as UTC − 5 hours
EDT	Eastern daylight saving time, as UTC − 4 hours
CT	Central time, either as CST or CDT, depending on place and time of year
CST	Central standard time, as UTC − 6 hours
CDT	Central daylight saving time, as UTC − 5 hours
MT	Mountain time, either as MST or MDT, depending on place and time of year
MST	Mountain standard time, as UTC − 7 hours
MDT	Mountain daylight saving time, as UTC − 6 hours
PT	Pacific time, either as PST or PDT, depending on place and time of year
PST	Pacific standard time, as UTC − 8 hours
PDT	Pacific daylight saving time, as UTC − 7 hours

Region/Acronym	Time Zone Name and UTC Offset
AKST	Alaska standard time, as UTC – 9 hours
AKDT	Alaska standard daylight saving time, as UTC – 8 hours
HST	Hawaiian standard time, as UTC – 10 hours
Australia	
WST	Western standard time, as UTC + 8 hours
CST	Central standard time, as UTC + 9.5 hours
EST	Eastern standard/summer time, as UTC + 10 hours (+ 11 hours during summer)

Table 30-4 lists an alternative method for referring to time zones, in which single letters are used to refer to the time zone difference from UTC. Using this method, the letter Z indicates the zero meridian, equivalent to UTC, and the letter J (Juliet) refers to the local time zone. Using this method, the international date line is between time zones M and Y.

TABLE 30-4   Single-Letter Time Zone Designators

Letter Designator	Word Designator	Difference from UTC
Y	Yankee	UTC – 12 hours
X	X-ray	UTC – 11 hours
W	Whiskey	UTC – 10 hours
V	Victor	UTC – 9 hours
U	Uniform	UTC – 8 hours
T	Tango	UTC – 7 hours
S	Sierra	UTC – 6 hours
R	Romeo	UTC – 5 hours
Q	Quebec	UTC – 4 hours
P	Papa	UTC – 3 hours
O	Oscar	UTC – 2 hours
N	November	UTC – 1 hour
Z	Zulu	Same as UTC
A	Alpha	UTC + 1 hour
B	Bravo	UTC + 2 hours
C	Charlie	UTC + 3 hours
D	Delta	UTC + 4 hours
E	Echo	UTC + 5 hours
F	Foxtrot	UTC + 6 hours
G	Golf	UTC + 7 hours
H	Hotel	UTC + 8 hours
I	India	UTC + 9 hours
K	Kilo	UTC + 10 hours

Letter Designator	Word Designator	Difference from UTC
L	Lima	UTC + 11 hours
M	Mike	UTC + 12 hours

Using Time Stamps

`Edmonton(config)#service timestamps`	Adds a time stamp to all system logging messages
`Edmonton(config)#service timestamps debug`	Adds a time stamp to all debugging messages
`Edmonton(config)#service timestamps debug uptime`	Adds a time stamp along with the total uptime of the router to all debugging messages
`Edmonton(config)#service timestamps debug datetime localtime`	Adds a time stamp displaying the local time and the date to all debugging messages
`Edmonton(config)#no service timestamps`	Disables all time stamps

Cisco IOS Licensing

This chapter provides information and commands concerning the following topics:

- Cisco licensing earlier than IOS 15.0
- Cisco licensing for the ISR G2 platforms: IOS 15.0 and later
- Verifying licenses
- Cisco License Manager
- Cisco Smart Software Manager
- Installing a permanent license
- Installing an evaluation license
- Backing up a license
- Uninstalling a license

Cisco Licensing Earlier Than IOS 15.0

Before IOS Version 15.0, the software image was selected based on the required needs of the customer.

Eight images satisfy different requirements in different service areas; see Figure 31-1.

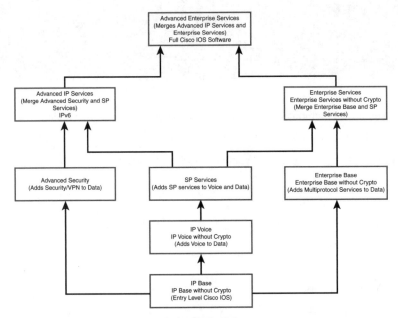

Figure 31-1   Cisco IOS Images Before IOS 15.0

Software Image/Package	Features
IP Base/IP Base without Crypto	IP data. This is the entry-level Cisco IOS Software image.
IP Voice/IP Voice Without Crypto	Adds voice to data: VoIP, Voice over Frame Relay (VoFR), IP telephony.
Advanced Security	Adds security to data: Security and virtual private network (VPN) features, including Cisco IOS Firewall, intrusion detection system/intrusion prevention system (IDS/IPS), IPsec, 3DES, and virtual private network (VPN).
SP Services	Adds service provider (SP) services to voice and data: Secure Shell/Secure Sockets Layer (SSH/SSL), ATM, Voice over Asynchronous Transfer Mode (VoATM), Multiprotocol Label Switching (MPLS).
Enterprise Base	Adds multiprotocol services to data: AT, Internetwork Packet Exchange (IPX), limited IBM support.
Enterprise Services	Merges enterprise base and SP services. Adds full IBM support.
Advanced IP Services	Merges advanced security and SP services. Adds IPv6.
Advanced Enterprise Services	Merges advanced IP services and enterprise services. Full Cisco IOS Software.

Cisco Licensing for the ISR G2 Platforms: IOS 15.0 and Later

Beginning with the Integrated Services Router (ISR) G2 platform (1900, 2900, and 3900 series), the router now ships with a single universal IOS image and corresponding feature set packages, as shown in Figure 31-2.

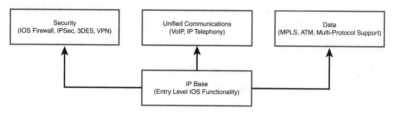

Figure 31-2   IOS Licensing for ISR G2 Platforms: IOS 15.0 and Later

Routers come with IP Base installed. You can install additional feature pack licenses as an addition to expand the feature set of the device.

Software Image/Package	Features
IP Base (ipbasek9)	Entry-level IOS functionality
Data (datak9)	Adds MPLS, ATM, multiprotocol support to IP Base
Unified Communication (uck9)	Adds VoIP and IP telephony to IP Base
Security (securityk9)	Adds IOS Firewall, IPS, IPsec, 3DES, and VPN to IP Base

NOTE   The IP Base license is the prerequisite for installing any or all of the Data, Unified Communications, or Security Package licenses.

Verifying Licenses

Router#**show license**	Displays information about all Cisco IOS Software licenses
Router#**show license feature**	Views the technology package licenses and features licenses supported on this router

Cisco License Manager

If you work in a large environment with a lot of Cisco routers, you might want to implement the Cisco License Manager in your workplace. This software can help you manage all your software licenses, including the following:

- Discovering your network
- Inventories license features

- Given a product authorization key (PAK), securely obtains device licenses from the Cisco.com license server

- Securely deploys licenses to activate the software features on your managed devices

- Enhances security using role-based access control

- Integrates Cisco licenses into existing license or asset management applications (if you have these installed)

- Provides detailed reporting capabilities

- Reduces failure recovery time by deploying licenses stores in its local database

- Automatically retrieves and deploys licenses for a given device

NOTE   Cisco License Manager is a free software tool available at Cisco.com.

Cisco Smart Software Manager

Cisco Smart Software Manager enables you to manage all of your Cisco Smart software licenses from one centralized website. With Cisco Smart Software Manager, you can activate your products, manage your entitlements, and renew and upgrade software.

Smart Software Licensing eliminates PAK installations for product activation and introduces license pooling. Now licenses don't have to be node-locked to devices; they can be used on any compatible device in your company.

Cisco Smart Software Manager does not need specialized software to be installed on your management device; you only need an Internet browser and access to the Cisco website (www.cisco.com).

Installing a Permanent License

NOTE   If you purchase a router and identify and purchase a permanent license at the time of ordering, Cisco will preinstall the appropriate license for you. You use the following commands if you want to update your router with new technology packages after purchase.

NOTE   To install a permanent license, you must have purchased that license from Cisco, and your license file must be stored on the flash of your router.

NOTE   Permanent licenses are perpetual; no end date is associated with them. After you have installed the license onto your router, the license never expires.

`Router#license install stored-location-url`	Installs a license file stored in the location identified by the *stored-location-url*
`Router#reload`	Reloads the router

NOTE   A reload is not required if an evaluation license is already active on the router. A reload is required only to activate a technology package license when the evaluation license for that technology package is not active.

| Router#**show version** | Verifies that the new license has been installed |

NOTE   Perform the **show version** command after a reboot to confirm that your license has been installed.

Installing an Evaluation License

NOTE   Evaluation licenses are temporary licenses, allowing you to evaluate a feature set on new hardware. These temporary licenses are limited to a specific usage period of 60 days. The 60-day limit may be extended through the Cisco Technical Assistance Center (TAC) under certain circumstances.

NOTE   Depending on the hardware on your router, some evaluation licenses might not be available; the UC Technology Package License is not available to install on any of the 1900 series devices, for example.

Router(config)#license boot module module-name technology-package package-name	Enables the evaluation license
Router(config)#exit	Returns to privileged EXEC mode
Router#reload	Reloads the router to allow activation of the software package

NOTE   Use the **?** to determine the *module-name* of your device. It should look like **c1900** or **c2900** or **c3900** depending on the platform.

NOTE   Use the **?** to determine which *package-names* are supported on your router.

| Router#**show license** | Verifies that the new license has been installed |

Backing Up a License

| Router#**license save** file-sys://lic-location | Saves a copy of all licenses in a device. The location can be a directory or a URL that points to a file system. |
| Router#**license save** flash:all_licenses.lic | Saves a copy of all licenses to the flash memory of the device under the name *all_licenses.lic*. |

NOTE   Use the **?** to see the storage locations supported by your device.

NOTE Saved licenses are restored by using the **license install** command.

Uninstalling a License

To uninstall an active permanent license from an ISR G2 router, you must perform two tasks: Disable the technology package, and then clear the license.

NOTE You cannot uninstall built-in licenses. You can remove only licenses that have been added by using the **license install** command.

`Router(config)#`**`license boot`** **`module`** *`module-name`* **`technology-`** **`package`** *`package-name`* **`disable`**	Disables the active license.
`Router(config)#`**`exit`**	Returns to privileged EXEC mode.
`Router#`**`reload`**	Reloads the router to make the software package inactive.
`Router#`**`show version`**	Verifies that the technology package has been disabled.
`Router#`**`license clear`** *`feature-name`*	Clears the technology package license from license storage.
`Router#`**`configure terminal`**	Moves to global configuration mode.
`Router(config)#`**`no license boot`** **`module`** *`module-name`* **`technology-`** **`package`** *`package-name`* `disable`	Clears the **license boot module** *module-name* **technology-package** *package-name* **disable** command that was used for disabling the active license.
`Router(config)#`**`exit`**	Returns to privileged EXEC mode.
`Router#`**`reload`**	Reloads the router. This is required to make the software package inactive.
`Router#`**`show version`**	Verifies that the license has been cleared.

Basic Troubleshooting

This chapter provides information and commands concerning the following topics:

- Viewing the routing table
- Clearing the routing table
- Determining the gateway of last resort
- Determining the last routing update
- OSI Layer 3 testing
- OSI Layer 7 testing
- Interpreting the **show interface** command
- Clearing interface counters
- Using CDP to troubleshoot
- The **traceroute** command
- The **show controllers** command
- **debug** commands
- Using time stamps
- Operating system IP verification commands
- The **ip http server** command
- The **netstat** command
- The **arp** command

Viewing the Routing Table

Router#**show ip route**	Displays the entire routing table
Router#**show ip route** *protocol*	Displays a table about a specific protocol (for example, Open Shortest Path First [OSPF] or Enhanced Interior Gateway Routing Protocol [EIGRP])
Router#**show ip route** *w.x.y.z*	Displays information about route *w.x.y.z*
Router#**show ip route connected**	Displays a table of connected routes
Router#**show ip route static**	Displays a table of static routes
Router#**show ip route summary**	Displays a summary of all routes
Router#**show ipv6 route**	Displays the entire IPv6 routing table

Router#**show ipv6 route** **X:X:X:X:X:X:X:X**	Displays information about route X:X:X:X:X:X:X:X
Router#**show ipv6 route** *protocol*	Displays a table about a specific IPv6 protocol (for example, OSPFv3 or EIGRPv6)

Clearing the Routing Table

Router#**clear ip route ***	Clears entire routing table, forcing it to rebuild
Router#**clear ip route** **a.b.c.d**	Clears specific route to network a.b.c.d
Router#**clear ipv6 route ***	Clears entire IPv6 routing table, forcing it to rebuild
Router#**clear ipv6 route** **X:X:X:X::X**	Clears specific route to network X:X:X:X::X

Determining the Gateway of Last Resort

Router(config)#**ip** **default-network** *w.x.y.z*	Sets network *w.x.y.z* to be the default route. All routes not in the routing table will be sent to this network.
Router(config)#**ip** **route 0.0.0.0 0.0.0.0** **172.16.20.1**	Specifies that all packet destinations not matching a specific entry in the routing table will be sent to 172.16.20.1

NOTE   The **ip default-network** command is for use with the deprecated Cisco proprietary Interior Gateway Routing Protocol (IGRP). Although you can use it with EIGRP or Routing Information Protocol (RIP), it is not recommended. Use the **ip route 0.0.0.0 0.0.0.0** command instead.

Routers that use the **ip default-network** command must have either a specific route to that network or a **0.0.0.0 /0** default route.

Determining the Last Routing Update

Router#**show ip route**	Displays the entire IPv4 routing table
Router#**show ip route** *w.x.y.z*	Displays information about route *w.x.y.z*
Router#**show ipv6 route**	Displays the entire IPv6 routing table
Router#**show ipv6 route** **X:X:X:X:X:X:X:X**	Displays information about route X:X:X:X:X:X:X:X
Router#**show ip protocols**	Displays the IP routing protocol parameters and statistics
Router#**show ipv6 protocols**	Displays the IPv6 routing protocol parameters and statistics

OSI Layer 3 Testing

Router#**ping** `w.x.y.z`	Checks for Layer 3 connectivity with the device at IPv4 address *w.x.y.z*
Router#**ping** `aaaa:aaaa: aaaa:aaaa:aaaa:aaaa:a aaa:aaaa`	Checks for Layer 3 connectivity with the device at IPv6 address *aaaa:aaaa:aaaa:aaaa:aaaa:aaaa:aaaa:aaaa*
Router#**ping**	Enters extended ping mode, which provides more options

NOTE   See Chapter 29, "IOS Tools," for all applicable **ping** commands.

OSI Layer 7 Testing

NOTE   See Chapter 29, "IOS Tools," for all applicable Telnet commands. See Chapter 25, "Device Hardening," for applicable SSH commands.

Router#**debug telnet**	Displays the Telnet negotiation process

Interpreting the show interface Command

Router#**show interface serial 0/0/0**	Displays the status and stats of the interface.
Serial 0/0/0 is *up*, line protocol is *up*	The first part refers to the physical status. The second part refers to the data link status.
...<output cut>...	
Possible output results:	
Serial 0/0/0 is *up*, line protocol is *up*	The interface is up and working.
Serial 0/0/0 is *up*, line protocol is *down*	Keepalive or connection problem (no clock rate, bad encapsulation, PPP authentication).
Serial 0/0/0 is *down*, line protocol is *down*	Interface problem, or other end has not been enabled.
Serial 0/0/0 is administratively *down*, line protocol is *down*	Interface is disabled, or shut down.

Clearing Interface Counters

Router#**clear counters**	Resets all interface counters to 0
Router#**clear counters** *interface type/slot*	Resets specific interface counters to 0

Using CDP to Troubleshoot

NOTE See Chapter 28, "Cisco Discovery Protocol (CDP) and Link Layer Data Protocol (LLDP)," for all applicable CDP commands.

The traceroute Command

Router#**traceroute** *w.x.y.z*	Displays all routes used to reach the destination of *w.x.y.z*
Router#**traceroute ipv6** *A:A:A:A:A:A:A:A*	Displays all routes used to reach the destination of *A:A:A:A:A:A:A:A*

NOTE See Chapter 29 for all applicable **traceroute** commands.

The show controllers Command

Router#**show controllers serial 0/0/0**	Displays the type of cable plugged into the serial interface (DCE or DTE) and what the clock rate is

debug Commands

Router#**debug all**	Turns on all possible debugging.
Router#**u all** (short form of undebug all)	Turns off all possible debugging.
Router#**show debug**	Lists what debug commands are on.
Router#**terminal monitor**	Debug output will now be seen through a Telnet/SSH (a vty line connection) session (default is to only send output on the console screen).

CAUTION Turning all possible debugging on is extremely CPU intensive and will probably cause your router to crash. Use *extreme caution* if you try this on a production device. Instead, be selective about which **debug** commands you turn on.

Do not leave debugging turned on. After you have gathered the necessary information from debugging, turn all debugging off. If you want to turn off only one specific **debug** command and leave others on, issue the **no debug** *x* command, where *x* is the specific **debug** command you want to disable.

Using Time Stamps

Router(config)#**service timestamps**	Adds a time stamp to all system logging messages
Router(config)#**service timestamps debug**	Adds a time stamp to all debugging messages

Router(config)#**service timestamps debug uptime**	Adds a time stamp along with the total uptime of the router to all debugging messages
Router(config)#**service timestamps debug datetime localtime**	Adds a time stamp displaying the local time and the date to all debugging messages
Router(config)#**no service timestamps**	Disables all time stamps

TIP   As a last resort, make sure you have the date and time set with the **clock** command at privileged mode so that the time stamps are more meaningful. A better solution is to have Network Time Protocol (NTP) enabled. See the section on NTP in Chapter 30, "Device Monitoring," for more details on configuring NTP.

Operating System IP Verification Commands

The following are commands that you should use to verify what your IP settings are. Different operating systems have different commands.

- **ipconfig** (Windows 10/8/7/Vista/2000/XP):

  From the Command Prompt:

  - C:\Users\Scott>**ipconfig**

  - C:\Users|Scott>**ipconfig /all**

- **winipcfg** (Windows 95/98/Me):

  Click **Start > Run > winipcfg**.

- **ifconfig** (Mac/Linux)

The ip http server Command

Router(config)#**ip http server**	Enables the HTTP server, including the Cisco web browser user interface
Router(config-if)#**no ip http server**	Disables the HTTP server

CAUTION   The HTTP server was introduced in Cisco IOS Software Release 11.0 to extend router management to the web. You have limited management capabilities to your router through a web browser If the **ip http server** command is turned on.

Do not turn on the **ip http server** command unless you plan to use the browser interface for the router. Having it on creates a potential security hole because another port is open.

The netstat Command

`C\>netstat`	Used in Windows and UNIX/Linux to display TCP/IP connection and protocol information; used at the command prompt in Windows

The arp Command

The **arp** Windows command displays and modifies entries in the ARP cache that are used to store IP addresses and their resolved Ethernet (MAC) addresses.

`C:\Users\Scott>arp -a`	Displays the entire ARP cache
`C:\Users\Scott>arp -d`	Clears the ARP cache, forcing the machine to repopulate with updated information

This chapter provides information and commands concerning the following topics:

- The **ip classless** command
- RIP routing: mandatory commands
- RIP routing: optional commands
- Troubleshooting RIP issues
- Configuration example: RIPv2 routing

The ip classless Command

`Router(config)#ip classless`	Instructs Cisco IOS Software to forward packets destined for an unknown subnet to the best supernet route
`Router(config)#no ip classless`	Turns off the **ip classless** command

NOTE: A supernet route is a route that covers a range of subnets with a single entry.

NOTE: The **ip classless** command is enabled by default in Cisco IOS Software Release 11.3 and later.

RIP Routing: Mandatory Commands

`Router(config)#router rip`	Enables RIP as a routing protocol.
`Router(config-router)#network w.x.y.z`	*w.x.y.z* is the network number of the *directly connected* network you want to advertise.

NOTE: You need to advertise only the classful network number, not a subnet:

Router(config-router)#**network 172.16.0.0**

not

Router(config-router)#**network 172.16.10.0**

If you advertise a subnet, you will not receive an error message, because the router will automatically convert the subnet to the classful network address.

RIP Routing: Optional Commands

Router(config)#**no router rip**	Turns off the RIP routing process.
Router(config-router)#**no network** *w.x.y.z*	Removes network *w.x.y.z* from the RIP routing process.
Router(config-router)#**version 2**	RIP will now send and receive RIPv2 packets globally.
Router(config-router)#**version 1**	RIP will now send and receive RIPv1 packets only.
Router(config-if)#**ip rip send version 1**	The interface will send only RIPv1 packets.
Router(config-if)#**ip rip send version 2**	The interface will send only RIPv2 packets.
Router(config-if)#**ip rip send version 1 2**	The interface will send both RIPv1 and RIPv2 packets.
Router(config-if)#**ip rip receive version 1**	The interface will receive only RIPv1 packets.
Router(config-if)#**ip rip receive version 2**	The interface will receive only RIPv2 packets.
Router(config-if)#**ip rip receive version 1 2**	The interface will receive both RIPv1 and RIPv2 packets.
Router(config-router)#**no auto-summary**	RIPv2 summarizes networks at the classful boundary. This command turns auto-summarization off.

`Router(config-router)#`**`passive-interface`** **`s0/0/0`**	RIP updates will not be sent out this interface.
`Router(config-router)#`**`neighbor`** *`a.b.c.d`*	Defines a specific neighbor with which to exchange information.
`Router(config-router)#`**`no ip split-horizon`**	Turns off split horizon (on by default).
`Router(config-router)#`**`ip split-horizon`**	Reenables split horizon.
`Router(config-router)#`**`timers basic 30 90 180`** **`270 360`**	Changes timers in RIP: 30 = Update timer (in seconds) 90 = Invalid timer (in seconds) 180 = Hold-down timer (in seconds) 270 = Flush timer (in seconds) 360 = Sleep time (in milliseconds)
`Router(config-router)#`**`maximum-paths`** *`x`*	Limits the number of paths for load balancing to x (4 = default, 6 = maximum).
`Router(config-router)#`**`default-information`** **`originate`**	Generates a default route into RIP.

Troubleshooting RIP Issues

`Router#`**`debug ip rip`**	Displays all RIP activity in real time
`Router#`**`show ip rip database`**	Displays contents of the RIP database

Configuration Example: RIPv2 Routing

Figure 8-1 illustrates the network topology for the configuration that follows, which shows how to configure RIPv2 using the commands covered in this chapter.

Figure 8-7   Network Topology for RIPv2 Routing Configuration

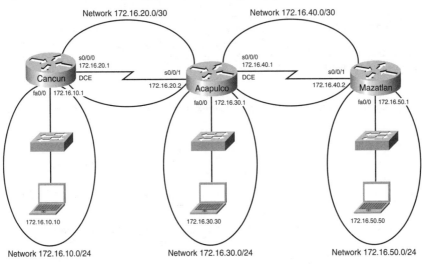

NOTE: The host name, password, and interfaces have all been configured as per the configuration example in Chapter 6, "Configuring a Single Cisco Router."

Cancun Router

Cancun>**enable**	Moves to privileged mode
Cancun#**configure terminal**	Moves to global configuration mode
Cancun(config)#**router rip**	Enables RIP routing
Cancun(config-router)#**version 2**	Enables RIPv2
Cancun(config-router)#**network 172.16.0.0**	Advertises directly connected networks (classful address only)
Cancun(config-router)#**no auto-summary**	Turns off auto-summarization

Cancun(config-router)#**exit**	Returns to global configuration mode
Cancun(config)#**exit**	Returns to privileged mode
Cancun#**copy run start**	Saves the configuration to NVRAM

Acapulco Router

Acapulco>**enable**	Moves to privileged mode
Acapulco#**configure terminal**	Moves to global configuration mode
Acapulco(config)#**router rip**	Enables RIP routing
Acapulco(config-router)#**version 2**	Enables RIPv2
Acapulco(config-router)#**network 172.16.0.0**	Advertises directly connected networks (classful address only)
Acapulco(config-router)#**no auto-summary**	Turns off auto-summarization
Acapulco(config-router)#**exit**	Moves to global configuration mode
Acapulco(config)#**exit**	Returns to privileged mode
Acapulco#**copy running-config startup-config**	Saves the configuration to NVRAM

Mazatlan Router

Mazatlan>**enable**	Moves to privileged mode
Mazatlan#**configure terminal**	Moves to global configuration mode
Mazatlan(config)#**router rip**	Enables RIP routing
Mazatlan(config-router)#**version 2**	Enables RIPv2
Mazatlan(config-router)#**network 172.16.0.0**	Advertises directly connected networks (classful address only)

`Mazatlan(config-router)#`**`no auto-summary`**	Turns off auto-summarization
`Mazatlan(config-router)#`**`exit`**	Moves to global configuration mode
`Mazatlan(config)#`**`exit`**	Returns to privileged mode
`Mazatlan#`**`copy running-config startup-config`**	Saves the configuration to NVRAM

Binary/Hex/Decimal Conversion Chart

The following chart lists the three most common number systems used in networking: decimal, hexadecimal, and binary. Some numbers you will remember quite easily, because you use them a lot in your day-to-day activities. For those other numbers, refer to this chart.

Decimal Value	Hexadecimal Value	Binary Value
0	00	0000 0000
1	01	0000 0001
2	02	0000 0010
3	03	0000 0011
4	04	0000 0100
5	05	0000 0101
6	06	0000 0110
7	07	0000 0111
8	08	0000 1000
9	09	0000 1001
10	0A	0000 1010
11	0B	0000 1011
12	0C	0000 1100
13	0D	0000 1101
14	0E	0000 1110
15	0F	0000 1111
16	10	0001 0000
17	11	0001 0001
18	12	0001 0010
19	13	0001 0011
20	14	0001 0100
21	15	0001 0101
22	16	0001 0110
23	17	0001 0111
24	18	0001 1000
25	19	0001 1001
26	1A	0001 1010
27	1B	0001 1011

Decimal Value	Hexadecimal Value	Binary Value
28	1C	0001 1100
29	1D	0001 1101
30	1E	0001 1110
31	1F	0001 1111
32	20	0010 0000
33	21	0010 0001
34	22	0010 0010
35	23	0010 0011
36	24	0010 0100
37	25	0010 0101
38	26	0010 0110
39	27	0010 0111
40	28	0010 1000
41	29	0010 1001
42	2A	0010 1010
43	2B	0010 1011
44	2C	0010 1100
45	2D	0010 1101
46	2E	0010 1110
47	2F	0010 1111
48	30	0011 0000
49	31	0011 0001
50	32	0011 0010
51	33	0011 0011
52	34	0011 0100
53	35	0011 0101
54	36	0011 0110
55	37	0011 0111
56	38	0011 1000
57	39	0011 1001
58	3A	0011 1010
59	3B	0011 1011
60	3C	0011 1100
61	3D	0011 1101
62	3E	0011 1110
63	3F	0011 1111
64	40	0100 0000

Decimal Value	Hexadecimal Value	Binary Value
65	41	0100 0001
66	42	0100 0010
67	43	0100 0011
68	44	0100 0100
69	45	0100 0101
70	46	0100 0110
71	47	0100 0111
72	48	0100 1000
73	49	0100 1001
74	4A	0100 1010
75	4B	0100 1011
76	4C	0100 1100
77	4D	0100 1101
78	4E	0100 1110
79	4F	0100 1111
80	50	0101 0000
81	51	0101 0001
82	52	0101 0010
83	53	0101 0011
84	54	0101 0100
85	55	0101 0101
86	56	0101 0110
87	57	0101 0111
88	58	0101 1000
89	59	0101 1001
90	5A	0101 1010
91	5B	0101 1011
92	5C	0101 1100
93	5D	0101 1101
94	5E	0101 1110

Decimal Value	Hexadecimal Value	Binary Value
95	5F	0101 1111
96	60	0110 0000
97	61	0110 0001
98	62	0110 0010
99	63	0110 0011
100	64	0110 0100
101	65	0110 0101
102	66	0110 0110
103	67	0110 0111
104	68	0110 1000
105	69	0110 1001
106	6A	0110 1010
107	6B	0110 1011
108	6C	0110 1100
109	6D	0110 1101
110	6E	0110 1110
111	6F	0110 1111
112	70	0111 0000
113	71	0111 0001
114	72	0111 0010
115	73	0111 0011
116	74	0111 0100
117	75	0111 0101
118	76	0111 0110
119	77	0111 0111
120	78	0111 1000
121	79	0111 1001
122	7A	0111 1010
123	7B	0111 1011
124	7C	0111 1100
125	7D	0111 1101
126	7E	0111 1110
127	7F	0111 1111
128	80	1000 0000
129	81	1000 0001

Decimal Value	Hexadecimal Value	Binary Value
130	82	1000 0010
131	83	1000 0011
132	84	1000 0100
133	85	1000 0101
134	86	1000 0110
135	87	1000 0111
136	88	1000 1000
137	89	1000 1001
138	8A	1000 1010
139	8B	1000 1011
140	8C	1000 1100
141	8D	1000 1101
142	8E	1000 1110
143	8F	1000 1111
144	90	1001 0000
145	91	1001 0001
146	92	1001 0010
147	93	1001 0011
148	94	1001 0100
149	95	1001 0101
150	96	1001 0110
151	97	1001 0111
152	98	1001 1000
153	99	1001 1001
154	9A	1001 1010
155	9B	1001 1011
156	9C	1001 1100
157	9D	1001 1101
158	9E	1001 1110
159	9F	1001 1111
160	A0	1010 0000
161	A1	1010 0001
162	A2	1010 0010
163	A3	1010 0011
164	A4	1010 0100
165	A5	1010 0101
166	A6	1010 0110

Decimal Value	Hexadecimal Value	Binary Value
167	A7	1010 0111
168	A8	1010 1000
169	A9	1010 1001
170	AA	1010 1010
171	AB	1010 1011
172	AC	1010 1100
173	AD	1010 1101
174	AE	1010 1110
175	AF	1010 1111
176	B0	1011 0000
177	B1	1011 0001
178	B2	1011 0010
179	B3	1011 0011
180	B4	1011 0100
181	B5	1011 0101
182	B6	1011 0110
183	B7	1011 0111
184	B8	1011 1000
185	B9	1011 1001
186	BA	1011 1010
187	BB	1011 1011
188	BC	1011 1100
189	BD	1011 1101
190	BE	1011 1110
191	BF	1011 1111
192	C0	1100 0000
193	C1	1100 0001
194	C2	1100 0010
195	C3	1100 0011
196	C4	1100 0100
197	C5	1100 0101
198	C6	1100 0110
199	C7	1100 0111
200	C8	1100 1000
201	C9	1100 1001
202	CA	1100 1010
203	CB	1100 1011

Decimal Value	Hexadecimal Value	Binary Value
204	CC	1100 1100
205	CD	1100 1101
206	CE	1100 1110
207	CF	1100 1111
208	D0	1101 0000
209	D1	1101 0001
210	D2	1101 0010
211	D3	1101 0011
212	D4	1101 0100
213	D5	1101 0101
214	D6	1101 0110
215	D7	1101 0111
216	D8	1101 1000
217	D9	1101 1001
218	DA	1101 1010
219	DB	1101 1011
220	DC	1101 1100
221	DD	1101 1101
222	DE	1101 1110
223	DF	1101 1111
224	E0	1110 0000
225	E1	1110 0001
226	E2	1110 0010
227	E3	1110 0011
228	E4	1110 0100
229	E5	1110 0101
230	E6	1110 0110
231	E7	1110 0111
232	E8	1110 1000
233	E9	1110 1001
234	EA	1110 1010
235	EB	1110 1011
236	EC	1110 1100
237	ED	1110 1101
238	EE	1110 1110
239	EF	1110 1111
240	F0	1111 0000

Decimal Value	Hexadecimal Value	Binary Value
241	F1	1111 0001
242	F2	1111 0010
243	F3	1111 0011
244	F4	1111 0100
245	F5	1111 0101
246	F6	1111 0110
247	F7	1111 0111
248	F8	1111 1000
249	F9	1111 1001
250	FA	1111 1010
251	FB	1111 1011
252	FC	1111 1100
253	FD	1111 1101
254	FE	1111 1110
255	FF	1111 1111

Create Your Own Journal Here

H

I

CISCO

Connect, Engage, Collaborate

The Award Winning Cisco Support Community

Attend and Participate in Events

Ask the Experts
Live Webcasts

Knowledge Sharing

Documents
Blogs
Videos

Top Contributor Programs

Cisco Designated VIP
Hall of Fame
Spotlight Awards

Multi-Language Support

https://supportforums.cisco.com

ı|ı.ı|ı.
CISCO.

Cisco
Press

NEW
CCNA Routing & Switching
(100-105 / 200-105 / 200-125)

Special Offers and New Learning Materials

Cisco Press is pleased to provide you with special offers to save up to 70% on complementary learning materials. Each code is unique and only applies to the products specified in the grid below. Coupon details are located in the CD/DVD sleeve in the back of this book. Each product includes at least three of the special offers below.

OFFER	ISBN	TITLE
Single-use code **70% OFF** one Premium Edition	9780134440972	CCENT ICND1 100-105 Official Cert Guide Premium Edition
	9780134441009	CCNA ICND2 200-105 Official Cert Guide Premium Edition
Single-use code **60% OFF** one Complete Video Course	9780134580722	CCENT ICND1 100-105 Complete Video Course
	9780134580739	CCNA ICND2 200-105 Complete Video Course
	9780134580708	CCNA 200-125 Complete Video Course
Single-use code **50% OFF** one Simulator Product	9780134575728	CCENT ICND1 100-105 Network Simulator
	9780789757814	CCNA ICND2 200-105 Network Simulator
	9780789757814	CCNA 200-125 Network Simulator
Single-use code **50% OFF** one Reference or Late-Stage Exam Prep Product	9781587205880	CCNA 200-125 Portable Command Guide
	9780134466170	CCNA 200-125 Portable Command Guide eBook
	9781587205903	31 Days Before Your CCNA 200-125 Certification Exam
	9780134466194	31 Days Before Your CCNA 200-125 Digital Study Guide

REGISTER YOUR PRODUCT at CiscoPress.com/register

Access Additional Benefits and SAVE 35% on Your Next Purchase

- Download available product updates.

- Access bonus material when applicable.

- Receive exclusive offers on new editions and related products.
  (Just check the box to hear from us when setting up your account.)

- Get a coupon for 35% for your next purchase, valid for 30 days.
  Your code will be available in your Cisco Press cart. (You will also find
  it in the Manage Codes section of your account page.)

Registration benefits vary by product. Benefits will be listed on your account
page under Registered Products.

CiscoPress.com – Learning Solutions for Self-Paced Study, Enterprise, and the Classroom
Cisco Press is the Cisco Systems authorized book publisher of Cisco networking technology,
Cisco certification self-study, and Cisco Networking Academy Program materials.

At CiscoPress.com you can
- Shop our books, eBooks, software, and video training.
- Take advantage of our special offers and promotions (ciscopress.com/promotions).
- Sign up for special offers and content newsletters (ciscopress.com/newsletters).
- Read free articles, exam profiles, and blogs by information technology experts.
- Access thousands of free chapters and video lessons.

Connect with Cisco Press – Visit CiscoPress.com/community
Learn about Cisco Press community events and programs.

Cisco Press

What Do You Want to Do Today?